TWAYNE'S WORLD LEADERS SERIES

EDITOR OF THIS VOLUME

Hans L. Trefousse
*Brooklyn College, The City University
of New York*

Ferenc Deák

Ferenc Deák

Ferenc Deák

BÉLA K. KIRÁLY

Professor of History
Brooklyn College of The City University of New York

TWAYNE PUBLISHERS
A DIVISION OF G. K. HALL & CO., BOSTON

Library of Congress Cataloging in Publication Data

Király, Béla K   1912–
     Ferenc Deák

     (Twayne's world leaders series)
     Bibliography: p. 221–35.
     1. Deák, Ferencz, 1803–1876. 2. Hungary—Politics and
government—19th century.
DB933.3.D2K57   943.9'04'0924 [B]   74–20558
ISBN 0–8057–3030–3

To Robert A. Kann

Contents

About the Author

Béla K. Király, Professor of History at Brooklyn College and the Graduate School of the City University of New York, is a graduate of the Ludovika Military Academy and the War (General Staff) Academy of Hungary. General Király commanded the War Academy of Hungary where he taught military history, and commanded the Hungarian National Guard during the 1956 revolution.

After receiving his M.A. and Ph.D. degrees at Columbia University, the author lectured in American, European, Asian and Latin American universities, and in 1959 became an honorary member of the Staff and Faculty at the U.S. Army Command and General Staff College. In 1969 he received the "Teacher of the Year" award from Brooklyn College.

His account of the Hungarian revolution of 1956, was published in 1958 by the Institute of Foreign Affairs, Tokyo, Japan, under the title *The Hungarian Revolution of 1956*. The author of *Hungary in the Late Eighteenth Century: The Decline of Enlightened Dispotism*, Professor Király has also published in various learned and popular magazines.

Preface

Ferenc Deák was a towering figure in the Habsburg Empire of the nineteenth century. In keeping with his stature, the Hungarian, and to a lesser extent the German, literature on him is extensive and varied. It would be idle to expect a short English biography of him to add much new data to what is already known to those who read Hungarian. Yet a few new facts were found in Vienna in the *Haus-, Hof- und Staatsarchiv* and, surprisingly, in the *Kriegsarchiv*.

Regardless of any new information, every author interprets his subject his own way; so does the writer of this work. It is meant to fill a gap for the English-speaking reader. The only other English biography of Deák, which is amazingly accurate in many respects, is both incomplete and very dated: *Francis Deák, Hungarian Statesman: A Memoir* by Florence Foster-Arnold (London: 1880).

Since the great majority of the documents, memoirs, and studies quoted in this book are in Hungarian or German, complete footnote references to them for English readers would be pedantic. Only the most important sources and a scattering of secondary material are therefore mentioned in the footnotes, the Hungarian ones in abbreviated form. The abbreviations are explained in the Selected Bibliography.

The map shows all the counties and other self-governing territories of the Kingdom of Hungary in detail. It was planned by the author, and the cartographic work was executed by Edward J. Krasnoborski of the United States Military Academy at West Point, N.Y. As he has for all my other English publications, Peter J. Beales favored me with what is most needed by those who write in other than their native tongues: he revised style. To both gentlemen I am grateful.

Warm thanks are due to my friend and colleague Hans L. Trefousse, Professor of History at Brooklyn College and chief editor of this series, for his invitation to write the biography. It was completed on the ninety-eighth anniversary of Ferenc Deák's death.

This study was made possible by grants from the American Philosophical Society and the Research Foundation of the City University of New York. Without their help it may never have been completed.

BÉLA K. KIRÁLY

Highland Lakes, N. J.

Chronology

1665   Mihály Deák (Ferenc's great-great-grandfather) ennobled by Leopold I, December 22.

1792– Francis I.
1835

1803   Ferenc Deák born in Söjtör (Zala county), October 17.

1808   Death of father; ward of his brother Antal and sister Klára in Kehida (Zala county).

1808– Elementary school in Kőszeg.
1811

1811– Secondary education (at Keszthely Premonstratensian
1817   Gymnasium, 1811–12; at Pápa Benedictine Gymnasium, 1812–13; at Nagykanizsa Piarist Gymnasium, 1813–17).

1811– Last Hungarian diet of the Napoleonic era, August 29–
1812   June 1.

1817– Law school in Győr.
1821

1820   Revolutionary spasm through Europe.

1821   Troppau Protocol, Congress of Laibach (Ljubljana).

1821   Watched Győr County Assembly defy absolutism, November.

1821   Declared of age, December 17.

1822– Articled in Pest, November 16, 1822–December 19, 1823,
1823   Established lifelong friendship with Mihály Vörösmarty.

1823   Called to the bar, December 19.

1823   Watched Zala County Assembly challenge absolutism, December 23.

1824   Honorary deputy public attorney, August 29.

1824– Notary to the Zala County Committee for Orphans, De-
1832   cember 13, 1824–March 26, 1832.

1825   Honorary public attorney, June 6.

1825– First Hungarian diet of the pre-revolutionary era, Septem-
1827   ber 11, 1825–August 18, 1827.

1829 Zala county magistrate.

1829– Appointed to defend József Babics against charges of
1831 highway robbery and murder, September 10, 1829–January 28, 1831.

1830 July revolution in Paris.

1830 Publication of István Széchenyi's *Hitel* ("Credit") opens Reform Era.

1830 Diet in session, September 8–December 20.

1830– Insurrection in Russian-controlled [Congress] Poland,
1831 November 1830–September 1831.

1831 "Plague" revolt in northern Hungary (Slovakia).

1832 Deputy high sheriff surrogate of Zala county, November 5.

1832– Diet in session, December 16, 1832–May 2, 1836.
1836

1833 Elected junior deputy to the diet for Zala county, April 15.

1833 Established lifelong friendship with Ferenc Kölcsey.

1834 Senior deputy to the diet for Zala county, April 1.

1835– Ferdinand I (V of Hungary).
1848

1835 Political trials of Wesselényi, Kossuth, and Youth of the Diet.

1836 Report on the diet to Zala County Assembly, June 22.

1836 Recognized as leader of the liberal opposition. Elected honorary magistrate by several counties.

1837 Deputy high sheriff of Zala county.

1838 Memorandum demanding freedom of expression and assembly circulated by Zala county throughout Hungary, written by Deák, April 15.

1839– Diet in session, June 6, 1839–May 13, 1840; Deák senior
1840 deputy for Zala county and leader of the liberal opposition.

1839 Honorary member of the Hungarian Royal Academy of Sciences, November 21.

1840 Secret negotiations with Vienna's agent in March lead to first "compromise" by which political prisoners are released on April 29.

1840 Report on the diet to Zala County Assembly, July 27.

1840 Elected honorary magistrate by 23 counties.

Chronology

1841   Liberal daily *Pesti Hírlap* launched by Lajos Kossuth, January 2.

1841–   Diet Committee on Reform of the Criminal Code in ses-
1843   sion, December 1, 1841–March 19, 1843; Prof. E. J. Mitter-maier of Heidelberg cooperates with Deák in drafting recommendations.

1842   Death of Antal Deák, June 20; Ferenc emancipates his serfs and takes over management of family estate until 1854.

1843   Diet committee's Minority Reports completed, March 15.

1843   Bloody election campaign in Zala county returns Deák as senior deputy; Deák turns down "blood-stained" mandate and refuses to attend diet, even though no substitute elected.

1843–   Diet in session, May 18, 1843–November 13, 1844.
1844

1844   Delegation of liberal lgeislators visits Deák in Kehida where he heals liberal rifts, June 4–5.

1844   Kolovrat imposes despotic new regime on Hungary, November.

1845   Deák leads county resistance to absolutism; his move to organize pro-regime reform party turned down.

1845   Speech supporting Kossuth's "Protection Association," February 9.

1846   Conservative Progressive Party founded, November.

1847   Liberal "Opposition Circle" founded, January.

1847   "Statement of the Opposition" published, June 5.

1847–   Last feudal diet in session, November 12, 1847–April 11,
1848   1848; Deák elected senior deputy for Zala county but refuses mandate.

1848   Revolution in Paris, February 24.

1848   Kossuth calls in diet for radical reforms, March 3.

1848   Revolution in Vienna, March 13.

1848   Revolution in Pest, March 15.

1848   Batthyány appointed prime minister of Hungary, March 17.

1848   Deák reaches Pozsony; acceptance of ministry of justice, March 20.

1848   Batthyány ministry installed, April 7.

1848– First popularly elected Parliament in session, July 5,
1849 1848–August 11, 1849; Deák member for Zala county.

1848 Draft compromise with Croats endorsed by Batthyány
ministry, August 27.

1848 In Vienna with Batthyány seeking settlement with the
royal court, end of August.

1848 Batthyány ministry resigns, September 10.

1848 Jelačić crosses Drava and invades Hungary, September 11.

1848 Parliament begins debate on Deák's agrarian reform bill,
September 15.

1848 "Not for a single hour could I identify myself with the
court's policy," Deák writes to brother-in-law, September 22.

1848 Ferdinand abdicates; Francis Joseph proclaimed emperor,
December 2.

1848 Parliamentary peace delegation to Austrian supreme commander fails in mission, late December.

1849 Deák returns to Kehida, January.

1849 Hungarian army lays down its arms at Világos, August 13.

1849– Deák under investigation by military tribunal in Pécs,
1850 December 1849–May 1850.

1850 Turns down invitation to take part in Imperial Legal
Committee, April 25.

1850– Passive resistance.
1860

1854 Kehida estate purchased by Széchenyi, July 31; Deák
moves permanently to Hotel Angol Királynő, Pest.

1859 Battle of Magenta, June 4.

1859 Battle of Solferino, June 24.

1859 Laxenburg Manifesto, July 15.

1859 Protestant Patent, September 1.

1860 Suicide of Széchenyi, April 7.

1860 October Diploma, October 20.

1861 Deák takes part in the Lord Chief Justice's conference,
January 23–February 26, cooperating with regime for
first time since 1848.

1861 February Patent, February 26.

1861 First post-revolutionary Parliament in session, April–

August; Deák member for Central Pest and leader of the Party of Petition.

1861   First petition presented to Parliament, May 13; passed by Lower House, June 5.

1861   Francis Joseph rejects amended petition, July 8.

1861   Second draft petition passed by Lower House.

1861   Beginning of provisional neo-absolutist regime and renewed passive resistance August 22.

1862– Conservatives' efforts to reach settlement with court fail.
1864

1865   Publication of Prof. Wenzel Lustkandl's pamphlet attacking Deák's role in 1861; publication of Deák's response in *Budapesti Szemle*; press polemics triggered by exchange.

1865   "Easter Article" published April 16, and "May Program" in series of articles in *Debatte* during May.

1865– Second post-revolutionary Parliament in session, Decem-
1868   ber 10, 1865–December 1868; Deák member for Central Pest and sole leader of the liberals.

1866   Advises Parliament March 3 to elect Committee of Sixty-Seven which in turn elects Committee of Fifteen to prepare Compromise with the dynasty; both committees dominated by Deák.

1866   Outbreak of Austro-Prussian war, June 17.

1866   Battle of Custozza, June 24.

1866   Draft of Compromise endorsed by Committee of Fifteen, June 24.

1866   Parliament adjourned, June 25.

1866   Battle of Königgrätz (Sadova), July 3.

1866   Assures Francis Joseph Hungary will not increase demands following the defeat at Königgrätz, July 19.

1867– Ministry of Gyula Andrássy, February 7, 1867–November
1871   14, 1871.

1867   Compromise codified as Act XII, May 29.

1867   Francis Joseph crowned king of Hungary, June 8.

1868   First defeat in Parliament by his own party during budget debate on question of subsidizing the Hungarian and Serbian national theaters.

1869– Third post-revolutionary Parliament in session, April

1872   1869–April 16, 1872; Deák member for Central Pest.
1869   Health begins to deteriorate rapidly.
1869   Second parliamentary defeat on question of modernizing judiciary, July 8.
1870   Parliamentary defeat of his candidate for Hungarian state comptroller.
1871   Death of József Eötvös, February 2.
1871   Boldizsár Horváth, a loyal supporter, resigns ministry of justice, May.
1871   His foe Menyhért Lónyay succeeds Andrássy as prime minister, November.
1871–   Ministry of Menyhért Lónyay, November 14, 1871–De-
1872   cember 4, 1872.
1872–   Fourth post-revolutionary Parliament in session, Septem-
1875   ber 1872–May 1875; Deák member for Central Pest.
1872–   Ministry of József Szlávy, December 4, 1872–March 21,
1874   1874.
1873   Last major speech in Parliament on subject of church-state relations, June 28.
1874–   Ministry of István Bitto, March 21, 1874–March 2, 1875.
1875
1875   Fusion of the Deák and Left Center Parties into the Parliamentary Liberal Party; Deák nominal first member but without influence.
1875   Ministry of Béla Wenckheim, March 2–October 20.
1875–   Ministry of Kálmán Tisza, October 20, 1875–March 19,
1890   1890.
1875   Elected member for Central Pest for the last time.
1876   Death on January 28.
1876   Memorial to him codified as Act III/1876, February 24.

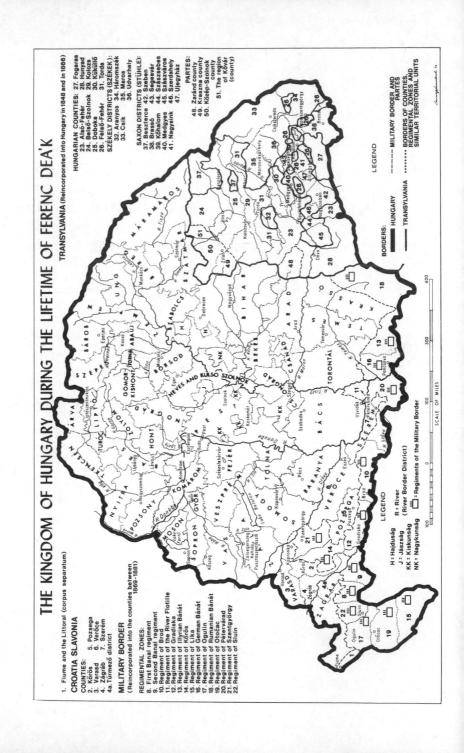

THE KINGDOM OF HUNGARY DURING THE LIFETIME OF FERENC DEÁK

CHAPTER 1

The Young County Gentleman

I *Overview*

FERENC Deák died in Pest on January 28, 1876. Although he had been a nonpracticing Catholic, it was the Roman Catholic Primate of Hungary who officiated at his funeral. On February 3, a cold, foggy winter's day, Deák, followed by hundreds of thousands of mourners, was laid to rest with such pomp and ceremony as had never before been seen in Hungary.[1]

Seldom had there lived a Hungarian so widely respected in his own lifetime or whose counsel had been so carefully heeded. Most of Deák's biographers attribute his unsurpassed esteem to his extraordinary success in negotiating and drafting the Compromise of 1867; his accomplishments when younger had been lost to memory, overwhelmed by the magnitude of his later triumphs. But in fact, the fame of the maker of the Compromise was rooted in his achievements before 1848. His place in history would be assured as much by the progressive legislation he sponsored as by the pact of 1867.

Three vignettes of different stages of Deák's life point to the essence of his statesmanship. One is his maiden speech in the Lower House of the Hungarian Diet, another is his last major speech in Parliament in 1873, and in between is his own assessment of the Compromise at the end of the year of its promulgation. Vignettes may not always be enlightening in an historical essay because they highlight a colorful salient point, while history and human affairs are a continuum mostly in shades of gray. But they are well suited to an introduction to a man like Deák, in whose statesmanship they reveal certain unchanging qualities—qualities so ingrained that he was often accused, and probably correctly, of being too legalistic, too dogmatic, too inflexible.

Deák entered national politics on May 1, 1833, when he first took his seat in the Lower House as a deputy for Zala county. On his second day there, disregarding what has become a modern convention that freshmen be seen and not heard, he asked for the floor. The diet record reads: "Ferenc Deák referred to the custom ... of flogging village headmen as a punishment and demanded that the communes be stripped of their authority to punish village headmen and vineyard wardens by flogging or any other means."[2]

It is characteristic that Deák's first intervention in the national legislature should have been an effort to move the law in a liberal, humane direction. His request was a call to abolish a feudal relic, the right of administrative bodies to order corporal punishment and mete out sentences. He wanted the rights restricted to legally constituted courts. He thus set the precedent he was to follow as a legislator. At this time, anticipating the revolution of 1848[3], he earned a national reputation as a reformer by backing, sponsoring, and drafting proposals and legislation to grant freedom and equality to all religious denominations without exception, to establish the supremacy of the legislative over the executive, to abolish the entail system (the greatest obstacle to the country's economic advance), to secure the freedoms of assembly, expression, and the press, to separate church and state, to overhaul the criminal code and the judicial system, and to emancipate the serfs and endow them with as much land as possible.

Deák, then, was a liberal reformer. His speeches, his legislative drafts, his moral standards and behavior were all based on the four pillars of liberal thought: the stern moral standards of the ancient Hebrews, the Hellenistic tradition of free speculation and beauty for beauty's sake, the Roman respect for the rule of law, and Christian teaching of the brotherhood of men, classes, races, and nations. Deák must have been happy to have lived in an age when these concepts were still the foundation of the value judgments of many, himself included.

Deák's philosophy and basic political ideas were relatively constant, unlike his energy and will to engage in political activities. The latter ebbed and flowed. In the realities of political life, he suffered several sharp setbacks. He was often morbidly pessimistic, and he put off necessary decisions, a quality that earned him the nickname of *Fabius Cunctator*. He would present a pitiful sight, sitting idle in his none too splendid country house, puffing on his pipes, while others were bursting with plans for action. He was often sickly and rarely out of debt until 1854 when he sold his lands. Yet basically he was a contented man, and his satisfaction reached its peak in 1867 with the promulgation of the Compromise. On December 17 of that year, when the effects of that settlement were already beginning to be felt, he spoke to a delegation of citizens from Hungary's twin capital city, Pest and Buda:

It may be stated that never since the disaster of Mohács have the lands of the Crown of St. Stephen been so united as they are now. It may be stated that never in the reign of the Habsburg dynasty has such trust existed between king and nation. It may be stated that never before has there been so little division and bitterness between Austria and Hungary. It may be stated that the foreign capital that used to be reluctant even to approach the border is now pouring into the country much more plenteously and readily. Our people are skillful and talented enough to use it for the good of the country. . . .

If we wanted to overturn all this, then we must strike at its root, the Compromise, and it will probably all come to an end.[4]

Deák always gave the impression of saying only what he believed to be true, and this statement most likely reflects his actual feelings. Convinced of so much, he must have been experiencing an immense sense of fulfillment. He had achieved a lifelong ambition: a truly self-governing Hungary was a fact, and fundamental laws embodying his ideas had been promulgated. Yet, for Deák, the settlement with the dynasty was not an end in itself; it was rather a means to enable him to get back to work on the new laws that were still needed to complete what the liberals of Hungary's great Reform Era (1830–48) had begun. In December 1868, at the conclusion of the epochal Parliament of 1865–68, Deák said: "Our work is not yet finished . . . Our program cannot but be to uphold the fundamental laws we have just created, to advance our constitutional life and institutions, and to promote the nation's economic and spiritual interests while safeguarding the people's rights and full equality before the law."[5] In short, Deák looked to fashion a democratic government and society out of the classic liberal form of government established in 1867.

The passage of progressive laws was still Deák's prime concern when he delivered his last major speech in Parliament on June 28, 1873. By chance the members were debating church-state relations. In the spirit of the liberals' program, Deák advocated the separation of the two. He likewise criticized the Hungarian system in which the prelates of the Roman Catholic and Orthodox churches were *ex officio* members of the House of Lords.

If we want to establish the equality of the rights of all churches and we want to do so on the basis of common sense, this anomaly, this discrimination, cannot be continued. There are two roads open to us: either to extend those privileges to all churches or to remove them from all of them. . . . Both the Protestants and the Jews would be grateful and would appreciate such an act. . . .

Our agenda include reform of the House of Lords and in that context it would be appropriate to announce that no one should sit in the legislature as a lawmaker by virtue of his office, including bishops and county high sheriffs. If the House of Lords is to be reformed so that its members are elected or appointed, or some combination of the two, then those who will have the right to elect or appoint should be permitted, if they wish to name a bishop, to do so, or a superintendent, or a rabbi, or anyone else, but he would sit as an elected or appointed peer of the land.[6]

The circle was complete. Deák's active political life came to a close on June 28, 1873, when as a seventy-year-old elder statesman he stood on the rostrum of the Lower House of Parliament and delivered an address that was in perfect harmony with what he had first said as a freshman forty years earlier. Both speeches were keyed to the ideas of liberalism. Indeed, the most constant feature of the whole of Deák's career was his unflagging effort to implant liberalism in semifeudal Hungary by peaceful means—through legislation. His first English biographer, Florence Foster-Arnold, was essentially correct in saying: "Deák . . . was no cosmopolitan; his life was spent in and for Hungary; he was a genuine Magyar character, in another light than that which we are accustomed to associate with the 'nation of hussars.' . . . And yet whoever has looked closely into the deeds and words of Francis Deák will allow that there was nothing provincial in this Hungarian politician, who was cast in the same metal of which some of the world's heroes have been made."[7]

II *Early Life: 1803–33*

Ferenc Deák was born at Söjtör, Zala county, on October 17, 1803.[8] His birth came at a time when the precarious European peace established by the Treaties of Lunéville (1801) and Amiens (1802) was already falling to pieces. Napoleon had invaded Hanover, the German state ruled by the King of England, and had massed at Boulogne the Grand Army, the most magnificent armed force he ever commanded. Before Deák was a year old, a process had begun, inspired by Napoleon, that was to eliminate Habsburg power in Germany. It began with the fading away of the Holy Roman Empire and Francis I's proclamation of the Austrian Empire in August 1804. It was to be completed in 1866, during the turmoil which culminated in one of the greatest achievements of Deák's life, the Compromise of 1867.

At the time of Deák's birth, relations between the Hungarians and the Habsburg dynasty were peaceful, as they had been ever since the crisis of 1790.[9] The outward sign of this internal peace was the free functioning of the two focal institutions of the Hungarian gentry's power: their domination of country administration went unchallenged, and, more significantly, the Habsburg kings regularly summoned Hungary's national diet.[10]

Such was the situation in Habsburg Hungary when Ferenc Deák was born. He was the fourth generation of the noble branch of his family. Leopold I (1657–1705) had granted a patent of gentility to Mihály Deák, a colonel of the hussars, and his younger brother Péter, a legal scholar, on December 22, 1665, for loyalty to the crown. It was a time when Hungarian opposition to absolutism was growing almost daily, and an anti-Habsburg Fronde known as the Wesselényi Conspiracy was taking shape. Yet, despite the unrest and the widening rift between the

Hungarians and the throne, the Deáks had remained true to the dynasty, a family characteristic that was long to endure.

Péter was Ferenc's great-grandfather. His son Gábor added to the family's prestige and wealth by marrying Anna Hertelendy, the rich heiress of another gentry family. Their son, Ferenc senior, did the same by marrying the daughter of the deputy high sheriff of Győr county, Erzsébet Sibrik of Szarvaskend. Ferenc junior was the youngest of six children, four of whom grew to maturity: Antal, Józéfa (who married József Kiss of Nemeskér), Klára (who married József Oszterhuber-Tarányi), and Ferenc himself.

Deák's mother Erzsébet died in giving birth to him. His father was inconsolable and could not even bear to lay eyes on the infant. The baby was put in the care of his uncle József Deák, the squire of Zala-Tárnok, who hired a wet nurse to look after him. His older sister Klára would anxiously visit him there and one day, finding him infested with lice, took him back home with her and thereafter brought him up virtually as her own child.[11] Since his father found living in the same house where his wife had died intolerable, the family soon moved to Kehida, where the Deáks had another home. There on January 25, 1808, Ferenc Senior died and Antal, young Ferenc's senior by fourteen years, became the child's guardian. A relationship developed among the brothers and sister that would delight a psychiatrist, were enough details available. Hated by his father, Ferenc was adored by his sister-mother and his older brother, and all three of them remained linked by the closest bonds of affection to the end of their lives. After their father's death, Antal and Ferenc did not divide the estate as was customary; instead it was run as a single joint estate. They lived under the same roof, and neither of them ever married.[12]

It is a valid question what Ferenc Deák's relationship was with women. So little information is to be found, however, that it is an unrewarding inquiry. Lajos Kossuth took a political approach to Deák's capacity to love and hate. It hardly illumines Deák's relations with women but it is an interesting starting point, for he was above all a political animal. Deák, Kossuth wrote, "could get along with everybody both to the right and to the left. Such a character has always been blessed and is a valuable substitute for intellectual responsibility in public life. Yet, since he hates no one, whoever has such a nature cannot love anyone either."[13] Was Kossuth right? Was Deák incapable of loving? Deák once confessed to his lifelong friend, the poet Mihály Vörösmarty, that on one occasion he had nearly fallen in love but he had been able to "reason" how to end the affair in time and never become emotionally attached to any woman seriously.[14] This womanless man of great physical strength and personal charm, who loved company and cherished above all the time he spent with his own family, has remained a puzzle to his biographers. Amazingly, he was only twenty-three when he wrote to Vörösmarty with such finality about never becoming involved with a woman and yet he kept to this for the whole of his life. Károly Eötvös, a contemporary biographer who left no stone unturned in investigating Deák's relations with women, came up with nothing positive. He speculated that two reasons may have persuaded Deák not to bind himself to a woman. One was to evade the constant machinations of the Austrian secret police who could have done him much damage if he had been compromised in an affair with a woman. He wanted to avoid any association that might have influenced him to abandon his political goals. There could certainly have been some truth to this during the diet of 1832–36 when a group of the most beautiful ladies of Pozsony, the seat of the diet, made a concerted but unsuccessful effort to capture Deák's fancy. The Austrian secret police kept voluminous dossiers on everyone of interest to the the regime in which were recorded even the most trivial personal data. Deák was among those under the closest surveillance. Exhaustive search through the dossiers failed to uncover any hint of an unconventional relation between Deák and any woman or of any other exceptionable feature of his life.[15] It is out of the question that anything that could have been used to blacken Deák would not have been reported in the secret police files.

Eötvös's second reason is far more speculative. He suggested that Deák may have fallen in love with a woman who was either already married or whose rank and social station were too much above his own. Of this there is no evidence at all, so one is left with nothing more reliable than anecdotes about Deák. These do, however, often contain Deák's own answers to serious questions.

Deák, for instance, used to spend several weeks every summer either at Balatonfüred, one of the loveliest watering places in Hungary, or at the Bohemian spa of Marienbad. One summer a group of politicians were taking their ease at Balatonfüred and lightheartedly discussing whether marriage was sensible. Unable to agree, they sought out Deák to decide the issue. "With the same solemnity you put the question to me," he told them, "I answer: Honest men marry, wise ones don't."[16]

In 1868 after a banquet in honor of Deák's sixty-fifth birthday, a group of friends and admirers escorted him back to his suite at the Hotel Angol Királynő in Pest. At the door he turned and said in farewell: "See, had I been married, I would now have been welcomed by some old crone, probably in her night clothes. What sort of pleasure could she have given me? And for that matter, what joy could I have brought her?"

The cynicism of such quips could be taken as a cover for bitterness rather than evidence of felicity, and indication that he was disillusioned by his state and missed the warmth of a woman's love.[17] Yet Kossuth went so far as to imply that Deák was incapable of deep feelings for anyone at all. In this he was wrong. Deák was devoted to his brother Antal and, after his death in 1842, turned these feelings to his brother-in-law József Oszterhuber-Tarányi, who returned them in kind. Deák evinced an extraordinary depth of friendship for the poet Vörösmarty and, after he died in 1855, for the poet's son Béla, who was Deák's godson. He was close friends with the liberal statesman Baron Miklós Wesselényi, the jurist László Szalay, the politician Antal Csengery, and others. These relationships were based on complete mutual trust and shared ideals, on a man's respect and appreciation of the talent and character of another. Only in one case is it unclear what the elements were in Deák's association with another man. Practically nothing is known about the character, ideas, or abilities of Deák's companion of perhaps longest standing, Count János Mikes.[18] Mikes took up residence in a back room of Deák's suite at the Hotel Angol Királynő when Deák first moved there in 1854 and stayed until the very end. It was he who

kept watch at the bedside when Deák lay dying and who closed
his eyelids when he breathed his last. Who was this man? What
was the source of the unparalleled bond between the two men
is one of the unsolved mysteries of Deák's affective associations
with other people.

Ferenc Deák was given the thorough education that was
usual for the sons of the gentry in early nineteenth-century
Hungary. By that time, a substantial number of the common
folk were also literate. For there were 9,717 teaching clergy and
lay instructors for Hungary's 11,367,000 people (excluding the
population of Transylvania). If private tutors are included, the
number would be in excess of 10,000. That is, there was one
teacher for every 1,140 inhabitants, a fairly high ratio for an
agrarian country at that period.[19]

Deák's schooling began under a private tutor, a Franciscan
friar. In the fall of 1808, after his father's death, he started
regular elementary education at a church school in Kőszeg. From
there he went on to church schools in Keszthely and Pápa, and
graduated from the gymnasium in Nagykanizsa in 1817. He was
thus in school when Napoleon's Italian army advanced into
western Hungary in 1809, and he probably saw units of it marching through Kőszeg. It is also likely that he was well aware of the
excitement caused by Napoleon's Proclamation to the Hungarian
Nation of May 13, 1809. His brother Antal, meanwhile, as a
captain of the noble levy,[20] took part in the Battle of Győr,
where the Hungarian irregulars were mauled by Napoleon's
troops. Deák's family was thus personally involved in the quixotic
and ill-starred final appearance in battle of the feudal levy of
the Hungarian nobility.

From 1817 to 1821 he attended the Royal Law Academy at
Győr. He was by then fluent in German and Latin, both of
which remained working languages for him as well as Hungarian.[21] The school records do not indicate that he was especially
industrious but show that he excelled at history and constitutional
law, both of which interested him greatly. He was characterized
by his power of retention rather than his diligence. He was
known for his good humor but not as a sportsman, and even

less as a dancer,[22] for even in his youth he was thickset and not very agile. His oratorical talents, on the other hand, were highly esteemed early on, and he was his school's first choice for a speaker whenever the occasion arose.

He finished his law studies in August 1821 and on December 17 of that year Zala County Assembly declared him legally of age, and as his very first act as his own man, Deák emancipated his former wet nurse from all servile obligations and dues.[23] In November 1822 he left his home in Kehida to become articled in Pest. He passed his bar examinations with distinction on December 19, 1823. Only twenty years old, he had completed all the educational requirements to go into law practice or to start a political, administrative career.

During the years that Deák was in school the alliance between the dynasty and the Hungarian gentry had been breaking down. It had worked well from 1790 to 1811, both sides keeping their part of the bargain. The monarch had convoked the Hungarian diet regularly: it sat five times between 1795 and 1811. The gentry had drafted one million peasant youths as cannon fodder for the Habsburg army and had squeezed thirty million florins out of the serfs as Hungary's contribution to the war effort. But tension between the dynasty and the Hungarians began to mount.

Even during the Napoleonic wars it had become clear that the Habsburg government was tolerating Hungarian constitutional government simply as an expedient to strengthen its military potential. Once the imminent danger receded, the dynasty reverted to its customary absolutist, centralist, Germanizing policies. The antagonism surfaced as early as 1810. As soon as Francis I became Napoleon's father-in-law and the immediate threat from France was past, his despotism began to show itself. In Hungary, reaction did not even wait till 1815 as it did in the rest of Europe. The diet was prorogued by Francis on July 1, 1812. It was the last Hungarian diet of the Napoleonic period, for no new session convened for a decade and a half. This absolutism was much resented by the counties of Hungary and met with continual resistance. In the meanwhile the court was more than doubling Hungary's taxes,[24] and to collect them, it had to send in a massive number of troops. As the empire's

domestic difficulties increased and European revolutionary sentiment showed itself much less ready to subside than was anticipated, the dynasty was forced to have second thoughts about
taking such a hard line in Hungarian affairs.

Gradually the Metternichian system's grip on Hungary was
eased, and the counties' resistance increased at the same pace.
By the time Ferenc Deák was a young man, the Hungarian
counties were opposing the regime vigorously. One of the
revelations to the political tyro was the county system's potential
for resisting tyranny, for it had already shown that it could
challenge Metternichianism with success and was to score a
major political victory over absolutism at the diet of 1825–27.
During this period of Deák's life, three factors profoundly
influenced his thinking and the course of his future career.[25]

First, while still at the Royal Law Academy, he watched the
Győr County Assembly refuse to execute an unconstitutional
royal decree.[26] It is interesting to note that the first recorded
political experience of this champion of law and order was to
break the academy's rules by attending sessions of the county
assembly. He went in defiance of a typical repressive absolutist
regulation that forbade students to attend any political gathering,
including official meetings of the county assembly. For a law
student the assembly's action must have been an eye-opener.
Even more significant, he was back home in Zala county before
he began his articles when the county assembly twice defied Metternichian absolutism. On both occasions the local gentry mounted
an outspoken opposition campaign and gave the regime a very
hard time.

The second influential factor was Deák's adored brother
Antal, who was the leader of Zala county's constitutionalist opposition to Habsburg absolutism. Ferenc in fact grew up with
a family tradition of resisting despotism regardless of loyalty
to the dynasty. The third factor was that his home was in Zala
county, one of the bellwether Hungarian counties in challenging
absolutism and demanding a return to constitutionality.

Zala County Assembly's two acts of defiance were directly
related to the European troubles of 1820–21. The Habsburg
government wanted to use its subjects' resources for the suppression of others. In April 1821, after conferring in Laibach

with his fellow monarchs on the suppression of European revolution, Francis issued an order to the Hungarian counties to conscript 35,000 recruits for the army and another one to raise new taxes. Both measures were prerogatives of the Hungarian diet, not of the king. Antal Deák at once began a campaign in Zala against the ordinances, arguing that, since they were unconstitutional, not only did the county have a right but also a duty not to comply. Very soon a second rescript reached Zala, ordering the county to execute the Laibach decrees forthwith. On November 21, Ferenc Deák witnessed the meeting of the county assembly at which it defied the second command. Its stand made a lasting impression on him.

Faced with continuing opposition, the court threatened force. Antal Deák spearheaded the county's counterthreat that, if force were used, all the local officials would resign so there would be no one to implement the king's orders. At first Francis suspended the county's autonomy, but in due course he had to allow the county assembly to convene again. Ferenc Deák was again present at its dramatic session on December 23, 1823, just four days after he had passed his bar examinations. Under his brother's leadership, the assembly refused even to discuss the royal decrees. It solemnly denounced them as unconstitutional and ordered its resolution to this effect to be made known to all the other counties of Hungary. Antal Deák's reputation became known throughout the country and Zala county's steadfast resistance set a pattern that was followed elsewhere.

Metternich was at a loss to know how to deal with the tide of opposition. There were, in fact, only two alternatives. The opposition could be crushed by military force, but only at the risk of rekindling the Italians' barely suppressed revolt and possibly fanning German discontent into open rebellion. Even at this period, news traveled across Europe fast, and events were becoming increasingly interdependent. The other alternative was to compromise with the Hungarian estates by reestablishing Hungary's constitutional feudal government. The Habsburg government opted for the latter course and to that end summoned a new diet in the belief that a pacified Hungary could become a dynastic power base rather than a powder keg.

On August 9, 1824, a new royal commissioner, Count Imre

Batthyány, appeared before the Zala County Assembly. He was charged with making peace between the crown and the estates. If he were successful in Zala, it was hoped that the rest of the country would follow suit. Batthyány accomplished his mission, and soon thereafter the election campaign for the diet of 1825–27 was in full swing everywhere. It was to reestablish constitutional government in Hungary. What no one could foresee was that Hungary's Reform Era would gradually take shape in its wake.[27]

It was the reconciliation with the Zala County Assembly that brought Ferenc Deák into his first public office. He was appointed as a gesture of recognition that his brother had changed from a leader of resistance to the crown into an official loyal to the dynasty. Ferenc Deák's career began at a moment when the power of the counties and constitutionalism had just defeated absolutism, at a moment when the crown and the estates were extending the hand of friendship to each other. Its beginning was also associated with convoking the diet and reestablishing the rule of law, two subjects that were to dominate the rest of Deák's life.

When Deák took up his office in 1824, he was already a cultured young man.[28] He had a good and substantial education, sophistication acquired during his years in Pest, Hungary's cultural center, and very close connections with the leading cultural organizations and intellectuals of his day. The most important of the latter were his association with the *Auróra* Circle, the meeting place of Hungary's most progressive thinkers, and his lifelong friendship with the country's foremost intellectual, Mihály Vörösmarty.[29] This friendship contributed much to Deák's intellectual development.

Of Deák, Vörösmarty wrote to Baron Miklós Wesselényi: "The existence of such a man is very necessary, not just for the sake of the country, but also so that in our hours of misfortune we may not forget the claim that man was created in God's image."[30]

These are the words of a poet, but Vörösmarty was also a liberal intellectual whose judgment, poetic or not, was shared by many. There was another reason, too, for his high esteem of Deák. Many members of the Hungarian gentry in the early nineteenth century were still very unsophisticated, uncivilized, narrow-minded, stubborn, ruthless, coarse, and provincial rustics. Deák, though he was a typical county man in the early stages of his career, was an exception—one of a group of progressive, liberal men who cared about the deprived mass of people and looked for reform.

The gentry's commitment to reform or reaction was a determining factor in Hungary's policies in this period. In fact it became the backbone of the struggle against the dynasty's absolutist rule. The lesser nobility, the third estate, was extremely numerous in Hungary. In 1840 there were 500,000 lesser nobles in Hungary in a population of 11,367,091. This meant that there was one nobleman for every 20 commoners, while in Bohemia the ratio was one to 828, in German Austria one to 350, in Lombardy-Venetia one to 300, and in Galicia one to 68. Political power in the county administrations and the Lower House of the diet was supposed to be shared among Hungary's huge third estate, but in practice this was very seldom so. It was exercised almost exclusively by the upper stratum of the lesser nobility, the gentry.[31]

Only a few of these families lived in each county, and they supplied the top county officials and the deputies to the diets. These families had medium-sized estates with several tenant villages and some thousands of serfs. The Deáks owned 1,238 yokes (approximately 1,220 acres) of arable land. Typical gentry, their menfolk had high county offices and deputation to the diet open to them.

The county office Ferenc Deák held longest was that of notary to the County Committee for Orphans, to which he was elected on December 13, 1824. During his seven and a half years' tenure, though unpaid, he performed numerous acts of goodwill for Zala's waifs. On April 24, 1829, he was elected county magistrate, another honorary office.[32] It was at this time that the Babics case occurred. Remembered by most of his biographers because the summation he made at Babics's trial was his first public speech to have survived in full, it afforded a glimpse of the philosophy of young Deák, the county official. The speech, it has often been remarked, points up Deák's humane qualities, but even more, it is a kind of ideological confession.

Deák was to defend József Babics, who had been charged with highway robbery, murder, and various related crimes. To appreciate what Deák said in his defense, it has to be understood that the County Court was a typical feudal institution, staffed entirely by gentry with legal training, for prosecuting commoners facing criminal charges. It was, in effect, an instrument of the lesser nobility's self-defense against the serfs, who were utterly exposed, particularly in this court, to their superiors' whims. Deák never accepted jurorship in the County Court, probably for that very reason.[33] Moreover, the organs of the county, including the court, functioned as a springboard for young members of the gentry who aspired to the highest national offices. There was no other channel open to them. If a young gentleman could pass the critical scrutiny of his peers, he could hope to be delegated by the county assembly as a deputy to the national diet, where he might try his luck in national affairs. Yet, even as a deputy, he was subject to his county peers' control, because he entered the diet with strict voting instructions. If he ignored these he could be recalled immediately, and his career would be at an end. The county administration, in short, could make or break a young man's career. Under such circumstances, it would not have been surprising if Deák with his political ambitions had tried to cater to the feudal minds of the court in the Babics case. But the path of least resistance was not his.[34]

Two points in his defense summation stand out. He questioned the capital sentence that was mandatory for highway robbery and murder. Aware of the limits of institutional authority, he realized that a criminal court exists to enforce the law, not to reform it. He did not therefore call explicitly for the abolition of the death penalty, but clearly stated which circumstances he considered warranted it and which did not. In what amounted to a spirited attack on capital punishment itself, he reminded the court that a law could not be all-encompassing and take into account all a criminal's motives and circumstances, which were what doomed or acquitted him. The immanent shortcomings of the law, he pleaded, had to be supplemented by the heart and humanity of the judge. The death penalty was warranted, in his view, only when the accused was incorrigible beyond shadow of doubt: "The purpose of the death sentence must not be

vengeance, for vengeance is a cruel impulse and true juris-
prudence must not give in to such an impulse. The death sentence,
after all, offers no compensation: the life of the murder victim
cannot be restored by any sentence or cruelty."

Deák made much of the fact that his client had repented,
had made a convincing pledge that he would mend his ways,
and therefore deserved to be spared.

Apart from this legal philosophy that evinces an attitude of
humanity rarely found in the early nineteenth century, Deák
made a second point of far greater significance to his future
political career. The gentry might easily have forgiven him as a
naïve idealist, a dreamer, while he was philosophizing about the
nature of capital punishment, but it was scarcely ready for what
was to come. With extraordinary diligence he pressed his
argument for something akin to an environmental and social
inquiry into József Babics's life, an idea that was well ahead of
his time. In his effort to save Babics, Deák pointed the finger
of accusation at the gentry and feudal society. Babics, he told
the court, had been born in a village with neither a place of
worship nor a school, a village never visited in all the years
he had lived there by priest, minister, or teacher. So poor were his
parents that they could not afford to send him to school elsewhere,
so he had remained completely uneducated through no fault
of his own. The blame was society's. Babics was apprenticed to
a herdsman, who happened also to be a highwayman. Criminals,
Deák claimed, did not tolerate innocence, so the hapless youth
was threatened, browbeaten, and ridiculed until he became the
highway gang's accomplice. It was, he said, Babics's environment,
his helpless social condition, his abject poverty that made him
a murderer, not natural evil.

Deák's passionate plea was in vain. Babics was sentenced on
January 28, 1831, to be broken on the wheel "as punishment
for his crimes and as a deterrent to others." The sentence was
modified on appeal to execution on the block, and finally the
Supreme Court of Justice on March 11, 1834, ordered Babics
hanged. The sentence was duly carried out. Deák had acted as
Babics's defense only in the court of the first instance, and his
effort was a failure. What else could it have been? But it did
show Deák to be completely uncompromising where he saw his

basic ideals at issue. Refusal to compromise was the key to the real Deák. The great paradox of his life is that although he was the maker of the Compromise of 1867,[35] he was totally unyielding on every basic moral, social and constitutional issue. In his defense of József Babics, as in other cases he handled, and whenever his counsel was sought, Deák strove for justice, pure and simple. Respect for the law he considered the backbone of society, and he bent all his efforts to encourage obedience to it.

The Babics trial was toward the end of Deák's career in the Zala county administration. In time he reached the top of the ladder of county offices, and on November 5, 1832, he was elected deputy high sheriff surrogate.[36] Before this position became permanent, his county career—and the first phase of his political life—was brought to an end by his election on April 15, 1833, as a deputy to the diet. From that day to the end of his life the Hungarian legislature became his sole preoccupation.

Deák's election to the national diet was founded on his services to his native county. At that time Hungary's fifty-odd counties engaged in a lively correspondence as they prepared common actions against Habsburg absolutism, coordinated their legislative drafts, exchanged views on matters of the moment, and kept each other informed about their officials' activities. So Ferenc Deák's name was not unknown around the country when he entered the diet.

The counties were the cornerstone of feudal constitutionalism in Hungary, and their importance cannot be overestimated.[37] "The county system has long been one of the most beautiful jewels of Hungary's constitution. It is an ancient institution, just as our constitution is. Both have evolved out of our national life. That is why the one like the other has been fashioned through the ages in harmony with the evolution of the very life of the nation."[38] So wrote Deák. Indeed no Hungarian institution was more independent of Habsburg power. It was within this remarkable institution that Ferenc Deák received his practical training in politics and refined his skills. The counties' traditional emphasis on constitutional rule taught him the power of law. The gentry's domination of the counties and the counties' control over the diet taught him the political realities of the country.

Deák became keenly aware that nineteenth-century Hungary would proceed along the road of reform only at the pace the Hungarian gentry saw fit. The deep roots he struck in county administration during his ten years in Zala made Deák a practitioner of *Realpolitik*, a statesman who refrained throughout his political life from overzealously soliciting support for his plans. He always went to pains to sound out the gentry to see what it was ready to accept, and by so determining what political goals were realistic, he generally managed to carry them through. For his tactics he has been compared to Fabius Cunctator. But the comparison is really fair, for in Rome's struggle against Hannibal, Fabius was not a loser.

CHAPTER 2

Leader of the Liberals
The Reform Diet of 1832–36

FIVE years after he began working in the administration of Zala county, Ferenc Deák was elected county magistrate, a coveted honorary office that involved the holder in a wide range of administrative, judicial, and police duties. On June 1, 1829, he was also sworn in as a county judge,[1] thus nearing the pinnacle of the career to which the gentry could aspire in local administration.

In July 1830 revolution broke out in Paris, and the political and social upheaval that followed was felt as far east as Poland and Hungary. It shook Hungarian society and had a notable effect on Deák. It was the same year that Count István Széchenyi published his momentous treatise *Credit*,[2] the fountain of Hungarian liberalism, just as elections to what was promised to be a reform diet returned Ferenc's brother Antal to the national legislature for the second time. By the time the diet sat, from September 8 to December 20, 1830, the alarm caused by the shock waves from Paris buried all thought of reform. The diet hastily crowned Francis's son Ferdinand king of Hungary, passed the most pressing items of legislation, and rose after receiving a royal promise that a real reform diet would be summoned within a year. The dynasty, however, had achieved its objective: while the Bourbons were being overthrown in Paris, the Hungarians had demonstrated their loyalty by crowning the Habsburg heir. Almost on the eve of adjournment the November Insurrection erupted in Poland, and the flame of revolution cast its shadows over the Carpathians. The Polish refugees fleeing into Hungary brought with them the plague, and in the wake of the epidemic that swept over northern Hungary the peasants of the area rose in revolt.

37

It was a typical peasant uprising, disorganized and lacking central leadership, operational knowledge, and modern arms. There was no concerted action, only outbreaks of local violence. With nothing but makeshift weapons, most of the peasants were content to exact vengeance on their own landlords; few collaborated with neighboring communities. The organized military forces of the state had no difficulty in putting the rebellion down, terrorizing the peasants into submission.

The nobility drew certain conclusions from the disaster. Conservatives became more reactionary out of fear and came to believe that the answer to future peasant discontent was to strengthen their own privileges and tighten control over the serfs. The liberals, of course, thought otherwise. They became even more convinced that their reform plans were urgently needed to head off further unrest. They had also been persuaded by the Polish experience that the nobility could not struggle for national independence with the millstone of a bound peasantry about its neck. The pre-condition for a fight for independence was cooperation with the peasants, and the price of that cooperation was thoroughgoing reform of the peasants' status in society. In this spirit the counties began discussing reform projects for the forthcoming diet.

As the progressive gentry became more vocal with its reform ideas in the county assemblies, the government began to retreat from its earlier, more tolerant stance, and Prince von Metternich warned the Hungarians: "I hold the dam in my hand. I shall let the flood overwhelm you. I shall let the peasants strike you down."[3] The court was well aware that the potential for peasant unrest all over Europe was a curb on the reformist estates. The regime used a similiar kind of pressure against the Galician Polish gentry in 1846.[4]

The Hungarian diet that was convoked for 1832 was destined to be one of the longest on record and the first national legislative body in which Deák would be involved. On January 24, 1833, his brother Antal resigned as the senior deputy for Zala. Before taking his leave, Antal suggested to the county that it should elect his younger brother to take his place. This smacks of nepotism, to be sure, but the top officeholders in the county, including its nominees to the diet, were after all drawn from the narrow circle of the gentry, and Ferenc Deák's stature in Zala made him a very likely candidate. Besides, Antal was convinced that his brother would go far. When friends tried to persuade him to retract his resignation, he wrote: "I shall send in my place a young man in whose little finger are hidden more talent and knowledge than in my entire being."[5] This may not have been the only reason, however. It is quite possible that Antal had decided that the management of their joint estate could not be left to Ferenc. When Antal was home, he ran it very well and enjoyed doing so. When he was away, it was left to Ferenc, who simply could not be bothered with such routine cares. Even as a schoolboy Ferenc had been lazy about his class work and, instead of using his notebook, would scribble jottings on scraps of paper. He would then lose them, and most of his reviewing had been done from notes and textbooks borrowed from his classmates.[6] Later, during his work in the county administration all the detail work had been done for him by the regular staff: all he had to do was make the decisions. His attitude toward farming was the same, and in consequence things became very neglected. So behind all the idealistic interpretations of why Antal stood down from the diet in favor of his younger brother may have been far less altruistic facts of economic necessity. Antal's proposal was accepted by the County Assembly, and Ferenc was sent to the diet. He arrived in Pozsony to take his seat on April 24, 1833, while Antal hurried back to Kehida to straighten out whatever mess had been left there.

The decade from the mid-1830's into the 1840's, when Deák first entered the national political arena, was a critical period for feudalism in Hungary. Hungary was in a state of political domination and economic subjection by a foreign dynasty; with an agrarian problem linked to the pauperization of the serfs, a faltering agricultural revolution, and scant industrialization; and with improverished estates, especially the gentry to which Deák belonged. A series of measures relegated Hungary to be a raw-material producer and a market for finished goods from the more industrialized Habsburg provinces such as Lower Austria and Bohemia. While Cis-Leithanian[7] industry flourished, Hungarian craftsmen were put out of business and remained unemployed because of the low level of industrialization in Hungary. On top of this were the devaluations of 1811 and 1816, the compulsory redemption of Habsburg bonds which imposed on agrarian Hungary a burden almost as great as that shouldered by the industrial Cis-Leithanian provinces, and the protection of Cis-Leithanian moneylenders' interests in Hungary against inflation and devaluation at the expense of the Hungarians.

The one relief in an otherwise bleak picture was provided by inchoate agricultural revolution and small-scale manufacturing, but even these were very limited. In the 1830's some aristocratic families (the Károlyi, Eszterházy, Festetics, Batthyány, Andrássy, Schönborn, and a few others) began introducing changes on their lands. They did away with the *corvée* and started hiring labor; they separated the lord's pasturage from the serfs'; they drained marshlands and irrigated grazing lands; they used systematic fertilization; they replaced free-range cattle breeding with stabling for their herds; they revised their crop rotation; they began training their bailiffs, putting up better buildings, and mechanizing their farms. As a result there was an increase in their production of potatoes, tobacco, maize, and sugar beet. Twenty new sugar mills started operation and there began to be a need for factory hands. The Cis-Leithanian provinces were too occupied with their own mechanization to supply all Hungary's light industrial needs, so local plants began manufacturing simple farm machinery. By the 1840's Hungarian demand had become so large that mass production and repair facilities had to be built. The big factories of the Röck, Schlick, Ganz, and Vidacs companies came into being. A new, highly mechanized paper industry was founded, and several flour mills were opened. Yet Hungary still lagged behind the industrial standards of the Cis-Leithanian provinces. Of all the capitalized manufactures of the Habsburg lands in the 1840's, only 10.5% were produced in the lands of St. Stephen's Crown. Fifteen times more steam engines were in use in Austria than in Hungary, although an embryonic industrialization was on its way in Hungary.

Gradual industrialization brought with it the same social changes that accompanied industrial revolution elsewhere. A proto-working class slowly took shape. The number of skilled workers increased by 136% between 1828 and 1846; during the same period the unskilled labor force increased in strength from 63,500 men to 150,000. Urbanization began at the same time. The population of major towns like Debrecen, Miskolc, Szabadka, Temesvár, and Kassa grew by 70% to 100%. The number of inhabitants of Pest rose from 32,000 in 1787 to 110,500 in 1848. The slow accumulation of domestic capital made a modern credit system both possible and necessary. Credit legislation was passed in 1840, and the following year the Hungarian Bank of Commerce was founded in Pest. By the early 1840's 32 steamships were sailing on the Danube, and the first railroads connected Pest and Vác and Pest and Szolnok. Though this development was hampered by Hungary's feudal institutions, it also eroded them and so contributed to the growing tensions in Hungary's feudal social structure. These are, then, the economic factors which contributed to the dynamism of the first decade of Deák's career in national politics.

The agenda of the diet Deák first attended included a program of substantial reforms. The order in which the recommendations, which appeared as royal propositions, were listed in the agenda showed which ones the throne attributed most importance to and which it hoped would become law. Reform of serfdom headed the list. The draft, which provided for the serfs' economic betterment, included no measures to improve their political or social lot. Improving their economic conditions was of interest to the dynasty for several reasons. The peasants in the Cis-Leithanian lands were already better off than those in Hungary, and the reform aimed to close the gap. The court hoped that such a reform would enhance the government's standing among the serfs because credit would go to the government rather than to the estates. And of course, if the serfs were better off, they would be able to provide more tax revenue.

The liberals in the diet, whom Deák now joined, certainly did not object to the government's intentions, but they wanted to go much further. The reformers wanted to introduce social, political, and judicial changes in the serfs' conditions as well. Not only would such reforms make the Hungarian peasants better off than those in the Cis-Leithanian provinces, they also ran counter to the government's social conservatism. The court was afraid that such a quantum jump in the Hungarian peasants' circumstances would trigger demands for similar reforms in all the Habsburg provinces and was ready to block all reforms in Hungary that had not already been granted in the Cis-Leithanian lands. The government and the liberal opposition were thus on a collision course. The floor leaders for the government were the Palatine in the House of Lords and the Speaker[8] in the Lower House, where, though the government's supporters were in the minority, they had the extra weight given them by the government's control of the offices of the house and the dynasty's prestige and power. They were more cohesive, better organized, and more highly disciplined than the liberals in the Lower House and posed a formidable challenge to their less coordinated opponents, whom they had been able to defeat more than once without the court's ponderous intervention. Yet, had they not had the backing of the crown, the officers of the government and the House of Lords in the diet of 1832–36—backing that occasionally even took the form of a royal veto—the liberals with their public support would have succeeded in turning the session into a momentously progressive one.

The liberals, led by Ferenc Deák's close friend Baron Miklós Wesselényi, attacked the draft on servile reform on the grounds that it tended to preserve the peasants' status rather than improve it, that it damaged rather than protected Hungary's economy, and that it hindered the building of a unified nation on a basis of equality of citizens' rights. The liberals sought to enlarge the scope of the draft fundamentally and, to facilitate this, they accepted all seven sections of the government bill with few amendments and tacked their own proposals on in condensed form as a single eighth section. This Section VIII was already drafted before Deák joined the diet. It contained all the social, political and judicial changes the liberals wanted: the right of the serfs to sell their plots of land and so secure freedom of movement; and compulsory, permanent settlement of their obligations to their lords under contracts that would permit the serfs to redeem them either with a lump-sum payment or through annual payments over a fixed term. The liberals wanted to make the serfs the owners of the land they worked. The jurisdiction of the manorial courts was to be sharply curtailed, so that the lords could no longer try cases to which they were a party, only cases between serfs. The serfs' personal and property rights would thus be embedded in the laws of Hungary.[9]

Ferenc Deák joined the Lower House of the diet on May 1, 1833, amidst these debates. He threw himself instantly into the debate on section VIII of the draft legislation. The enactment of this section would have realized all the liberals' wishes, but such a revolution by consent of the privileged aroused the ire and opposition not only of the throne, the lords, and government officials, but also of the conservative elements in the Lower House. Ferenc Deák argued that the changes were demanded by the laws of nature, that they were no favor or act of clemency but the redress of an injustice eight hundred years old. Spurred by Deák's eloquence and persuasiveness, the liberals managed to get the whole reform package through the unofficial session of the Lower House[10] at which the deputies discussed all matters before the diet in the absence of the court-appointed diet officers and agreed how they would vote on them in the official session. On July 16, 1833, the bill was presented in Latin and Hungarian to the official session of the Lower House,[11] which debated it and voted on it section by section.

Deák reminded the house—quite correctly—that the court's real intention in proposing to reform the serfs' economic circumstances was to increase its tax base, nothing else. What Deák wanted, he said, was "to right an 800-year-old wrong incorporated in our 800-year-old constitution."[12] "The freedom of the individual and the right to property," he declared, "are not privileges of the few but are primordial rights that may be demanded by all citizens, and our first obligation is to secure them for all citizens."[13] The conservatives answered that the provisions of the *Tripartitum* [the compendium of the rights of the nobility][14] stood for all time, so that the serfs could not be brought within its protection. Despite the conservatives' objections, the first section of the bill was adopted. It was the first substantial liberal victory, inspired by Deák.

During this debate an interesting feature of Deák's character came to the surface. He was not so much a man of creative or inventive mind, but rather a logical analyst. When and if an idea seemed to him logically serving general advance, his liberal convictions and his goals, he adopted it and promoted it with all his faculties. So when a proposition was presented in the diet that the right to own land be extended to all inhabitants, Deák promptly lent it his support. Denial of the peasants' right to property was one of the greatest obstacles to national progress and contrary to common justice, Deák said.[15]

The Lower House opened debate on Section VIII on September 21, 1833, and on November 19, 1833, a joint session of both houses passed the eight-section reform bill and sent it to the King for promulgation.[16]

It seemed that liberalism had won out in Hungary, and Deák had the lion's share in the victory. The bill emancipated the serfs and raised them to the status of full citizens, enabling them to own land freely and abolishing the basis of the feudal system. Francis now showed his true colors, demonstrating that his benevolence toward the serfs was no more genuine now in the 1830's than it had been in the past. The lords had in fact finally passed the bill on instructions from Francis so that he could veto it himself. He was not content simply to see social reforms frustrated but wanted to defeat them personally. Karl Friedrich von Kübeck, president of the Imperial Court Chamber in Vienna, recorded in his diary that when the topic came up Francis had literally shouted that he would put a stop to any attempt to change the Hungarian serfs' status. He would not have the Palatine waste the lords' time in opposing the Lower House's reform measure; "the Emperor in person will cut short any such projects...."[17]

For nine months nothing was heard. Then on August 30, 1834, the royal rescript reached Pozsony. In it Francis vetoed all provisions for social change, all political concessions, and the whole of Section VIII. Maria Theresa's *Urbarium*[18] and the Josephian reforms remained in force. The only substantive progress was a law on urbarial contracts that permitted the serfs to conclude irrevocable agreements with their lords "exclusively on their debts, services and tithes." It contained no provision for the serfs' compulsory manumission, however, nor did the contracts it referred to abolish their servile condition, as the liberals had wished.

Although the plenary session had endorsed the rescript, an unofficial session was called at Deák's insistence to discuss what could be done. On January 25, 1835, Deák introduced to the unofficial session a new draft to replace the vetoed Section VIII. It was a brilliant stroke. He picked up a sentence in the royal rescript in which Francis had stated his intention of protecting the serfs against arbitrary actions and a similar assurance in the address from the throne delivered at the opening of the diet. "Whatever the two branches of the legislative [crown and diet] agree on," Deák told the deputies, "is the common property of the people and our homeland shall never be deprived of it."[19] In this spirit Deák presented his draft amendment, which was inserted into the preamble of the new law on the serfs (Act X, 1836, Sect. 5): "In order that the serfs collectively and singly shall in every respect, and hence also in their relations with their lords, be free from any arbitrary treatment, and in order that they shall be free in their persons as well as in their properties, it is hereby decreed. . . ."[20]

This was no guarantee of an immediate improvement in the serfs' conditions, but it was a statement of principle with the force of law that really put the peasantry's social and political situation on the legislative agenda. It was a fillip that lifted the liberals' morale at a crucial moment and established Deák as a master among his peers. In fact, from that time until the adjournment of the diet, all the diet papers, minutes, reports give evidence that Deák had been informally recognized as the leader of the Lower House of the Diet.[21] In reference to the success of Deák's amendment, Kossuth wrote: "So, out of the shipwreck of our high hopes, at least the sacred and glorious principle made it to shore."[22]

But the forces of reaction were gaining strength in the diet. The conservative deputies' tactics were to cause as much delay as possible while they were gathering their forces. The court's strategy was to muzzle the diet liberals by persuading the counties to change their original instructions to their delegates for more reactionary ones. For this purpose, the government in the fall of 1834 ordered all the county high sheriffs[23] to leave the House of Lords, where they sat by virtue of their office, and to return to their counties to organize conservative sentiment there. The most willing assistance in this grand design was rendered by the "slippered" nobles,[24] the impoverished majority of the lesser nobility. They gathered in strength at the county assemblies called by the high sheriffs in late 1834 and were instrumental in altering the instructions to the deputies of county after county. These new, retrospect instructions made the liberals' work in the diet ever harder. Deák complained in a letter to Wesselényi: "Our position becomes more difficult every day. Although our prospects were never splendid, we now shudder to see our hopes fade with every day."[25]

By the new year of 1835 reaction had most of Hungary under its sway. On March 2 Francis I died, but nothing changed with his son Ferdinand's ascent to the throne. To put teeth into the conservative threat, the new regime began a campaign of intimidation. The most celebrated instance was the trial of Miklós Wesselényi. A Transylvanian aristocrat, Wesselényi was a member of the Hungarian aristocracy by virtue of a small estate he owned in Hungary. At the opening of the diet of 1832–36, he was the most respected liberal leader. With the new turn of events he bent his every effort to turn back the tide of conservatism. For this reason, he and Kölcsey had hurried back to Szatmár county to try to persuade the county assembly to retract its new conservative instructions and go back to its earlier, liberal ones. The assembly met on December 9, 1834, and was addressed by both Kölcsey, who was born in Szatmár, and Wesselényi, whose Hungarian estate was there.

Wesselényi's speech was an impassioned one. At issue was the status of the serfs. He graphically described the misery of their condition and criticized a government that pretended to be their protector while really endeavoring to pit them against the nobility. He said this was why the court was misleading the estates into opposing reform of serfdom, and he called on the assembled nobles to defy the regime. He warned them that if they did not they would incur the wrath of an embittered peasantry, and even though the regime would suppress any revolt, "then woe betide our national independence!" His speech failed to move the assembly and Kölcsey resigned as the county's deputy rather than accept its new conservative instructions. "Kölcsey's loss is a very severe blow. No one could take his place," Deák wrote to Wesselényi.[26] Wesselényi for his pains was accused of *lèse majesté* and suffered prosecution, and subsequent imprisonment and great hardship.

The Wesselényi case became a *cause célèbre* between the liberals and the court-conservative alliance. Deák's part in it thrust him into greater prominence as a national leader of the liberals. Because of his close personal and political relationship with Wesselényi, Deák brought his considerable legal talents to bear in preparing his defense. Besides this, he also campaigned to convince his diet colleagues that the writ against Wesselényi was not a purely personal matter but also a natural issue. It was, Deák claimed, an unconstitutional violation of Wesselényi's freedom of expression, because he had made his statements at a constitutional meeting of a county assembly: "The county assembly is the institution that permits direct and personal participation in the legislative process and in administration through free expression by all those who enjoy that constitutional right."[27]

Deák vigorously denied that Wesselényi had offended the person of the king by his denunciation of the regime, as was charged. Criticism of the government in a constitutional system was inevitable, he said, and if it were illegal, then even orderly consultations on political questions would be impossible without the risk of *lèse majesté*.[28] In the spirit of the freedom of expression that he was defending, Deák himself drafted a "Petition of Grievances" for the diet to present to the king. The petition sought assurance that liberal principles would be respected and that Wesselényi's civil rights would be protected. Deák's purpose was to make of Wesselényi's trial a constitutional issue, and his work on the petition was an important step in his career as a codifier of laws and drafter of state documents.

The petition proved to be one of those defeats that seemed only to enhance Deák's prestige. Archduke Joseph, the Palatine, threatened to abdicate his office immediately if the diet endorsed Deák's petition. He also threatened to arraign anyone who infringed the law, just as had been done to Wesselényi, but many liberals ignored his warning. János Balogh, a deputy from Bars county, formally declared that he agreed with everything Wesselényi had said in the Szatmár county assembly; the court responded by charging him, too, with *lèse majesté*. Such a pitch did things reach that Deák began to fear that the diet would be dissolved before it could achieve anything meaningful on the serf issue, so he bowed to defeat and withdrew his peition. To ease tension further, he persuaded Balogh to withdraw temporarily from the diet on the excuse of having to visit his son, who happened to be ill. By taking the path of realism, Deák compromised none of his principles. He simply deferred direct action by the diet and thwarted the court's probable intention of dissolving it.

His next move was to try to mobilize public opinion in support of the liberals to strengthen his hand in pushing for reforms, especially reform of serfdom. Encouraged by him, Bars county published a circular denouncing Balogh's indictment as a "public grievance" and retained a lawyer to defend him at public expense. Both the county and Deák hammered away at the question of freedom of expression, a concept that found wide popular support. A royal decree was finally issued on October 31, 1835, annulling the charge against Balogh. This was no gesture of conciliation, however. The court merely wished to be rid of a highly sensitive and popular issue at a moment when it was having to deal with another, equally touchy problem.

The secret police had intercepted circulars sent out by Békés county to other Hungarian counties, appealing for support for a new draft bill on the redemption of serf obligations and the establishment of their personal and property rights. The government suspended the autonomy of Békés, placed it under a royal commissioner's administration, and denounced the circulars as incitement to subversion. "If even this is subversive incitement," Deák told the diet, "then the estates may as well put out their hands to be manacled individually and collectively, for there is scarcely a man among us who has not at some time spoken out on one problem or another equally or even more openly."[29] Feelings rapidly began to run high, and the two houses of the legislature exchanged several extraordinarily sharply worded messages. At the same time, in the absence of both Wesselényi and Kölcsey, Deák's stature as leader of the liberals grew.

With remarkable legal dexterity Deák was able in 1836 virtually to predetermine the amount of redemption the lords would be paid for serf holdings when the serfs were finally emancipated by the April Laws of 1848. This groundwork was laid in a bill on compensation for land expropriated for the construction of railroads, which was written by Deák and promulgated as Act XXV, 1836, Sect. 6.[30] The bill stipulated that for the railroads' right-of-way the landowners would receive only "the value of the servile payments and services" that they lost through the expropriation of their land and no other assessment. As a result, in 1848 the legislators' hands were tied, for it was not feasible to demand from the serfs a higher rate of reparation than the state itself had paid only twelve years previously.

The debate in the closing months of the long diet had brought Deák to the forefront of the liberal leadership where he now stood unchallenged. He was a veritable dynamo, exerting all his efforts to help the serfs and break the back of feudalism in Hungary. The supremacy of the Lower House over the House of Lords, the diet's independence from domination by the dynasty, the exclusion of royal appointees from the working committees of the Lower House to free them from executive tutelage—Deák subscribed to every such concept. He strove to increase the diet's control over the budget in order to end the medieval practice whereby the diet was obliged to vote tax revenues for the crown to spend as it saw fit. In this he had some measure of success by taking a leading part in the defeat of a government bill that would have enabled the crown to collect indefinitely the same amount of tax as the diet approved for the current year.

Deák's final success in the diet of 1832–36 was to extract concessions on the very sensitive legislative procedure of phrasing the adopted bills.[31] In the Middle Ages the members of the estates were an active part of the Hungarian production system and could not afford to be absent from their home districts for unlimited periods to attend the diets. For this reason medieval diets debated and adopted draft laws without taking time to attend to the fine points of legal wording. The final phrasing of adopted bills was entrusted to the king, on whose behalf the Royal Chancellery elaborated the final texts of laws for promulgation. This practice had survived under the Habsburg kings who often abused it by proclaiming laws, the texts of which differed in substance from what the diet had passed. The diets tried to obviate this by having the final texts of enacted laws drafted jointly by the Royal Chancellery and an *ad hoc* diet committee. Even this did not prevent the Habsburg kings from promulgating laws that contradicted the intent of the diet. Deák's sense of legality was outraged by the practice, and throughout the diet of 1832–36 he fought for repeal of the law which allowed it.

Despite the opposition of the Royal Chancellery, he eventually succeeded in getting through a bill that made the wording of the final text of adopted laws the prerogative of the diet without interference from the court. In cases where the two houses passed differently worded versions of the same bill, a joint committee elected by secret ballot produced the final text. This important legislative privilege was won for the diet by Deák almost single-handedly.

The liberals had no formal party organization, no discipline to ensure concerted action, no clear distinctions along party lines, no caucuses. Wesselényi had tried to introduce them and failed. Deák's leadership came not from consuming ambition or technical arrangements, but from the fact that, as the diet progressed, more and more deputies heeded him. In their efforts to defeat reform projects, the conservatives did their best to confuse men and issues, but the more confusion they generated, the more deputies listened to Deák, who had a remarkable facility for clarifying issues and suggesting the most rational solutions. Deák entered the diet skilled in county politicking and firm in his liberal beliefs; he ended it a statesman.

His experience in county administration had given him a good grasp of legal procedures and of all the problems—economic, social, and political—that the lesser nobility faced. He had a masterly knowledge of constitutional law, legal codification, and local government. He had made an exhaustive comparative study of Hungarian law and that of various Habsburg provinces, as well as of Prussian and French law. He was exceptionally well versed in the records of earlier diets. His personal philosophy was based on the concept of legality, and he was devoted to the highest ideals of the rights of men. He was convinced that for Hungary's prosperity political, social, and economic reform was necessary, and his sense of *Realpolitik* enabled him to construct a viable synthesis of liberal ideas and western models suited to Hungarian realities.

On May 2, 1836, after all the newly enacted laws had been promulgated, the diet was prorogued and Ferenc Deák returned to his home in Zala. Traveling home as he had come to the diet at his own expense, he turned down the spans of serfs on his route, a privilege of members of the diet. His efforts to improve the lot of the serfs in the legislature was matched by his small deeds.[32] On June 22 he presented to the county assembly a three-hour report[33] on the diet, which the following day was discussed paragraph by paragraph and unanimously approved. It included a polished definition of one of his cardinal principles: "Legality should be rigorously observed at all times in our commissions and our omissions: in our deeds so that the estates may adhere strictly to the law and do everything that is not against the law to promote progress; in our omissions so that we may not implement unlawful decrees."

Despite his acknowledged leadership of the liberal opposition, Deák was still at heart a county politician. He held to the traditional view of the counties as the guardians of Hungary's constitution. Although the concept had no basis in law, the counties considered themselves entitled to refuse to execute any royal decree that they believed clashed with pre-existing laws or the constitution. Deák considered this attitude a necessary defense against any resurgence of absolutism; other liberals rejected it as a shield for feudalism.

If future legislation were to be successful, he told the assembly, the forces of liberalism would have to overcome reaction by concentrating selectively on the most urgent reforms first. If too much were attempted at once, there was a risk that the reformers might be fragmented and achieve nothing. Aware of the strength of the forces of reaction, he noted: "Every step forward is a gain to him desirous of progress"—however small a step it might be.

Deák proposed a program, the most important point in which was to strive to enfranchise as large a segment as possible of those who still enjoyed no political rights. Moved by Deák's eloquence and logic, the estates promptly passed a resolution setting the aim of the county's future legislative initiatives:

"Representatives of the commoners should have the citizen's right to contribute to legislation." As he closed his report, Deák reminded the assembly: "Everything depends on us, on how we take advantage of present circumstances." As he had taken advantage of the spirit of the times to press for social reforms, so would he again in 1867 in negotiating the Compromise.

Deák's report reverberated across the country. The county assembly had it printed and mailed to the other counties of Hungary. Kossuth published extracts from it in his periodical *County Assembly Reports*,[34] until the latter was banned by the increasingly reactionary regime. The Hungarian Viceregal Council reprimanded Zala county for allowing the report to be published without prior clearance by the censor, who on government orders seized all available copies of it. The county in response rejected the reprimand, reaffirmed its satisfaction with Deák's report, and defended its publication as a manifestation of the freedom of expression. Not only in Zala but throughout the country Deák became the symbol of progressive ideas. According to Széchenyi, Deák's "preeminence was recognized on all sides." County after county followed the lead set by Borsod on August 29, 1835, and honored him by electing him a magistrate.

Deák did not court popularity, prestige, or influence. Had he done so his career would have been different. He was driven by his belief in the need for liberal reform, he fought for it, and he was repeatedly defeated. A self-seeking man could never have borne to expose himself to such failures for the sake of principles. There is little doubt that at this early stage Deák would have preferred to have led a quiet life in the country rather than be caught up in the hurly-burly of national politics. He indicated as much in a letter he wrote to Kossuth when reactionary ideas began to take root in Zala, which had been one of the most liberal counties:

You should not be too happy with Zala county and its assembly, my friend, for here too an army of hissing serpents have raised their heads at us. . . . I fear for the resolutions just passed because it takes so much less brain to stir up the blind and savage aristocracy than it does to still them. As for me personally, I do not care, I am even glad to some extent for all that has happened, because it gives me not only an excuse but also a right to retire to the solitude I so desire, should our ideas be defeated.[35]

Deák has been described as a clever tactician because, among other qualities, he never considered a case closed or an issue defeated for good if he believed in the justice of the cause. Whenever he was in difficulties and had to yield ground, he did so step by step, fighting all the way in an effort to exhaust his opposition and salvage whatever he could. He was always eager to hear the views of others, even of his opponents, and this enabled him to maintain his composure against all odds, however overwhelming. His way was never to humiliate another or force his ideas down another's throat. His diligence in attending all diet sessions and his performance at his first diet made it clear that his life was to be in national politics and legislation, he was to be a statesman in other words. Yet in his own eyes he was no more than a codifier of progressive laws.

CHAPTER 3

Deák's First Attempt at Compromise
The Reform Diet of 1839–40

DEÁK's complaint to Kossuth in September 1836 that "an army of hissing serpents have raised their heads at us," which meant that reactionary trends had gained more and more power in Zala county,[1] was in fact true as regards the central government also. On March 2, 1835, Ferdinand I (already crowned King of Hungary as Ferdinand V some four and a half years earlier) became Emperor of Austria. Since Ferdinand was epileptic and feeble in both mind and body, Francis on his deathbed had signed a testament naming a Council of Regency.[2] Its president was Archduke Ludwig; the other members were Archduke Franz Karl, Metternich, and his equally conservative archrival, the Bohemian Count Franz von Kolowrat. This arrangement ensured the preservation of the principle of primogeniture and also secured a new lease on life for Metternich's conservative system, for the Council, in principle, only advised Ferdinand; in fact it governed. The Council decided that an all-out offensive had to be conducted against the forces of progress in Hungary by means of censorship, secret police action, and the Roman Catholic Church. To inaugurate the new policies, on July 7, 1836 the highest officials of the Hungarian government were replaced by ultraconservatives.

Two months earlier several leaders of the fifteen-hundred Youth of the Diet, young noblemen chosen to accompany and serve the deputies, who attended the diet of 1832–36 had been arrested and, after a secret trial at which they were denied the benefit of legal counsel, were sentenced to long prison terms. Baron Miklós Wesselényi, who had first been arraigned on May 5, 1835, was indicted on May 2, 1836, immediately after the diet adjourned and his parliamentary immunity came to an

54

end. Deák drafted two petitions for Zala county, the second of
which was taken to Vienna on January 9, 1837, by a delegation
that he himself headed. Since the King refused to receive the
delegation and Deák refused to hand the protest to anyone else,
the delegation returned to Zala without accomplishing anything.
During the night of May 4–5, 1837, Lajos Kossuth was arrested
on a charge of publishing his *County Assembly Reports*.[3] His journal had been printing news of what the liberal reformers were
planning and doing in the county assemblies now that the diet
was over. The prosecution of Wesselényi and Kossuth kept
Hungary in uproar.

Zala now tried a new line of action to defend the freedoms
of assembly and expression and to secure the release of Wesselényi and Kossuth. A memorandum prepared by Deák on April 15,
1838, was sent to all the Hungarian counties. The embodiment
of Deák's policies, it stood firm on principles but also offered
to strike a compromise with the crown on practical matters
if a stop was put to violations of the law. It warned that political
trials undermined Hungary's constitutional liberties, and that
the appointment of commissioners to administer the counties and
the rejection of the counties' numerous petitions of grievances
to the crown were violations of the Hungarian constitution. Deák
explained that the court had nothing to fear from the Hungarian
estates. The accusations of stirring up revolution and colluding
with foreign powers against the dynasty were pure fabrications.
The estates, he said, were accused with overstepping their
privileges and demanding unconstitutional changes in the state's
economic and social organization. But what had they really
done? "Openly and constitutionally they have requested the
king to redress wrongs, and that is his duty. The nation treads
a constitutional path." The counties have openly discussed reform
projects, but the open discussion of changes is no violation of
the law. Rather, the violations were the unlawful acts instituted
by the regime. "What the counties have done was only a constitutional self-defense in reaction to the unlawful measures of
the government."[4]

To remedy the situation, Deák proposed the reestablishment
of sincerity and trust between king and nation, the redress of
constitutional grievances, the frank and open expression of

opinions by the king and Hungary to pave the way to cooperation, the setting aside of old grievances to foster cooperation,
and amnesty for all illegally condemned prisoners. His platform
boiled down to a plea for communication on the basis of the
crown's respect for the law and the nation's pledge to stop
its policy of endless petitioning and to start cooperating with
the King. Deák's memorandum did not lack backbone, however;
he emphasized that on the nation's fundamental liberties nothing
would be yielded. "If our request is again denied, we shall
stand by our rights and defy anything done against our laws
and rights. All such actions will be considered unlawful and so
not binding on us; they will be considered acts of violence. . . .
Whatever happens, we shall then continue the defiance we have
begun, and our belief in our inalienable rights, justice, and
innocence will not be shaken. We shall then look to the future
in numb silence, aware that force may crush our happiness but
cannot destroy our rights. We shall remain confident that under
any burden only our shoulders may bow but our souls will
never falter."

Throughout his career Deák believed there were only two
possibilities for relations between the court and the Hungarians.
Either the dynasty would respect Hungary's constitution and
laws, and reign accordingly, in which case Hungary would
remain loyal to the dynasty, or else Hungary's constitution and
laws would be suppressed, and the Hungarians would follow a
line of unyielding passive resistance. It was to be his belief
during the trials of the Bach era; it was his declared attitude in
1861 when the crown still refused to restore Hungary's constitutional rights; and it was the essence of his approach to the
Compromise of 1867.

When Deák drafted his memorandum in 1838, offering himself
as peacemaker between the crown and the nation, Hungary
may have been ready for a compromise, but the court was not.
The international dangers and internal upheavals of the "hungry
'40's" had yet to persuade the dynasty to countenance a compromise arranged by Ferenc Deák.

Instead of accepting Deák's proposal to negotiate on the basis
of the release of political prisoners, the Metternich-Kolowrat
government responded by pressing its case against Wesselényi.

The defense was ordered to present its arguments in writing to the District Court on August 21, 1838. The plea was framed by Deák, who contended that the suit was unconstitutional because it was taken out against a legislator during a session of the diet. Since the charge was based on a speech given before a properly constituted county assembly, there was no cause for indictment, let alone prosecution for *lèse majesté*. Wesselényi had criticized the government, not the King, in connection with a draft bill before the diet, and this could not be the grounds for any legal action. On February 1, 1839, the charge of *lèse majesté* was dropped, but Wesselényi still was sentenced to three years. On February 9 the Supreme Court of Appeal[5] confirmed his sentence. The government also pressed the case against Kossuth, who on February 23 was sentenced to three years by the District Court. On appeal, the Supreme Court increased his sentence to four years' imprisonment.

Just two days after Wesselényi was sentenced by the District Court, Deák sought an audience with the King, engaging his personal prestige in a second attempt to reach an accommodation with the court. He was received by Archduke Ludwig, then by Metternich and Kolowrat, and finally by Ferdinand himself. Deák wanted to calm the dynasty's dread of the possibility of revolution in Hungary. He stressed that no one in Hungary, apart from a few extremists, wanted any violence. As he was so often to do later, he pleaded for the dynasty to put its trust in Hungary. If the government would stop prosecuting Hungarians who were inspired only by a sense of patriotism, it could count on the Hungarians' loyalty. It must realize that only a handful of oligarchs wanted Hungary's medieval political and social system to continue unchanged; the rest of the nation desired fundamental reforms. It would be vastly to the crown's benefit to lean on this overwhelming majority rather than work through that minuscule oligarchic group. The implementation of liberal reforms would secure for the crown a government supported by a loyal majority. Deák assured them that if only the government would be open and straightforward in its dealings the dynasty could be sure of popular backing. The Hungarians, he said, were very apprehensive about the Russians' power, especially since the ruthless suppression of the November Insurrection in Poland.[6]

A little goodwill from the dynasty would allay the Hungarians' fears. Deák even offered to help organize a majority party to support the government if the court would sponsor liberal reforms of its constitutional, national, and economic policies at the next diet. If it did so, he added, Hungary would be the cornerstone of the Habsburg domains instead of a stumbling block. Finally, Deák begged for the release of Wesselényi, whose eye ailment had become so bad in prison that there was a risk he might lose his sight altogether.

Had Deák's earnest arguments been heeded, had the government possessed vision and foresight, a compromise between the Hungarians and the monarch might have been struck in February 1839, thus sparing the dynasty's subjects a great deal of distress. The Hungarians might then have turned their attention to settling problems with their national minorities instead of expending all their energies in fighting the court's threats to their national, constitutional, and individual freedoms.

Was Deák really the skilled politician he is reputed to have been if he honestly expected the court to listen to him? Széchenyi called him a politician who viewed the world from the window of Zala County Hall. There is little doubt that his outlook was still provincial, even naïve. He never really grasped international affairs, which frightened him. Yet they were the court's major concern. He could not understand how the government could be scared of gradual, peaceful change carried out according to liberal principles. The dynasty for its part, could not understand how Deák could be concerned exclusively with internal affairs when the Empire faced such serious problems in Europe. Hitherto Deák had never been west of Vienna. Széchenyi on the other hand knew England, France, Germany, and much of the rest of western Europe, as well as Greece and the Near East. Széchenyi was also more familiar with the Habsburg lands than Deák was and knew what the dynasty's primary concerns were. He may not have agreed, but he understood that the dynasty was unwilling to allow change for fear that a chain reaction could shake the Empire to its very foundations. It was incomprehensible to Deák how the King could flout a law he himself had promulgated and should be expected to uphold. In the 1830's, in fact, Deák was acting according to a very different set of precepts from the court.

It was hardly surprising, though it came as a shock to Deák, that the only result of his pleas was that Wesselényi was temporarily released to have his eyes treated. Unswayed, the regime pressed ahead with its political crackdown, including the sentencing of Kossuth. In the midst of the government's campaign, the royal summons was issued to assemble the diet on June 6, 1839. Repression, however, did not scare the Hungarians into silence; it fired them to apply as much pressure as they could against the government's policy. Counties that had been strongholds of reaction, such as Esztergom, the permanent seat of the Roman Catholic Primates of Hungary, and Heves, espoused the liberal cause. The counties' correspondence with each other dealt mainly now with suggestions for reforms. Meetings were held in clubs,[7] reading rooms, and social organizations to promote liberal ideas.

Many of the reform projects took the traditional form of grievance petitions to the crown, but more and more of them contained plans of an unquestionably liberal character. In the wake of the political trials the demand for freedom of expression grew, and more and more references were made to the governmental systems of western Europe. Széchenyi told the Pest County Assembly that freedom of the press was the foundation of national culture and progress. Deák expressed the same concept in a laconic statement: "Any press law needs but the promulgation of a single sentence: 'Do not lie.' "[8] There were appeals for an end to censorship. A popular idea was to form a national militia open to all to counterbalance the units of the standing army garrisoned in Hungary and to protect national independence. The presence of non-Hungarian troops on Hungarian soil and the use of Hungarian troops against the Italians were condemned. Political rights for the serfs and their representation in the diet, their right to own property, taxation of the nobility, equality for all before the law, emancipation of the serfs and the compulsory redemption of their obligations became increasingly popular themes. The main vehicle for these ideas were newspapers and magazines published in Hungary, which grew in number impressively during the first half of the century. Fifty-one different periodicals were published between 1801 and 1830, and 98 between 1831 and 1848; more specifically, in the year 1830, 23 were appearing regularly (10 in Hungarian, nine in German, three in Slavic, and one in Latin); by 1840, there were 54 (26 in Hungarian, 18 in German, six in Slavic, three in Romanian, and one in Latin).[9] The majority of these publications were progressive in outlook; subscriptions to the more conservative ones dwindled steadily. The liberal reformers, however, still had no properly constituted organization, and the liberal ferment tended to be local and uncoordinated, symptomatic of a general state of mind rather than indicative of vigorous concerted action.

Meanwhile, aware that the approach taken by Metternich and Kolowrat was achieving nothing positive, the government financed the formation of the Progressive Conservative Party[10] organized by Count Aurél Dessewffy. Its program called for the establishment of a credit bank with 100 million florins in state funds to issue loans to landowners, a modest redemption of servile obligations without actually abolishing the entail system, the extension of the vote to those intellectuals of non-noble birth[11] who had been in public service for a certain number of years, and the revocation of the privileges of nobles who had abused public office. Government support for the party was an acknowledgment that its inflexibly reactionary policies had to give way to some sort of modest reform program, but one initiated and controlled from above. The party's platform was intended to stabilize the social order, rather than effect meaningful change, and had very little to do with any sincere wish to improve general circumstances. The regime strove, not without success, to lure, bribe, and cajole the liberal right wing into the party. Yet the party did not become simply a tool of the government. It had a *raison d'être* of its own: to restore to the aristocracy its former political power.

Instructions were issued to the county high sheriffs to persuade the county assemblies to adopt conservative instructions for their deputies to the diet. Even Zala drafted conservative instructions that Deák found unacceptable. György Forintos, a poor local nobleman, tried to pack the county assembly with "slippered" nobles who would spike the liberals' guns. When finally the assembly was called to order, however, the 2,000 nobles present adopted a set of instructions that Deák could support, and on May 6, 1839, he was elected Zala's senior deputy by acclamation. The government's tactics, in fact, proved to have been, if anything, counterproductive and to have forced many liberals into more radical positions, much to Deák's distress.

The very idea of leaving home to attend the diet was painful to Deák. He loved the pleasures Kehida afforded. Nearly every day he had a dinner guest, most often the parish priest or his farm foreman, but his home was a favorite place to visit for many people, who especially enjoyed his endless fund of stories. Their earthy flavor and morals can be traced back to his childhood. By feudal tradition in Hungary the ownership of mills and butchers' shops had been a monopoly of landowners and, when Deák was a youngster, his family had owned several water mills. Deák had loved to stay around the millers and their apprentices and to mix with the peasants waiting for their grain to be ground. He would listen to their news and gossip, and, when these ran out, to the stories they told each other.[12] He was lucky because it was unusual for the children of gentry to be allowed to keep company with the peasantry. Thus he learned the peasants' way of thinking and their philosophy as expressed in their folktales in which justice was always done to the innocent. It may well be that the grounding of his tenacious belief in justice was laid while he was playing around these country folk. He had a good ear and an extraordinary memory for these moralities and became famous for quoting them throughout his life, whether to entertain, instruct, warn, or simply make a point.

Kehida was a place of complete relaxation for Deák, not work. True, he read whatever he could lay his hands on and kept up a diligent correspondence with friends everywhere, but his greatest delight was in handwork of all sorts. He was a keen gardener. He collected every kind of pipe not just to keep but also to use, for he was an inveterate smoker. But above all he enjoyed woodworking. He had his own workshop well equipped with tools where with considerable skill he would make furniture and household implements. He was fond of making figurines, canes, pipes, and ornamental articles as gifts for his guests.[13] It is not recorded how much they appreciated his "art" but much later, after he had become a national figure and had left Kehida, and his output had diminished because he could not take all his equipment with him to the Hotel Angol Királynő, it became highly prized.

In later years the place Deák most visited to relax was Zalaszentlászló, about twenty-five miles from Kehida, where his brother-in-law József Oszterhuber-Tarányi lived with his wife, Deák's "sister-mother" Klára. There was no diminution in her affection for Deák after her marriage, so that Zalaszentlászló became a second home to him.

Whenever Deák went to the capital or the diet in Pozsony, he always had a list of things not available in Zala to buy for his family and friends there. In addition he would show his love for Klára by sending her anything that caught his eye that he thought she would like, and so hats, fashionable accessories, seeds —things both useful and useless would come to her in a constant stream.[14]

Such was Deák's attachment to his family and home from which the diet would again cause him a long absence. He attended it out of a sense of duty, but that sense had always to be tempered by a belief that there was a reasonable chance of accomplishing at least part of what he wanted to do. Very much to the point, one of his contemporaries commented: "In Hungary there was no shortage of patriots, heroes, and martyrs like Batthyány [who was sentenced to death by an Austrian tribunal in 1849], Kossuth [who had to flee into exile in 1849 to save his life], or Teleki [who took his own life in despair in 1861]. But Deák was of another stripe. His goal was victory, not suffering."[15]

In the summer of 1839 Deák believed the liberals had a chance to realize part of their program, and so he went to Pozsony to take part in the diet.

The diet, when it assembled, turned out to be the first to be divided into groups along strictly ideological lines. The opposition liberals accepted Deák as their undisputed leader. The government's effort to consolidate the Progressive Conservative Party in the Lower House failed. In the House of Lords the liberals were led by Count Lajos Batthyány, and the government-sponsored Progressive Conservatives were headed by their party organizer, Count Aurél Dessewffy.

At thirty-six Deák was in his prime: experienced, trusted, vigorous, a motivating force not only for the liberals but for the whole Lower House, a man to be disregarded at one's peril. All during his political life, he respected existing laws, rules, and conventions, but he reached for modernity by aiming his ax at their medieval and feudal branches. The safeguarding of the constitutional roots of the land and their coordination with ideas of progress were the essence of liberal policy as represented by Deák.[16]

The diet opened at the height of the administrative despotism of Metternich and Kolowrat, but the formation of the Progressive Conservative Party was clear evidence that the Council of Regency was having second thoughts. The crown's legislative initiatives opened up the possibility of some sort of compromise by proposing that all petitions of grievance, old and new, should be taken up, that the strength of the standing army should not be increased, that the provisions and fodder that communities were required to supply to military garrisons[17] as well as the billeting of troops in Hungary (still the Habsburg logistical system in the absence of permanent barracks) should be brought under some sort of specific control to prevent abuses, and that the River Danube should be regulated. King Ferdinand himself opened the diet on June 6 and delivered his inaugural address not in Latin but in Hungarian—another conciliatory gesture.

The first item on the diet's agenda was a serious grievance, the Ráday case, a *cause célèbre* that helped to consolidate the liberals behind Deák. The liberal Gedeon Ráday had criticized the District Court for handing down unconstitutional sentences on the prosecuted Youth of the Diet and had presented to the Pest County Assembly a draft petition to the throne to remove the judges for exceeding their powers. A royal rescript issued on May 8, 1839, annulled Ráday's credentials, enjoined him from attending the diet, and ordered the county assembly to elect a new deputy.

Undismayed, Pest county refused to retreat and sent Ráday back to the diet, where he appealed for the legislature's protection. It also sent circulars to the other counties asking for their cooperation, though most of these missives were seized by the secret police. As soon as the diet convened for regular business, Pest county's junior deputy moved that the Lower House should take up no work as long as both Pest's deputies were not seated. Deák concurred in principle, but in order not to stop all meaningful activity he proposed that debate should begin on the proposals before the house but that no draft bills should be submitted to the throne until it had redressed all grievances, including the matter of Ráday. Deák was concerned not to give the King cause to prorogue the diet and return to undisguised absolutist ways in case tension should explode into violence. This would smash the movement for reform. He therefore decided on a tactical withdrawal in order to be able to advance further later. He persuaded Ráday to resign, and Pest elected another liberal in his place.

On October 31, 1839, the diet submitted a "petition of inquiry" to the King. It was based on Deák's interpretation of Act XIII, 1791, to the effect that all petitions of grievance had to be settled before the diet could begin discussion of the crown's legislative proposals. The House of Lords demurred, but after some hesitation passed the petition too. If the government wanted affirmative action on the budget and the draft, it had no choice but to concede. The crown assented to Deák's interpretation. In so doing it made an important change in Hungarian legislative procedure and gave Deák a significant parliamentary victory.

The diet then turned its attention to freedom of expression. "Freedom of expression," Deák told the deputies, "is the first condition for constitutional government, so our first obligation must be to defend it."[18] At issue was whether the executive branch of government and the person of the king were one and the same, in other words, whether criticism of the government was tantamount to an attack on the king's inviolability. This was the contention of the dynasty, the basis for Wesselényi's sentence, and the excuse for the prosecution of Ráday, Kossuth, and other liberals.

Deák claimed that the law had been violated when Kossuth was refused permission to conduct his own defense unless he remained in custody. He assailed the Supreme Court[19] for condemning the imprisoned Youth of the Diet for their part in founding clubs when no law forbade their action. Though no law gave the executive or the judiciary the right to censor private correspondence, Kossuth, he said, had been imprisoned for circulating in private letters speeches that had been delivered in properly constituted county assemblies. These cases, Deák declared, showed "how far the High Court has elevated itself above the legislature." He went on: "We face a situation in which the executive branch of government protects the judiciary, the judiciary protects the executive, and they both violate the law. We have no protection but the force of the law, which is not respected by either of the other branches. This is tyranny by both of them.

"In the past the country had the right to resist illegal acts by the crown.[20] The diet of 1687–88 renounced that privilege." The legislators of that day never dreamed that, once the privilege had been given up, the country would be forced into blind obedience to all the king's orders, even if they were against the law. Nor did they imagine that it would be forbidden to protest against such violations, Deák said. In place of that old right, it became established as a right that the counties could protest against illegal rescripts and petition the king for redress of their grievances.

The following day, prompted by Deák, the Lower House resolved that, notwithstanding the Upper House's view, the High Court had in fact violated the law and this was a grievance that the government had to redress.[21] At stake were freedom of expression, freedom of assembly, the inviolability of laws passed by the state's constitutional channels of legislation, the independence of the legislative from executive supervision and dictation, and the principle of the division of power and constitutional checks and balances. It was not a question of *Realpolitik* on which Deák could compromise; these were the very foundations of liberal government, and Deák would not yield an inch.

By the sixth month of the diet's session, there was no sign that the Lower House would give ground or that it would provide the regime with the money and the army recruits it needed until its main grievance, political persecution, was resolved. The liberals were confident of their strength and will. The regime was reluctant to push matters to the brink because neither internal nor external conditions warranted a return to absolutist repression. By the spring of 1840 the court was ready to compromise, and Deák was ready to make a third attempt to ar-

range it. Accepting an invitation to meet secretly with an agent
of the crown, some time during the second half of March 1840,
Deák stated the liberals' minimum conditions: the freeing of
the political prisoners, and a guarantee of the freedom of speech
and of the counties' autonomy. The agent assured Deák of the
regime's goodwill but made it understood that the crown could
not allow any change in the existing system of jurisdiction in
Hungary. Deák was invited to prepare a statement along these
lines, which the King would sign and send to the diet in the form
of a royal rescript. Deák felt he could not turn down this concession, limited as it was, and accepted. Twenty-four hours later
his draft was in the agent's hands, who rushed with it to Vienna.
The speed with which the court delivered Deák's draft in the
form of a royal rescript to the diet dramatized how urgent the
government felt it was to reach a compromise quickly. The
rescript reached the diet on March 24 and was read to both
houses the following day.

The script announced the king's intention to preserve freedom
of expression, as guaranteed under Hungary's ancient constitution, for the estates assembled in constitutionally established
bodies. Since it was the king's duty to rule, he reserved the right
to punish those who overstepped these bounds. The independence
of the judiciary had to be protected, both to maintain the
integrity of their offices and to uphold fundamental law. The
rescript ended by assuring the estates that they would not find
the sovereign reticent about exercising his prerogative to pardon.

Thus the first compromise reached under Deák's leadership
was neither a total victory for the crown nor a complete triumph
for the liberals, but then neither side could have expected it to be.
The liberals had realized their essential demands: the release
of those unjustly imprisoned, and the guarantee of freedom of
speech. The king, however, was not ready to yield to the legislature such slight control over the judiciary as would have been
implied by his accession to the demand to set aside unconstitutional sentences. This was the price the legislators would have
to pay if they wished to make good the two gains offered them.
It was steep, for with the antiquated judicial system unchanged,
repetitions of the Wesselényi, Kossuth, and Youth of the Diet
cases were possible. Deák contented himself with this compro-

mise for the moment, but he was never to forget those cases, which hung like a shadow over the liberals' meager gains. His more immediate problem, however, was how to make his own followers accept the rather tenuous bargain he had struck. He and his close associates had to use all of their persuasiveness to convince the majority of the liberals that they should endorse the royal rescript because it contained as much as they would get. It was not approved until it came up for a second vote. The Lower House then passed the tax and recruiting bills that the court wanted but limited their effect to the period from May 2, 1840, to May 2, 1843, in order to compel the king to call a new diet within the constitutional three years if he did not wish to run out of men and money.

On April 30, 1840, the diet received a royal rescript informing it that the political prisoners had been pardoned. Continuing in his role as peacemaker, Deák penned the text for the Palatine to read to a joint session of the legislature. In his text he omitted the word "pardoned" with its inevitable implication of guilt and announced simply that the prisoners were being released. The revised wording was read by the Palatine and published in the minutes of the diet, thus fulfilling the terms of the first compromise Deák concluded with the crown. All that was left for the Lower House to do was to act on a few smaller bills [excerpts].[22]

That the court was willing to concede the little it did in March was due in no small degree to the international situation. The Münchengrätz Convention of September 1833 had reaffirmed the Holy Alliance between Russia and the Habsburg Empire for the protection of their monarchs' divine rights; the following month Prussia, too, had subscribed to it. The convention also provided that, in the case of the likelihood of the dissolution of the Ottoman Empire, the signatory powers would act in concert. This possibility became a reality in July 1839 when Mohammed Ali and the Egyptians roundly defeated an attack by the Sultan's forces; for a while there seemed to be a real danger that the Ottoman Empire might fall. At the very time the Hungarian diet was heatedly debating the Ráday case, it looked as though the trouble in the Balkans might expand into a general war. For fear of Russian machinations, Metternich flirted briefly with France, Mohammed Ali's ally, despite the common interest of the Habsburg and the Romanov dynasties in preserving the status quo. The Ottoman crisis was at its height when the compromise of March 1840 was arranged, and it would not be too much to claim that, had it not been for the international situation, the Hungarians would probably have gained far less than they did, not unlike the relationship of the Compromise of 1867 to the defeat of the Habsburg forces at Königgrätz.

International crisis or not, the diet had to continue its work. The major bills it enacted were, of course, the budget and the draft, but it also chipped another piece away from the bastions of feudalism by permitting serfs to commute their obligations in perpetuity by mutual agreement with their lords, although it did not limit the lords' legal authority. Of greater significance were bills it passed liberalizing trade and commerce, freeing the financing of industrial enterprises from all restrictions, instituting an Austrian-type of credit system to facilitate purchasing, speeding the processing of suits against debtors, breaking the trade guilds' stranglehold on commerce, and regulating mercantile partnerships and corporations. The diet also improved conditions for Jews and passed a surprisingly progressive child labor bill that restricted the working hours of young people between the ages of 12 and 19 to nine a day and required them to be employed in healthy surroundings. Finally, the legislators adopted a measure that made Hungarian the official language of the state, a change that will be examined in greater detail later.

All this legislation was the outcome of the compromise between Deák and the regime's conservative forces, but it was also well in line with the liberals' policy on industrial development. It made notable inroads against the guilds and many other medieval, feudal restrictions, easing the way toward a *laissez-faire* economy. The gentry went far in dismantling their own privileges, even to the extent of permitting their property to be the object of suits for debt. The diet may not have achieved the liberals' every last dream, but it was a milestone of the Hungarian Reform Era.

The liberals' gratitude to Deák for his adroit leadership knew no bounds. On November 21, 1839, he was elected an honorary member of the Academy of Sciences, a position he was able to use to good effect during the Bach regime. On May 12, 1840, he was presented with a commemorative album bearing more than one thousand signatures, first among which was that of Count István Széchenyi. Several counties made Deák an honorary magistrate.[23]

Deák's legislative activities were conducted in the spirit of his own summation: "We can only survive if we are inspired by the great goals of humanity. Constitutionalism, popular education, political freedoms, these and similar concepts shall keep us going."[24] From other peoples' lips these words would sound like platitudes, but they were reinforced by Deák's disarming credibility and sincerity.

Zala called an extraordinary session of the county assembly on July 27, 1840, to hear its senior deputy's report on the diet. The minutes of that session read: "The estates expressed their complete and unreserved satisfaction with their deputies' actions. Ferenc Deák was given special acclaim for his exceptional talents, for his work for the benefit of the fatherland, and for conferring honor and prestige on his county before the whole nation."[25] The county set up a Ferenc Deák Fund. From the voluntary contributions 200 florins would be given every year to two youths, one noble and one a commoner, for their education. As long as he lived Deák could name the two recipients of the grants, and he was to be permitted to make his own arrangements for their award after his death.

Deák's "Report to the County Assembly"[26] was one of the most important documents he ever wrote. In it he embodied his philosophy, his sense of history, and his *Realpolitik*. Moreover, since he knew that it would be printed and circulated throughout the country, he included in it not only his own assessment of what had transpired during the diet but also his evaluation of what had yet to be achieved. It contained, in effect, the seeds of the liberals' program for continuing reform during the 1840s.

"The diet began work at a time of tribulation," Deák reported to his county peers. "Civil liberties were being violated, individual safety was threatened, and fellow citizens were being persecuted. There were moments when the enemy's strength grew and put into jeopardy not only our future progress but our present progress too. In these circumstances universal despair could be averted only by the justice of our cause and by the conviction that for a just cause one must put up a fight, even when there is no longer any hope of succeeding."²⁷ It was to this belief that Deák held even during the worst periods of the post-revolutionary despotism.

The lords, Deák said, had urged the Lower House to get on with passing new laws instead of dealing with petitions of grievance, "but violations of old laws could not be cured by passing new ones. Law restricts power, but the citizens are really seeking protection against tyranny by the law."

Deák noted that the most important element in the diet's act on the serfs was the provision for voluntary contracts of emancipation between the lords and either individual serfs or whole serf communities. "This law," he said, "involves no compulsion but it does away with a separating barrier. Its effects may be slow, but they will be sure, and its consequences will be great and irreversible. The law on manumission that the legislature has just passed has laid the foundation stone of one of society's most cherished qualities: freedom and the ownership of property. On this foundation a better future will be built. This law increases the number of those who may own property. The country can be strong only by virtue of such citizens, since freedom shared among many does not lose its value, but rather grows in strength and sureness."

Deák reported on the diet's efforts to relieve the oppressive conditions of the Jews. It was unjust that that sector of society which had fewest rights should have to bear the most burdens, in particular, that it should have to pay "toleration taxes" in addition to all the other taxes that everybody had to pay. Since the "toleration taxes" had no basis in law, they were arbitrary and objectionable. The diet considered it prejudicial that Jews should not have the rights of citizens. It therefore directed an Address to the Throne, emphasizing how unjust the situation was and listing the legal and political considerations that made an improvement necessary. The diet demanded a law that would do away with the "toleration taxes" and extend to the Jews all the rights enjoyed by gentile commoners.

The most significant provision of the act the diet passed was that which allowed Jews to settle without hindrance in the

Royal Free Boroughs. "We hope," Deák said, "that with the passage of time and easier circumstances the Jews will achieve what they have not yet been able to realize."

Deák also referred to the difference between the Habsburg system and other constitutional countries, that in the latter all national issues were discussed in the free press before they came up for legislative action. When the legislators took up a matter, every aspect of it had been discussed and explained and every shade of opinion had been heard. The nation's representatives were therefore able to adapt their actions to society's needs and the majority viewpoint. "Where there was no free press," Deák said, "the government and the legislators were groping in the dark, and one half of the country had no idea what the other half was thinking." This, he claimed, was the situation in Hungary. The next diet, Deák demanded, should pass a free press law that contains practical provisions to eliminate the numerous shortcomings in this area. The free press would then be the medium that would disseminate ideas of respect for the law and promote the progressive development of our country.

Deák was not complacent about his compromise with the dynasty. He concluded it to save the legislative process and to redress at least a few grievances, but the crown's decision not to permit any change in the Hungarian judicial system was a heavy price. No sooner had he bowed to the decision as inevitable for the time being than he turned his attention to the possibilities of effecting a change in Hungary's judiciary in the future in order to end its dependence on the will of the government. This was a major concern of his both before and during his tenure in the Ministry of Justice in 1848. Some of his concern was already clear in his "Report to the County Assembly." He stressed the need for general reform of criminal jurisdiction and for guarantees of citizens' freedoms in prosecutions for political crimes. He recalled that the King had given a pledge to respect *habeas corpus* and said that the legislative part of the King's pledge would be taken up by the next diet. His references to general criminal law reform were solidly based on liberal concepts. Existing criminal law, Deák said, was obsolete and insubstantial. In otherwise identical cases, the personality of different judges would lead to sharply dissimilar sentencing. The prisons were so bad they were a humanitarian outrage. "We have to confess with pain that in this country the jails are not places of rehabilitation but schools for crime," Deák said. In fact, up to 1849, besides his concern about the fate of the peasants, no other issue occupied a more prominent place in Deák's policies than his efforts to reform Hungary's judicial system. His role in the Babics case has already been discussed.[28] It showed the way he was going to take. The "Report to the County Assembly" reflected Deák's matured thoughts on the issue. His contribution to the labor of the diet committee on the reform of the judicial system of 1841–43[29] as well as his tenure as Minister of Justice in 1848 were the climax of this trend.[30]

The diet liberals, Deák said, had made proposals for the reform of education, but the crown had rejected them on the grounds that education had always been a royal prerogative. He found the crown's reaction unjust because the diet had been ready to vote taxes for educational reform, about which nothing had been done in the three years since the last diet.

It is imperative that the next diet should take the matter up again and apply itself tirelessly and resolutely to achieving whatever can be done by legislative action. . . . The noblest task is to educate the people. . . . Education makes men better and happier.

Deák concluded by calling for national unity and urging broad public debate of plans for reform.

Such was Deák's message to the nation. On it was built the decade of action that was to culminate in the revolution of 1848–49.

After Deák had delivered his report to Zala County Assembly, his supporters began a fund-raising drive for a torchlight parade in his honor. Within a few days they collected 3,000 florins. Deák was as dismayed at the idea of being publicly fêted as at the idea of spending so much money on flares and asked the organizers to abandon the project. They refused, forcing him to take another tack. "Wouldn't you feel ashamed to see such a large sum of money going up in smoke?" he asked them. "I have a better idea. I'll add a thousand florins of my own to your 3,000 and let's use the interest on 4,000 florins to put a poor youngster of talent through school." It was a proposal his liberal friends could not resist, and a scholarship fund was duly set up.[31]

CHAPTER 4

The Battle of the Pamphlets

FERENC Deák was not yet forty when the diet of 1839–40 was adjourned and he still had two-thirds of his life in national politics ahead of him. Yet he was already the leader of the liberals and laden with honors by his countrymen. He had audiences with the King to discuss domestic policies. He met for talks with the elder statesman of the age, Metternich. Every year he spent several weeks of the summer at Marienbad, one of Europe's most sophisticated spas, or at Balatonfüred, Hungary's most fashionable resort, and then returned to Kehida to dine with his farm foreman or the priest, chat with the villagers and play with their children. How did he look, this man who was at ease with the mightiest and the lowliest?

Ferenc Deák was neither imposing nor well groomed. He was short and burly and would comment deprecatingly about it. When a German lady had asked him as a young man to sign her autograph album, he had written:

> Kurz geschrieben, gut gemeint,
> Dicke Schrift, von dicken Freund
>
> [Briefly written, with good intent,
> Thick writing, from a fat friend.][1]

Both the self-derogating epithets were true. When he was young, his handwriting was atrocious, but with age it improved; his build was heavy, and with age got no better. But he was not flabby; rather he was muscular and stocky. Nevertheless, what struck people was not his physique so much as his eyes, which were generally described as hypnotic. It used to be said that with a look he could still an angry bull and quiet wild wolves. Such tales may be apocryphal but their popularity point to the power his contemporaries believed he had over others. There are also more likely accounts of how he could influence people. Bored by an adulator's prattle about how people were influenced by his clear, logical way of speaking, Deák cut him short: "Nonsense, my friend! My 'greatest achievement' of persuasion was not through logic but quite the opposite. Some supporters and opponents of the government were brawling ouside my office. They were waving big sticks, and it seemed to me it was only a question of time before they would be shedding blood, so I rushed out and shouted: 'Hey you, put those sticks down at once!' To my amazement, they all did except one defiant youngster. 'You heard me, lad. Drop it!' I yelled at him. 'Why should I?' he answered back. 'Why? Because a horsetail would look better in your hands than a stick.' He hesitated for a moment, then dropped the stick and the fight was over."[2]

The legal scholar László Szalay described Deák in a similar situation in the diet. "I saw Deák pitch into the turbulent waters, calm and strong, with one hand separating the conflicting currents and the other holding aloft the banner of justice, carrying it to victory above the surge."[3] The imagery may be fanciful but it was Deák to a tee, rallying and leading divergent political groups by his unflappable personality and the force of his ideas. Szalay's account also pointed up the appealingly human side of Deák's character. "An hour later he would be merrily and affectionately chattering with children as though he were a youngster himself or amusing his friends with a stream of jokes and stories."[4] Though he had none himself, Deák loved children, and Károly Eötvös observed how they made him as happy as he could make them. He would play games with them, tell them stories, spend hours joking with them round a bonfire, especially during the grape harvest season, or watching the silence of the night settle over the Zala valley as the fire burned down into ashes.[5] At such times there was a childlike innocence about Deák.

If Deák impressed his audiences, it certainly was not by his dress. Lőrincz Tóth, a journalist who wrote respectful reports of Deák's activities during the diet of 1839–40, noted: "His suit was anything but fashionably cut."[6] Eötvös wrote: "During the twenty-seven years that I have been seeing Deák he has always worn an easy-fitting black suit with a black vest. He must have had new ones sometimes but you could never tell from the look of them." He was always dropping ashes down his front and, absently sweeping them away, would brush more into his pants than off them so that his trousers seldom looked clean.[7] (He gave up his pipes after 1840 and chain-smoked cigars.) Outdoors Deák wore a wide-brimmed black felt hat and loose, comfortable overcoats.

On special occasions Deák would wear the black traditional Hungarian man's dress, never the colors, gold braid and plumes that were the fashion. He was no warrior and never unsheathed a sword in anger, but on occasions of high state he respected tradition and wore a Hungarian saber.[8] His one contribution to style was his fondness for a sleeveless, knee-length felt topcoat, which he wore whenever he had the chance and which became a favorite garment for young and old under the name *Deák szür*.[9]

He may have been "fat" but his eating habits were temperate. Though he took his food seriously, he ate only one main meal a day. He loved meat, but never touched alcoholic beverages. Once, invited to propose a toast at a social gathering by Count Manó Zichy, his host, knowing Deák's abstemiousness, told him: "You do the speaking and I'll do the drinking."[10]

Politics were his real staple. He considered his involvement in them a duty, and others were equally keen that he should be active in them, but after the diet of 1839–40 his eagerness waned for a while. It was not that he had grown complacent, but perhaps he sensed something of the tumultuous events that the 1840's were to lead to. For the time being the court continued the benevolent policy toward Hungary that was the result of its compromise with Deák in the closing weeks of the diet. An interesting account of the atmosphere in the imperial capital was given by Lajos Lederer, a publisher in Pest, when he returned from Vienna in December 1840. Lederer said: "I am happy to report that I had an opportunity to hear that the government is presently of the opinion that 'Hungary, being a constitutional country, should be governed differently from the Austrian hereditary provinces and the Hungarian nation with its long constitutional existence is mature enough for freedom of expression to be granted to all points of view within the limits of objectivity, legality and decency (which the censors have been commissioned to safeguard).' "[11]

In the wake of Deák's compromise with the dynasty, Kossuth was released from prison on April 29, 1840. It was a time of passionate discussion of ideas, plans, and policies, but the liberal movement still had not become a coherent, nationally organized force. There were in fact as many liberal groups as there were counties, and though their basic goals were the same and there was some regional cooperation, there were no concerted plans or actions. Under such circumstances, when Kossuth's daily, the *Pesti Hírlap*, began to appear on January 2, 1841, it was hardly surprising that it rapidly became the most powerful organ for disseminating and coordinating the liberal reformers' ideas. This was precisely Kossuth's goal: to create a uniform public opinion and mobilize it behind projects that he initiated or endorsed.[12] Batthyány and, above all, Count István Széchenyi, were incensed by its style, though in sympathy with many of its proposals. This division gradually elicited recriminatory speeches and correspondence and a flurry of pamphlets. Széchenyi became alarmed at Kossuth's rapidly growing influence and his tactics. He feared that Kossuth might lead the nation into revolution, which would not only destroy all the gains the reform movement had already made but might also jeopardize Hungary's very existence.

As soon as Kossuth heard about Széchenyi's impending attack on him and his newspaper, he turned to the other leading liberals, including Deák, for advice and protection. Deák readily gave him his support, and some time between March 20 and 30, 1841, wrote him a letter unequivocally upholding him and *Pesti Hírlap*. Kossuth was overjoyed at the warmth of Deák's letter and determined to hold it in reserve so that, if and when Széchenyi's attack came, he could publish it, pitting Deák's prestige against Széchenyi's.

Not only Kossuth but Wesselényi and even Széchenyi himself were much interested in Deák's views. On February 1, 1841, Széchenyi had written to Deák complaining that *Pesti Hírlap* was stirring up unprecedented agitation in Hungary and stating that he was determined not to let Kossuth endanger what the reform movement had so far accomplished. The letter was de-

livered by Ferenc Pulszky, who told Széchenyi on February 18
that Deák would be replying promptly.

Deák replied on February 20. Respectfully reminding Széchenyi
that the road Kossuth was taking had started with the publication of Széchenyi's own books in the early 1830's, he pointed out
that the agitation had been begun by Széchenyi to convince
the nation that fundamental reforms were necessary. "The main
question today is no longer whether reform is necessary, but
what should be changed and how," Deák wrote. Hungary's
unsolved problems were so numerous, the level of education so
low, and public opinion which is supposed to guide politicians
was so primitive that a free press was even more vital than in
other countries. "In our situation, to attack the paper for its
style, a paper that is only a few weeks old, an attack by those
who agree with its main line, would be disastrous," Deák wrote.
Széchenyi was utterly dismayed by Deák's letter. On June 23,
1841, while the debate was still raging, Széchenyi published
The People of the East.[13] He sent a copy to Deák as an answer
to his letter, making it quite clear that Deák's attempt at media-
tion had failed. The target of the book's devastating criticism
was not Kossuth's philosophy but Pesti Hírlap's style: "I have
no doubt whatsoever of the honesty of the intentions of the
editor of Pesti Hírlap. This I have emphasized again and again.
In general I share his ideas in their main outline. I have not
the slightest hesitation in stating here that I look on his general
lines like my own, indeed let me say I view them with the
sweetest fatherly feelings and consider most of them to be my
own. But I can and do object to the tone with which he presumes
to 'elevate the fatherland.' I believe 'he is pushing the Hungarians
into their grave.' "[14]

Kossuth, for his part, at once published Deák's March communication to him. Deák's letter solidly approved Pesti Hírlap
and the furore surrounding it on the ground that this was a
way to offer an opportunity to air ideas and explain plans and
to afford the politicians a rich vein to mine. Agitation in the
press, Deák wrote, was not in the least dangerous and was, in
fact, desirable. "Agitation in a newspaper simply opens the
way to free debate.... During a press debate every aspect of
an issue can be investigated and considered, and all its good and

bad sides can be mercilessly exposed. This makes it harder than in the past for assemblies to adopt ill-conceived resolutions."[15] The publication of Deák's letter shattered Széchenyi's dream of forming a middle-of-the-road group under Deák's leadership. It was also an immensely successful tactical move by Kossuth, for it confused his enemies, encouraged his supporters, and gave him time to prepare a pamphlet refuting Széchenyi's allegations. *Reply*,[16] Kossuth's response, was honeyed but did not fail to reject all Széchenyi's accusations. Kossuth rebutted the implication that the Hungarian nation was sick and feeble and that there was a single providential physician, Széchenyi, who was alone able to cure it. "I believe," Kossuth wrote, "that the nation is young, hale and hearty and has energy enough to correct the centuries-old defects in its institutions. I do not consider myself to be a doctor but a miniature part of that young, hale and hearty nation."[17] One by one Kossuth denied each of Széchenyi's charges and claimed that he was not courting personal popularity but popularizing ideas that Széchenyi had initiated.

The most dramatic support for Kossuth, however, came from Baron József Eötvös.[18] Like Deák, Eötvös deplored Széchenyi's allegation that Kossuth was following a revolutionary line, a charge habitually made by the court to reject Hungarian reform proposals, his call for censorship, and above all, his challenge to the freedom of the press. This last was a blunder of such magnitude that Eötvös felt compelled to write his pamphlet in defense of *Pesti Hírlap* and against Széchenyi.[19]

Such were the big guns in the battle of the pamphlets. Behind the scenes Deák continued his support for Kossuth, and the influence of his ideas was readily apparent both in Kossuth's and Eötvös's pamphlets. Both in his correspondence and his public utterances, Deák decried Széchenyi's encouragement to the court to curb the freedom of the Hungarian press and his support of charges that revolution was afoot in Hungary, especially since at the time there was evidence of a softening of the government's attitude. Deák wrote to Wesselényi on October 12, 1841: "I share your views about Széchenyi's book. You were giving tongue to my own thoughts in saying that if Széchenyi's accusations were true and there really was such an accumulation of revolutionary material in Hungary, then the paper's articles, even though they were screened by the censors, would soon stir up an outbreak like the French Revolution and the regime, which was using force and governing by terror until recently, could be excused at least politically. . . . Széchenyi has unwittingly given an excuse for the use of terror against us."[20] After the publication of his letter to Kossuth and of Eötvös's and Kossuth's own responses to Széchenyi, Deák felt that little purpose would be served by any dramatic public intervention by him. What had to be said had been said, though he wrote to Wesselényi: "I can only say that I would have given very much indeed if it could have prevented the publication of Széchenyi's book."[21]

The battle of the pamphlets left deep scars, some of which never healed, but it did contribute to the clarification of issues, the consolidation of the liberals, and the prestige of Eötvös and Deák and, above all, Kossuth, who was rising very fast. Deák tried to bind the wounds and close the breach. When he arrived in Pest on November 28, 1841, to begin work on the diet committee for a new criminal code, he was met at the Hotel Angol Királynő where he was staying by a torchlit parade of young people and speeches of welcome. While István Széchenyi watched from a balcony opposite, it was Deák the peacemaker who responded to the crowd:

Yes, the time for change has arrived, and indeed the most important moment in that time is at hand. Enthusiasm is no longer enough. What we need is cool reflection, tireless effort, for our country is in its time of greatest danger. We stand at the moment when a single false step could set the nation back and stop its progress. [This was a tilt at Kossuth.] . . . The most important part of this reflection is to have patience with each other's character, with each other's opinion, and this again is possible only if we avoid making accusations, which whether made by this party or that, are the meanest, most despicable sins that can be committed against the nation. [This sharper admonition was aimed at Széchenyi.][22]

The pace of events did not leave much time for licking the wounds inflicted by the pamphlets, and new issues and problems soon captured the attention of public and statesmen alike.

CHAPTER 5

Efforts to Reform the Criminal Code

THE last diet had set up a committee to draft a new criminal code for consideration by the next one.[1] The majority of its 45 members were conservatives, but it included a number of liberals, most notably Baron József Eötvös, László Pálóczy, Ferenc Pulszky, Gábor Klauzál, Dénes Pázmándy, and Ferenc Deák himself.[2] Regardless of their political inclinations, however, all its members were eminent scholars and statesmen. Their first session together took place on December 1, 1841; they adjourned, their work completed, on March 19, 1843. Their final recommendations were dated March 15, 1843, five years to the day before the outbreak of the revolution of 1848. Three subcommittees shared the actual work of deliberation and drafting: the procedural subcommittee, which dealt mostly with the organization of the courts system; the penal subcommittee, which considered the problems of prisons and correction methods; and the criminal subcommittee, which was concerned with the definition of crimes and the nature of the criminal courts. This last was under the chairmanship of Deák.

The inaugural session of the full committee endorsed several basic principles as fundamental to the new code, particularly the equality of all citizens before the law and an end to the legal differentiation of feudal law, and the abolition of the death penalty and corporal punishment. A number of other innovations proposed for the liberals by Deák were voted down by the committee's conservative majority. What disappointed Deák the most was the rejection of trial by jury and of the establishment of separate courts to hear political cases. The liberals, however, did not feel defeated and continued to press for these and other progressive measures in the subcommittees. In fact, the projects Deák and the liberals put forward during their sixteen months'

81

labor gradually became the most comprehensive liberal reform platform to be offered until the publication in 1847 of the Statement of the Opposition.[3]

The liberals' aim was to turn the committee into an organ for the fundamental reform of the state, an objective of which the conservatives were well aware. Had Deák and his supporters wanted to draft a thoroughgoing juridical reform, they would have had to contend with little opposition, for the conservatives were not in the least averse to modernizing the obviously obsolete legal system. The conservatives hoped that modernizing the judicial branch of the Hungarian feudal state would strengthen the whole state and give the Habsburg regime a more efficient means of exercising its control. The liberals by contrast had no wish to strengthen the government, but wanted instead to transform it into a liberal state. The fierce struggle in the committee thus did not concern the need for juridical reform and its shape alone, but ultimate control of the powers of the state—the same struggle that in the preceding diets had ranged the Habsburg court, government, and the Hungarian conservatives against the liberals. In the diet the liberals had always ultimately been outmaneuvered because the power of the dynasty was against them. Finding the main gate too well defended, they now sought to breach the fortress through the postern of the committee on reform of the criminal code. Every proposal they put forward for legal reform was double-edged, as they tried to inch toward a popularly elected parliament, an electorate based on minimal property qualifications, and the transformation of the feudal executive branch of government into a ministry answerable to the legislature. They were even ambitious enough to hope that their present oblique approach might bring the emancipation of the serfs a step nearer.

The conservatives, of course, refused to give them any help; the liberals refused to limit themselves to purely juridical reform. Deadlock ensued, as the majority conservatives either defeated the liberals' proposals or else watered them down beyond recognition.

The liberals' working methods under Deák were typical. On every topic each of them drafted his own plans, which were then considered at liberal caucuses chaired by Deák. Every proposal was discussed in depth, so that all sides of a question were well aired. Throughout, Deák would say little, but he would listen to the debate, come to his own conclusions, and then draft a proposal, which was translated into German by his highly trusted young associate Ferenc Pulszky. Pulszky would mail the translation to Dr. E. J. Mittermaier, professor of criminal law at the University of Heidelberg, the acknowledged authority of the day. He would comment on the draft and, once his opinion had been received, Deák would pen the final text.[4] The proposals that the conservatives continually turned down were thus modern and scholarly and incorporated very progressive legal thinking.

The liberals did not bow to these defeats. Instead, Deák wrote for them two minority reports to be presented with the majority draft to the forthcoming diet. These reports were signal documents that had a lasting effect on the Hungarian scene.

Three problems stand out among the many that Deák's minority reports dealt with: the definition of high treason, trial by jury, and the separation of political from criminal offenses. These issues in the reports were set forth in such a way that, were the diet to accept them, they would both modernize the law and move things a step nearer to a liberal form of government. They amounted to Deák's manifesto for a "legal revolution," which in the absence of political reform were meant to transform the feudal state through a nonviolent process of legal innovation. Such a revolution would have been a revolution by consent of the holders of power, the most beautiful and humane man can devise.

The minority reports' definition of high treason illustrates Deák's thinking and tactics clearly. What had been uppermost in Deák's mind was revulsion for the Habsburg concept equating the person of the king with the executive branch of government. Violation of the king's person was high treason, but to the Habsburg court so was spoken or printed criticism of the executive branch of government, the very antithesis of the liberals' cherished principles of the freedom of expression and freedom of the press. Kossuth, Wesselényi, Lovass, and the leaders of the Youth of the Diet had all been condemned for flouting the Habsburg concept of high treason. The remembrance of what happened to them during the 1830's guided Deák as he prepared his new definition of high treason. His version naturally encompassed such offenses as an attempt on the monarch's life and conspiracy to depose him, but the key phrase declared: "High treason is also committed by anyone who takes arms against the independence of the country and its civic constitution."[5] No mention here of verbal or written or any other kind of nonviolent attack on the king's person, let alone on the executive branch of government. Armed uprising was the essential precondition for an accusation of high treason. But Deák went further, virtually turning the Habsburg concept upside down. High treason, in his definition, was committed by "anyone who is party by his given counsel or by actual deed to the promulgation and execution of any royal decree that by force subverts any existing constitutional right, ... who is party to the collection of taxes or any other contribution in money or kind to public expenditure, or to the enlistment of recruits, in the absence of legislative acts for these purposes, or who in a county assembly advocates or votes for such illegal actions even if finally they are not put into effect."[6]

The Habsburg interpretation of high treason defended illegal acts by the executive branch of the government and hounded the liberal opposition. Deák's version lifted executive immunity and made members of the government accountable for their actions whenever they violated the laws of the land or the constitution. In answer to the conservatives' objections to this, Deák wrote: "We do not consider it necessary to expound at length on the universally accepted principle that in a constitutional state it is absolutely essential that the government should be held accountable for its actions by law, and on the fact that one of the basic principles of any free constitution is that no public taxes whatsoever or any other public contribution may be assessed without parliamentary approval."[7] In fact, Deák seems to have reached the same conclusion as the American colonists did when they revolted against the British crown two generations earlier, that there should be no taxation without representation.

The introduction of trial by jury into Hungary was proposed because in Deák's view it was the system best suited to Hungary's present circumstances. But it also fitted in well with his indirect approach to other reforms.

Whenever he could, Deák always justified his reform proposals by citing old laws and customs and any other precedents that might lend weight to what he was suggesting. His aim was to give the impression that he was not so much introducing something new as reviving something old, in order to pacify conservative fears and opposition and to appeal to the traditionalist sentiments of any wavering fellow liberals. In the case of the jury system, there was no precedent he could turn to. His only appeal could be to common sense and to the argument that the adoption of foreign patterns was not necessarily bad. Though he could refer to no legal precedent, he emphasized that individuals and groups traditionally borrowed and adapted alien forms for their own ends, so that even as revolutionary an innovation as trial by jury followed in a certain tradition. "Where would progress and human civilization be in our age, where would the institutions of nations be, had they not borrowed from each other what is good and beneficial?"[8] In the late twentieth century such a question may sound like a pretentious platitude, but it was far from that in an era of arrogant and insular East Central European nationalism.

Deák realized that he had to teach his compatriots the advantages of the jury system. He pointed out that the whole nation, not just the government, would exercise juridical power by electing jurors, who would return to the ranks of citizens once they had completed their trial duties; since jury duty was not a permanent office, it could not become the jurors' livelihood, so that they would not tend to become a distinct group separate from the rest of society; since jurors were not officials, they would be immune from interests connected with holding government office; juries were more resistant to government pressure than permanent courts were; and the jury system would not deteriorate into a tool to be used for political purposes by a tyrannical regime, so the jury system was a more effective guarantee of constitutional liberties than the ordinary permanent courts were. The degree of these advantages would be determined by the method by which the jurors were elected. Deák's proposal was that all males over the age of twenty-four with an annual income of one hundred florins or more should be eligible for jury duty. Such a minimum property qualification would have made the bulk of the serfs eligible, but would have excluded some of the slippered nobility whose incomes were even less than one hundred florins a year. Adoption of this reform would have been a major break in the feudal social system. For serfs to have been able to sit in judgment on the nobility would have amounted to a change of revolutionary proportions. Deák was convinced that, were serfs given the passive right of election to serve as jurymen, it would be but a short step for them to obtain the active right to elect juries, and from there general suffrage could not be far off. It was a characteristic move in his attempt at "legal revolution."

Deák did not expect this reform to be acceptable to the forthcoming diet, because the conservative gentry were particularly sensitive about basic changes affecting the rural population. They were far less concerned, however, about the burghers from the towns, who were already enfranchised and represented in the diet as the fourth estate. Since the extension of an existing right never seemed as radical as the creation of a new one, Deák made a particular effort to expand the burghers' rights. The conservative majority of the committee had already agreed to the principle of jury service in the towns but, in Deák's opinion, had set the property qualifications for the election of jurors and for eligibility to serve too high. Only the so-called *virilists,* the burghers who paid the highest taxes of all, were recommended for both rights. Deák criticized this concept. "The electorate should be such that all interests and all classes in it should be represented; no citizen should feel himself deprived of the direct and indirect exercise of his civil rights." He proposed that the committee's draft should be amended to enfranchise all citydwellers who owned a house or any real property, all municipal officials, all clergy and assistant clergy, and all teachers. This would have greatly broadened the jury franchise. The committee's narrow recommendation, Deák said in his minority report, was mistaken: "It is contrary to civic liberty to restrict the possession of any civil right to a closed class."[9]

Deák's definition of high treason would already have protected many who in the past had fallen victim to the Habsburg judiciary in Hungary for political reasons. But political cases had hitherto been heard by a division of the Supreme Court, the King's Bench,[10] where all the judges were appointed by the crown and held office during the king's pleasure. Such a court could hardly be expected to be objective and had tended to act in accordance with the court's wishes. Deák wanted this changed. "In the case of political offenses, neither the indictment nor the verdict should be entrusted to courts dependent on the government, but instead elected juries should be instituted to hear these charges."[11]

The legal revolution embodied in Deák's two minority reports was attacked without quarter by the conservatives who, like the critics of Britain's Second Reform Bill of 1867, saw them as a leap into the unknown darkness. "The whole populace with their wives and children," the conservatives claimed, "will feel the utmost agitation and we can have no idea where all these would lead." They warned of the unseen perils ahead were Deák's proposals ever to become law. "For new people to exercise new rights, to allow institutions to be administered by brand new men, certainly belong to the realm of experiments too daring by far."[12] Deák's minority reports really did advocate a daring experiment for his time. Even today's historians in Hungary, implacably hostile as they are to his role in the Compromise of 1867, are unexpectedly sympathetic toward his part in the committee on reform of the criminal code and his two minority reports. In the words of Béla Sarlós: "The two minority reports are among the finest products of Hungarian legal literature, they are two of its shining jewels; they are summaries of the principles of modern judicial procedure and jurisdiction that by their content and form as well as their style cannot be surpassed."[13] No less enthusiastic was Dr. Mittermaier, the Hungarian liberals' contemporary idol, who in 1845 wrote of the work of Deák and his colleagues: "The minority report for its spirit, logic, and clarity could be called a masterpiece."[14] The eminent German's plaudits, interestingly enough, were lost on Hungary's own traditional historians, who, though they could not entirely ignore Deák's work on the committee, almost damned with faint praise. Not so Florence Foster-Arnold, Deák's English biographer, who in 1880 could write: "As a piece of legal workmanship the rejected code met with high appreciation from com-

petent judges on the Continent and even in England; Mittermaier, the eminent German jurist, declared that he knew no
legislative work which satisfied so completely the progress of
the age, the requirements of justice, and the latest scientific
opinions."[15]

To draft laws, write dissenting opinions and put forward proposals that stir the commentators of later generations is one thing.
For his work on the committee Deák deserves high praise from
any objective historian, but as a lawmaker of the 1840's, he
was a failure. Not one of the committee's recommendations nor
any of the suggestions in either of the minority reports was
adopted and passed by the diet of 1843–44. What then is the
significance of the entire episode? Did it simply reveal Deák and
his fellow liberals as dreaming utopians? There was a kind of
utopianism in all that they did, but after all there never existed
a major innovator who did not tend toward some utopian maxi-
malism. But Deák also operated on a more pragmatic level.

For reasons that will become clear later, Deák had decided
not to attend the diet of 1843–44.[16] His absence notwithstanding,
he still wanted to influence its debates. He wanted to equip it
with the most comprehensive legal arguments possible for
judicial and constitutional reforms to be achieved by legal
rather than violent means. And indeed the diet debates did re-
volve around Deák's reports so that, though he was not present
in person, his ideas dominated the proceedings. On instructions
from the court, all the drafts were shelved by the House of Lords,
but the minority reports had a remarkable impact on liberals
and conservatives alike and went far to help crystallize the
ideology of the revolution of 1848.

Deák's reports also had a more direct impact as well in the
longer term. They remained in the files of the diet, available
to future legislators. Eventually the minority report on political
offenses with only minor editing became the law of the land as
Act III, 1848. The draft on procedural regulation of the criminal code, which was drafted by Deák, became the Press Act of
1848 and formed the basis of the executive order establishing
juries to hear press offenses issued by Deák when he became
Minister of Justice. Though the Upper House on the crown's
orders shelved the committee's drafts, it did not alter the fact

that the Lower House, the elected representatives of the political nation, endorsed and passed Deák's reports in full, indicating that the majority of the legislators accepted Deák's ideas for a legal revolution.

Deák had correctly sensed the mood of the public and was not a utopian dreamer after all. With a constitutional parliamentary system, Deák's drafts would have become law as early as 1844. They were blocked only by Habsburg despotism. Had the House of Lords not obeyed the court's instructions, had the wish of the people expressed through its representatives in the Lower House of the diet of 1843–44 been honored, the legal revolution might have settled Hungary's outstanding social and political problems by peaceful, gradual change, and the bloody revolution of 1848 might not have been necessary or have happened at all.

CHAPTER 6

The Death of Antal Deák
The Diet of 1843–44

H IS work in committee drafting the new criminal code kept
Ferenc Deák away from home longer than ever before,
from December 1841 to March 1843. It was a great sacrifice
because he loved his family and his home. It was his delight to
sit under the trees outside the family home at Kehida, with the
valley of the River Zala stretching away in one direction and
in the other the majestic forests of the Bakony Mountains rising
to the ancient castle of Rezi, which could be clearly seen in
fine weather.[1] The sweep of his view thus took in a symbol of the
historic past and the reality of the present as peasants toiled in
the fields of the fertile bottomland and the vineyards and
orchards on the hillsides. No sight brought him greater pleasure.

Deák's behavior was not what was expected of a middle-
sized landowner. He ought to have been busying himself around
his estate, planning and supervising and taking an active part in
running it. But in such matters he was downright idle and
readily admitted it in writing or speech. There was another
side to his nature, however. In affairs of state or local government, or when there was business to take care of for a friend,
he was convinced that he alone could handle it and he would
begin working like a dynamo, producing as few other men
could. This was the case during the long months of work on
reform of the criminal code and again in 1855 when his best
friend Mihály Vörösmarty died and left his orphans penniless.
On that occasion he wrote 800 letters in their behalf in 51 days,
some of them dictated but many of them in his own hand.[2]
During the first and second post-revolutionary Parliaments, in
1861 and 1865–68, Deák to all intents and purposes was the sole
leader of the Hungarian constitutionalists and showed amazing

90

energy in producing the Compromise of 1867. But for his own affairs or when faced with a problem incapable of realistic solution he would seldom lift a finger. "My idleness comes from my being fat," he told Vörösmarty in 1827.[3] "My mood is generally depressed; I'm inept and lazy about work," he wrote in 1846.[4] And in 1862 he confessed: "I'm old and lazy.... In the country I don't want to write or read or even think."[5] "My passion," he wrote that same year, "is what is called among gentlemen the comfortable life but what is included by the Christian Church among the seven deadly sins: sloth. This passion of mine has been challenging my own will as well as the resentment of others for the last half century. I have struggled against it for too long with no success, so I've given up the fight and ever since I did we (my laziness and I) have lived in peace with each other."[6] Such comments were written tongue in cheek, of course, but in essence they are true: Deák was lazy, hated administrative work, loathed managing his estate, and could not stand daily routine. He would even hold aloof from state and county business until he had persuaded himself that he alone could handle it. What he really liked, what was the very stuff of life for him, was conversation, meditation, the exchange of ideas and opinion.

Ferenc Deák's favorite conversation companion was his elder brother Antal. Antal was immensely proud of his brother's talents, and Ferenc admired Antal's common sense. Whatever the brothers did, they did only after thorough discussion. Antal, like Ferenc a bachelor, ran both their estates, relieving Ferenc of what would have been the misery of day-to-day responsibilities. Their mutual love and trust made Antal an integral part of Ferenc's life; Antal's able handling of their affairs made him indispensable. This cornerstone of Ferenc's life died on June 20, 1842, in the prime of life. He was only 53 years old.

Immediately after the funeral, Deák summoned his serfs and announced: "I am your landlord and you are my serfs. The law sets forth my rights over you and your obligations to me. However, I have no wish to exercise my rights, and I shall not demand that you fulfill your obligations. Should you come of your own free will to help me cultivate my land, I shall be grateful for your generosity and I shall reward you for your honest work."[7] Thus no sooner had Ferenc Deák become sole owner of the family lands than he freed his serfs of their feudal dues, making them free wage laborers if they chose to work for him. He practiced in his private life what, as a liberal politician, he preached was a necessary social reform. He may indeed have been a very incompetent farmer, but there is no question that he lived by his principles.

Deák's painful loss of his brother coincided with the vexing problems of the "hungry forties." Deák agonized over whether he should actively lead the liberals in a period of confrontation among ideas and political parties that virtually ruled out a peaceful, evolutionary solution of Hungary's problems. Such circumstances were the absolute opposite of those in which Deák would readily have accepted leadership and prepared policies. It was not that he was afraid of the radical ideas that were current, for they were his own, but he feared that a single tactical error by the reformers might be used by the court to turn the liberal tide. His consternation grew from his sense of impotence in the face of an increasingly complex situation. He could not properly comprehend it, so he could not and would not try to give any practical lead. Discussion in the press, the clubs, and the county assemblies gradually became more radical, and the positions of the opposing sides became ever more extreme. Yet it was a curious fact that, as Deák was being scared into complete inaction, his "Report to the County Assembly" was being increasingly used by the radicals to scourge the feudal system. It began to acquire a momentum of its own, so that Deák's ideas continued to have active influence even while his personal hesitancy was forcing him onto the political sidelines.

Under the direct influence of his report, Vas, a county neighboring Deák's own county of Zala, on August 31, 1840, issued a circular addressed to all the other counties of Hungary. It urged them to follow its example and appoint a committee to draft proposals for reform and to prepare instructions for their deputies to the forthcoming diet. Many counties followed Vas's advice, and the most notable result was Szatmár's "Twelve Point Program" that advocated the transformation of Hungary's feudal regime into a liberal form of government. It was stated that this platform was based on the tasks that Ferenc Deák had set for the immediate future of the nation in his report to the Zala county assembly.

In Zala, as elsewhere in Hungary, the central question was how far the gentry would go in support of liberalism and how far it could go without prejudicing its own interests. The predicament of the Hungarian reform era, now apparent to all, was how liberal reform could be wrought by the gentry, a feudal class that in the process would destroy its own time-hallowed constitutional privileges in exchange for gains of only limited selfish benefit. It demanded a high degree of motivation and altruism of the gentry, and many of them did not have these qualities. Reactionary demagogues played hard on the doubts of the hesitant, trying to cloud the issues and woo them away from the liberal cause. The "slippered" nobles were easy to rally against liberal reforms which would mean the repeal of their ancient privileges, among them their tax-exempt status. In this case the same awkward alliance of the sophisticated Habsburg court, the aristocracy, and the Roman Catholic hierarchy, together with this impoverished, uneducated, and conservative "slippered" nobility took shape now just as it did in the mid-1830's, when then too it had wrecked the liberals' plans. In Zala this alliance sometimes brought together as many as 6,000 "slippered" nobles for meetings of the county assembly. So huge was this unusual throng that the assembly had to meet in the open air because there was no hall large enough for it in Zalaegerszeg.

Ferenc Deák, the obvious prime choice for Zala's senior deputy, announced that he would not accept election if his instructions did not include a commitment to the obligation of the nobility to contribute to the domestic [county] taxes. The county assembly on February 13, 1843, elected a committee of 96, including Deák, to frame the instructions for the deputies. On March 20 the assembly was called into session to consider the committee's draft. Deák gave a spirited speech in support of taxation of the nobility. Thereafter the tone of the debate became increasingly vehement. Deák told the assembly: "I shall not be diverted from my convictions either by denunciations or by threats on my life."[8] He was in fact threatened by several of the "slippered" nobility, who were well aware that he was the guiding force behind liberal reform. The "slippered" nobility were led in their resistance to taxation by a fire-eater of their own number, György Forintos. When the assembly met for the final vote on April 4, 1843, the 22 speakers included Forintos, who declared: "We shall not let ourselves be taxed, we shall not permit the extinction of the privileges we acquired through our bloodshed." The assembly finally passed every section of the draft except that relating to the nobility's payment of the domestic[9] taxes. After it was over, a group of excited "slippered" nobles on their way back to their villages tried to burn down Deák's home. One of them, Gábor Kun of Büki, shot dead József Mészáros, a servant of Deák's, who had tried to stop the fire attack.[10] Deák kept his word. He turned down the assembly's election as Zala's senior deputy, thus precipitating not only a major crisis in the county and for the liberals but also perhaps the greatest in his own life.

The repercussions of Deák's decision were swift. The liberals in Pest county, alarmed at the prospect of Deák's absence from the next, crucial diet, begged him to accept nomination as Pest's deputy. Both the county's deputies offered to resign if he would accept election by Pest, which had already endorsed highly progressive instructions for its delegates, including taxation of the nobility. Thus if he had wished, Deák could have attended the diet on a platform entirely to his liking, but he declined the offer out of hand and announced that he would stand as the deputy for no county but Zala and only on his own conditions. His determination implies that he had decided not to attend the diet under any circumstances. His reasons had to be more than the momentary victory of the "slippered" nobility in Zala, for he certainly knew in advance what their reaction would be.

Zala itself was in complete confusion. No one would accept deputation unless Deák was the senior deputy. The high sheriff's frantic efforts to find a solution were fruitless. The county faced the possibility of being fined for failing to send deputies to the diet. The county administration therefore also set aside the recently adopted instructions for the county's deputies and the results of the county assembly's elections for them, and ordered new ones. The new campaign was an essay in corruption. Substantial sums of money were used in agitating for the liberal cause and to bribe susceptible "slippered" nobles to vote to deputize Deák and to accept instructions on the lines he had laid down.

The electoral assembly met on August 31 in an atmosphere of almost electric tension. Feelings were running so high that the high sheriff posted troops between the two sides and Zalaegerszeg took on the air of a town under siege. The liberals' machinations paid off, however. Of the 5,000 members of the nobility assembled in the main square, 3,000 voted for a progressive platform. And ironically, even the 2,000 who opposed such instructions and the very idea of taxing the nobility voted in favor of Deák as a deputy. Still Deák refused election. He deplored the corruption of the campaign and the fact that many liberals had aided it while their opponents had veered away from such practices. He lamented the fact that on the very day of the election several persons had been killed in political brawls and a number of others were badly hurt. The unrestrained demagogy and the intervention of Habsburg troops in the concluding stage of the campaign had made the whole procedure too unpalatable for him to accept nomination, he said.

Reaction to Deák's refusal was bitter. Friends who had put money and time into securing his election felt let down and accused him of going against both God and his country. The high sheriff ruled that, since Deák had been elected, he had no choice on pain of being fined. In protest, Deák stalked out of the assembly and turned a deaf ear to all entreaty. No other deputy was elected in his place, however, in the hope that he would change his mind. He did not, and at the diet of 1843-44 Zala was represented by only one of its two deputies.

Deák's behavior has puzzled historians ever since. Some have accepted at face value Deák's explanation that as a man of honor he could not accept a mandate stained with blood and corruption. Yet the diet had been seen as the legislative culmination of Hungary's reform era and was to have taken a decision on the recommendations of the committee on reform of the criminal code, including Deák's own minority reports and the cherished ideas of his that they contained. *Pesti Hírlap* had been mobilizing public opinion so that a larger segment of the nation than ever before was involved in the political struggle.

An all-out drive by the diet might have been enough to over-come the court's resistance and force it to enact further reforms. The whole future of the liberal movement in Hungary was thought to be at stake and this might have been expected to seem of far greater importance than even the most scrupulous man's qualms about the conduct of an election campaign, de-plorable as it had been. The reason for Deák's refusal to attend the diet lay elsewhere.

In 1843 Deák was the liberals' acknowledged leader so when he first began considering whether to attend the diet, he had to think about problems he as the liberal leader might face in the prevailing circumstances. For all his civility, modesty, and appar-ent lack of ambition, Deák was a man of great strength of will. He would accept leadership only on his own terms, and these were both stern and idiosyncratic. He summarized his principles two decades later, after the Compromise of 1867, and they may well have been in his thoughts in 1843. On May 30, 1867, he wrote:

> Does anyone dare to claim that I have tried to impose my will on others either with cajolery or reproaches? Did I ever press anyone to join the party I belonged to? Did I ever hinder anyone from following his own convictions? Did I ever seek a commitment, by asking for a man's word of honor or his hand, to join us and never leave us? Have I ever had recourse to the methods of party organization, which are so common elsewhere but which I have never endorsed? . . . If, despite all this, the majority's opinion and mine have coincided, it can be simply explained by the fact that their convictions and mine were the same.[11]

For Deák such were the essentials of effective leadership. If they were lacking, he simply would not accept the position of leader. The summer election campaign in 1843 had convinced him that the diet was not going to be smooth running. The con-servatives were out to balk reform and in reaction a further radicalization of tone, tactics, and even objectives could be anticipated. To keep the liberals on course would require strict party discipline and a great deal of persuasion to make the faint hearts hold out and not jump ship. Deák would not work in such an atmosphere, so alien to his leadership style and taste.

Besides, there was another precondition to leadership for Deák. He was apparently unwilling to play second fiddle or to share first place; he wanted to be the one man in command. Another episode in 1867 sheds light on this aspect of his decision. In a conversation about Kossuth's open letter condemning the Compromise Deák told an anecdote about two men traveling by coach. Their horses suddenly run wild and the driver is unable to hold them in check. In fear, the other man grabs hold of the reins, whereupon his companion says: "Let me handle this and we may survive. If we both try, we are certainly doomed." Deák likened himself and Kossuth to the two men. In the late 1840's, including the revolution of 1848, he had stood aside and left the leadership to Kossuth, giving him his full support. He therefore resented what he considered Kossuth's interference in 1867 and felt that Kossuth should have followed the example he had set twenty years earlier. And the fact is that Kossuth's strategy and tactics were admirably suited to the increasing radicalization of 1843, while Deák's were not. Deák believed that the legislators were likely eventually to come round to supporting Kossuth's approach rather than his own. At such a critical juncture he wanted to have no hand on the reins, especially when they were already in the charge of someone he trusted anyhow.

Though Deák turned down the leadership of the liberals in 1843, he did not rule out the possibility of taking over in the future when the conditions were right. No doubt he had this in mind when he wrote letters of explanation to all the progressive leaders of the day.[12] His eagerness to inform them of his views on the issues and his unblemished image imply that he still had his eye firmly on the leadership of the liberals.

So why could Deák not attend the diet as an ordinary legislator? It would have been impossible. As soon as he had shown his face in Pozsony, the liberals would have flocked around him and would never have let him be simply one of themselves. And in any case, Deák had personal reasons not to accept his mandate as a deputy. His explanations, both verbal and written, of his decision were sincere. He was really dismayed at the bribery and corruption of the election campaign and the intervention of the military. When he described his mandate as bloodstained, that is exactly what he meant. In addition, there was a political reason for declining the mission of a deputy. In 1843 the deputies were still subject to explicit instructions on how they were to vote, instructions that could be, and often were, changed by their home counties while they were away at the diet. Deák was afraid that that was what would happen during this diet. On September 3, 1843, he wrote to Gábor Klauzál: "I was able to be effective during the last diet only because I was convinced that there was no power at home that could persuade my county to change its mind and no one who could shake its confidence in me . . . , but in this case the deputy cannot be sure whether even the most sacrosanct cause might not be defeated in his county and all his attention, which ought to be concentrated on the solution of national problems, has to be diverted to keep an eye on what might be happening [at home]. . . . In these circumstances, his position is agonizing and his effectiveness is questionable if not impossible."[13] To a man of Deák's temperament, the fact that his effectiveness might be in doubt made it impossible for him to accept deputation.

Although he refused to attend the diet, Deák did not give up all political activity. He continued to attend sessions of the county assembly, proposing and pushing through liberal amendments and additions to the instructions to Zala's single representative at the diet. On May 17–18, 1844, Deák negotiated an accommodation between the two opposing sides in the county and restored a workable atmosphere in the county administration. Nor was his activity confined to the county. When the liberals at the diet reached an impasse, several of them, including Gábor Klauzál from the Lower House and Count Lajos Batthyány from the Upper House, visited Deák at his home in Kehida on June 4–5, 1844. It was Deák who then drafted an Address to the Throne that Klauzál and Batthyány took back to Pozsony, where it was unanimously passed by both houses. Such was Deák's authority among the liberals.

At the diet the liberals showed cohesion, political maturity, and parliamentary skill, but they still lacked the strength they needed because they had no formal organization and also perhaps because Deák was absent. True, they inched forward, but they achieved no major advance toward a liberal government or bourgeois society. The alliance of the court, the prelates, the aristocrats, and much of the nobility was powerful enough to thwart any major reforms. The strength of the reaction showed that the liberals had no chance for a breakthrough without much better organization. In the meanwhile three significant trends can be discerned in the period immediately before the revolution of 1848: a growing rift between Hungarian nationalism and that of the minority peoples; a vigorous effort to marshal the forces of opposition and give them a consolidated platform; increasing reaction in the court, greater radicalization of the reform movement and the emergence of Young Hungary, the most radical group of intellectuals of all. These were the makings of the revolution.

CHAPTER 7

Nationalism
The Question of a Hungarian State Language

FERENC Deák, though he lacked the sophistication of Giuseppe Mazzini, was really a Mazzinian nationalist in at least two respects. His nationalism was based on the dignity and rights of the individual, and it was not aimed against the national minorities. There was therefore no contradiction between his nationalism and his liberal beliefs. By the time he entered political life, however, there were already differences between the nationalisms of Hungary's various nationalities dating back to the 1790's. The growing rift was augmented by the divide and rule policies of the Habsburg dynasty.

In the protracted struggle against absolutism, the liberals could make only piecemeal progress toward a modern government and society. The more difficult the court made this advance, the more radical Hungarian liberalism became and the more intolerant, Hungarian nationalism. Likewise the more moderate a liberal a statesman was (Széchenyi, for instance), the more tolerantly he behaved toward the minorities and the more inclined he was to seek a fair solution to their relations with the Hungarians; the more intransigent he was (Kossuth and the radicals, for instance), the more he believed the minorities to be allies, or even tools, of the Habsburg dynasty and the more intolerantly he treated them. Deák's position was paradoxical: though in domestic reforms he was ideologically close to Kossuth, he was as tolerant as Széchenyi toward the minorities. To find a *modus vivendi* between the Hungarians and the national minorities was an extremely complex task, though a vital one, for Hungary was a multinational state.[1]

100

From the beginning of Hungarian nationalism at the end of the eighteenth century, its champions saw the evolution of the nation, the progress of its education, and the development of its own language as interdependent. In their view all three were being crushed by Habsburg absolutism, the dynasty's Germanizing efforts, and the continuation of Latin as the language of state and education.

Deák assigned first priority to abolition of Latin and introduction of Hungarian as the official language of state. He considered this to be a part of nation-building because Latin separated the nobles and prelates who could speak it from the rest of the population who could not. He also considered it too antiquated to be a medium of modern education. On June 28, 1836, Deák launched his attack: "In the Middle Ages it was the general European pattern to use Latin as the language of education and of the state, and so it also became Hungary's official language." While the other countries abandoned it long ago, it had endured in Hungary. "This foreign yoke" had almost expelled the "sweet native tongue" from legislation, the courts, administration, and education. What was even more absurd was that Hungary used a distorted Latin coined in the Dark Ages which "so differed from the beautiful, concise language of Rome that even Rome's most wretched rabble would have shied away from it and not recognized it as its own."[2] Not only had this misbegotten Latin squeezed Hungarian out of the affairs of state and education, Deák declared, but the problem had been compounded by Joseph II's repeal of Latin and imposition of German as the language of state and education. His action was a breach of law and had simply substituted one yoke for another. "At that time, however, the nation with feelings of pain raised its voice in protest," Deák said.[3] The six years that German remained Hungary's official language after its introduction on May 11, 1784, he said, increased the Hungarians' devotion to their native tongue as never before and convinced them that "the continuation of our national existence is inexorably bound up with the fate of our language."[4]

The repeal of German as the official language of Hungary did not, however, open the way to the free development of Hungarian. On the contrary, Latin was reinstated, and the court took pains to obstruct Hungarian. The effort to repeal Latin as the language of state gradually became a bone of contention between Croats and Hungarians also. The Croats claimed that the repeal of Latin was subject to their consent in the Hungarian diet. They were not about to give it but insisted instead that Latin should continue to be the language of state and education in both Croatia and Hungary proper. Deák contested their interpretation of the legislative system. "The drafting of laws in Latin is founded on custom not on law," he stated.[5] This being so, the Hungarian diet and the government could at any time introduce another language as the language of the state without the need even to pass legislation to do so. For Deák and the liberals it was most natural that the language of the largest nation, that is, Hungarian, should be adopted as the language of the state. They much resented the Croats' insistence on the continuation of the use of Latin. In an address to the diet on April 15, 1840, Deák conceded the Croats had a right to try to introduce the use of Croatian in Croatia but denied that they had any right to compel the Hungarians to retain Latin in Hungary proper.[6]

Since it was impossible to make legislative headway on the use of Hungarian, other approaches were taken. The Hungarian National Museum was founded in 1808 to "cultivate the Hungarian language and literature." The Hungarian Academy of Sciences was established in 1825 "not only to disseminate the language but also to refine it to be applicable to the arts and sciences."[7] Both institutions at once set about rejuvenating and modernizing the Hungarian language It needed these changes, although it was in no way so primitive as the court and some aristocrats pretended.[8] The opinion that the language was primitive was so widespread when Deák entered the diet that he felt it necessary to tell the Zala County Assembly in his report of 1836: "Many have claimed that Hungarian is unsuitable for use for legislation or administrative purposes. It is the claim of those who are hobbled by centuries-old custom, those for whom Latin has become an imaginary necessity. . . . Yet the number of those who have sensed the harmful consequences of centuries of neglect and have encouraged the development of our native tongue has grown. . . . The groundless accusations have been corrected. Every day the general feeling is stronger that it is both possible and necessary to publish laws in Hungarian."[9]

The real beginning of the legal acceptance of Hungarian in the administration was in 1830 when the Habsburg dynasty was again confronted with a revolutionary upheaval in Europe and needed Hungarian money and recruits. An act expanded the use of Hungarian in various branches of government and provided facilities for future public officials and lawyers to learn it.[10] Deák was already the leader of the liberals when in 1836 it was ruled that in the parallel Latin and Hungarian versions of laws, the Hungarian one was the authoritative text. In parishes where the preaching was in Hungarian, the registries, which were both ecclesiastical and state records, were to be kept in Hungarian.[11] The diet of 1839–40 introduced Hungarian as the official language of central, county, and ecclesiastical administration in all of Hungary except Croatia[12]–a blunder in a multinational state.

The laws of 1843–44 (the diet Deák did not attend) established Hungarian as the sole language of legislation, excluding Latin even as a secondary language.[13] The central executive branch of government, however, was to translate all laws into the vernacular of each of the nationalities of Hungary, just as the urbarial laws of 1836 had been, so that they should be easily accessible to all the minorities.[14] Hungarian was to be the sole official language for administrative, judicial, and ecclesiastical affairs. The Croatian deputies were to be allowed to address the diet in Latin for six more years and the Hungarian authorities would accept communications in Latin from the Croatian authorities, but Croatia would receive communications from the Hungarian authorities in Hungarian. Hungarian was to be the language of instruction in all public schools in Royal Hungary, but the non-Catholic church schools could continue to teach in the vernacular languages, so that in fact the vast majority of the children of non-Hungarians continued to be taught in their mother tongues.[15] In Croatia, Hungarian was to be a regular curricular subject but not the language of education.

In practice no serious effort was made to enforce the new regulations, and practically everything remained as it was. Militant Hungarian nationalism was thus tempered by administrative

inertia. Yet the law remained on the books and provided the
basis for a widespread movement of protest against the inept
campaign to assimilate the non-Hungarians. At the same time
it must be admitted that the language issue was the outcome of
the protracted struggle to free Hungarian education from the
yoke of Latin and German. It is extraordinary that it took a half-
century of nationalist pressure for Hungary to acquire the right
to teach in Hungarian in its high schools, colleges, and the University of Pest. Yet many of its central governmental institutions
that were directly under royal supervision, such as the Hungarian Royal Court Chancellery, the Hungarian Chamber, and
the armed forces, were directed by non-Hungarians, and their
administration remained either in Latin or German up to 1848.[16]
Every step toward the general use of Hungarian in Hungary was
the result of immense political effort, especially since the court
had openly set itself against Hungarian liberal nationalism. Little wonder, then, that the state's official language should have
become such an explosive issue in relations between the Hungarians and the national minorities, that the revolution of 1848–
49 degenerated into a bloody ethnic war in Hungary.

After the revolution the dynasty rewarded the national minorities for their loyalty with the same treatment it meted out in
punishment to the Hungarians. When Hungary regained its
home rule in 1868, the Act on the Equality of Nationalities was
promulgated. Elaborated under the general political direction
of Ferenc Deák, by then leader of the majority party in the
parliament, and drafted by the brilliant mind and pen of Deák's
old friend and fellow liberal, Baron József Eötvös,[17] it finally
brought to fruition the long-held wishes of such moderates as
Széchenyi and Eötvös and of Deák himself.

CHAPTER 8

Deák as Fabius Cunctator
The Liberals and Their Platform
(1844–47)

ONCE the diet of 1843–44 had adjourned, several nobles, Deák included, added their names to the lists of taxpayers, voluntarily accepting taxation from which they were exempt by right. Similar other liberal reforms were carried out all over the country. Although he promoted them, Deák was not satisfied with these purely voluntary piecemeal social actions, but sought to get local and national laws passed to lay a firmer foundation for substantial liberal reforms. At a meeting of the Zala County Assembly on September 26, 1844, he urged the nobility to tax itself to raise subsidies for a railroad that would connect the county with the sea at Fiume[1] and boost Zala's economic interests. The "slippered" nobles tried to shout him down with cries of "We shall give nothing." They were too strongly attached to this last shred of their social privilege to accept taxation voluntarily. Deák refused to be intimidated and replied that his lips could be sealed by force alone and that he would resist to the last. "I have respected the freedom of expression of others. I demand it for myself." The railroad was indispensable for the self-help of the nation and "a nation that does not help itself deserves its fate," he told the assembly.[2]

As liberal demands were aired throughout the country, the court decided to take action before it was too late. Kolowrat moved to prevent "anarchy" in Hungary. Under his prompting, a royal rescript was issued on November 10, 1844, on the future administration of the counties of Hungary.[3] The ostensible purpose of the rescript was to make the administration of the counties more reasonable and effective, but the real aim was to restrain the counties' autonomy, to undermine their constitutional

105

right to administer themselves. To circumvent constitutional local governments, many county high sheriffs were replaced by conservative officials called "administrators."

In Zala county, the popular high sheriff, Count Imre Batthyány, was replaced by Count Leo Festetics, who was appointed "administrator" of Zala county. When the royal rescript was read to the county assembly on May 26, 1845, Deák deplored the appointment, which meant a flat rejection of the county's wishes and its petition to the crown that Batthyány should be retained in his position. Deák added his voice to the nationwide chorus of protests against the system of "administrators." He proposed that the county should appeal to the next diet to repeal this arbitrary system that had supplanted the constitutional one. He grasped that the court's intention was to bring the county administrations to heel by authoritarian methods, having failed for centuries to do so by constitutional means. In view of this he never flagged in his opposition to the new system. Soon he and other liberals were given the perfect opportunity to press their point.

In Hont county, in northern Hungary, the "administrator" repeatedly violated law and constitution. The outraged county assembly declared his actions unlawful and petitioned the King to remove the "administrator" and the Palatine and the Lord Chief Justice to uphold the constitutional government of the counties. Circulars were sent to all the Hungarian counties appealing for their support.

Zala County Assembly took up the matter of Hont's circular on November 10, 1845, with Ferenc Deák as the main speaker. He reminded his colleagues that the appeal for support was both legal and just, for the county "administrator's" actions were high-handed and unconstitutional. Such violations of county autonomy, he warned, "would lead public affairs into chaos"[4] and could not be tolerated. The realist in Deák added, however, that, since Hont county had petitioned the highest executive and judicial authorities in the kingdom, their investigation should be left alone and its results awaited. The assembly acted on his recommendation to pass a resolution of support and take no further action.[5]

Deák used the occasion to express his philosophy of practical politics, particularly his concepts of good government, fair play in cooperating with a foreign-dominated government like the Habsburg regime in Hungary, and the role of an opposition party. He stated his view that in essence the royal rescript on county "administrators" was proper as far as its intention to improve the governance was concerned. "Had that been the government's sole intention, I should have endorsed it gladly." But what the "administrators" had done in various counties had caused dissension and dismay and had done nothing to solve the problem of efficient government, he said.

Although Deák condemned the system of "administrators," he did not censure Hungarians who accepted office under the Habsburg regime, even as "administrators." "There is nothing objectionable about anyone accepting office," he said. "The more men of integrity serve the government, the more likely it is that the administration will improve. What is despicable is the man who takes office in violation of his own conscience."[6] Deák's efforts to protect the honor and prestige of men who held office during the 1840's and later during the Bach regime are among the admirable qualities of the man who never himself accepted a position save on his own terms. That explains why he was so seldom inside the executive branch of the government and sat instead in the opposition benches of Parliament. His view on the role of the opposition, then, is of interest. Deák explained:

> Opposition in its healthy political sense is not an abstraction. The opposition should not oppose all the acts of the government simply because they are the government's acts. The opposition's duty is to scrutinize all government measures carefully. It should in particular keep a watchful eye that the force of the law is carefully preserved free of any violation. Every error, every violation of the law has to be attacked without personal considerations. The opposition should uncover all the government's shortcomings and speak out against them without reservations or partisan interest. In accord with the law, justice and its own conscience, knowing not fear nor despair nor self-interest, it must be concerned at all times with the interdependent interests of constitutional liberty and legal order and protect them both. This is the opposition's noble task, its most sacred duty.[7]

Assessing the chances of the liberals in the forthcoming struggle with the conservatives, Deák was skeptical about the support of the public. He told the Zala County Assembly that neither the government with its reactionary policies nor the opposition with its liberal platform would be able to enlist the majority of the political nation. "The majority," he said, "belongs to those who win the support of the undecided who are inspired not by causes but purely by selfish motives. The number of such men, alas, is very large in every country. They are won by those who promise the most."

In the political contest between Hungarian liberalism and court reaction, political, administrative, as well as economic issues were involved. In the guise of economic reforms the crown set out to repeal the tariffs between Hungary and the other Habsburg provinces. This move would expose Hungary to an unrestricted flow of manufactured goods. Industrialization in other areas, particularly in Bohemia, Moravia, and the Alpine provinces, was far advanced, fostered by a mercantile policy of state subsidies paid for out of general tax revenues from all the Habsburg lands, including Hungary. During the period of industrial development a tariff wall had been maintained around Hungary so that it could serve both as a market for manufactured goods and as a cheap source of raw materials. This tariff system also included features that afforded some protection for certain areas of Hungary's own slowly evolving industry. Repeal of the tariffs would wipe out this meager protection and any chance of further Hungarian industrial development. The diet of 1843–44 had tried to forestall such an eventuality by voting a protective tariff law, which was then weakened by the House of Lords and finally vetoed by the crown. If Hungary was ever to remedy its disadvantageous economic status in relation to the rest of the Empire, it had to resort to self-help.

Lajos Kossuth initiated such an effort—the Protection Association[8]—and he also coined a slogan for it: "Every patriot should raise a protective tariff at his own doorstep."[9] The members of the new organization pledged themselves to satisfy all their needs by purchasing only Hungarian-made goods.[10] Deák, though he found fault with the project, felt its merits outweighed its demerits and gave Kossuth his wholehearted backing. Since it would have been out of character for him not to have let Kossuth know his misgivings, he sent him a letter from Kehida on

November 2, 1844. Pointing out that it was a mistake to have members pledge not to buy foreign goods when Hungary was incapable of manufacturing everything the nation needed, Deák insisted that it would have been wiser to boycott certain key manufactures. All the funds the association could raise would be enough to build a few factories but not enough to subsidize the manufacture of all Hungary's needs. The money would be wasted if it were tried. Deák was convinced the Protection Association could never achieve the success of the American colonists' Protective Tariff Association before their War of Independence.

In America, Deák wrote, "the Protective Tariff Association was set up not so much to subsidize industry but with the political object of defying the British." He pointed out that the colonists boycotted only British merchandise and let in goods from elsewhere. Even then, though most of the colonists were "stable, persevering, highly moral people," they looked for ways round their pledge and when in 1770 Britain repealed all the objectionable revenue acts except the duty on tea they were quick to restrict their boycott to tea alone. "That is what was done by the American people who already had a free press and complete equality of rights among all citizens." Hungary, on the other hand, Deák noted, was neither a simple nor a stable society, had no free press to keep everybody informed, and did not enjoy equality among all its citizens as America did. Yet these were prerequisites much needed for the success of Kossuth's campaign.[11] Nevertheless, Deák did not withhold his support. "I shall not desert you," he assured Kossuth, and he kept his word.[12] Nevertheless, he asserted that the task of the new campaign was to overcome the vicious circle that was crippling Hungary's economy: "We buy foreign goods because our craftsmen are not skilled enough and our craftsmen are not skilled enough because we buy foreign goods."[13] To break out of this cycle, all citizens had to unite, regardless of social position, religion, profession, or political persuasion, in the Protection Association, so that one day they could say: "I and one million Protection Association members saved the country on its deathbed."[14]

Politically the Protection Association was an enormous success but it failed to realize its economic objectives. It flourished until

1846, when other purely political affairs absorbed the liberal leaders' attention. Leaving an important heritage in the involvement of the masses in a joint action with those who enjoyed political privileges, it was the first mass movement in Hungary that took in every stratum of society. It gave the liberals experience in mass organization. It allowed the populace to sense its collective strength and to take part in the shaping of policy. It was the dawn of the age of mobilizing the masses for political action, an ill omen for feudalism and a harbinger of the convulsion of 1848.

Another salient event of the years immediately preceding 1848 was the publication of the Statement of the Opposition,[15] the ideological climax of Hungary's pre-revolutionary era.[16] During the 1840's the liberals matured, but they also became divided into three distinct groups: the left-wing radicals, the center, and the moderate constitutionalists. This division reduced their efficiency. In the meanwhile the regime organized and consolidated its own supporters into the Progressive Conservative Party[17] which brought forward a program of limited reforms. Anticipating the liberals, this party published its platform on November 12, 1846. It contained certain elements of reform; nonetheless, it was obvious that the party's main goal was the entrenchment of the prevailing social and political order rather than its reform. The only field in which the platform advocated advancement was the economy.

The consolidation of the liberals into a unified party and the publication of their own reform program was a far slower process. The conservatives' success, however, was a spur. Kossuth had urged an immediate start on a single liberal program as soon as the diet adjourned in 1844. He also wanted it drafted by Deák, who enjoyed the greatest standing among all liberal factions. Kossuth knew Deák's ideological progressivism and trusted his aims and principles more than many others'.

Deák declined to write a joint platform for all the liberals on the grounds that it was dangerous, if not impossible. If the draft dealt in generalities, it would be acceptable to all factions because it would transgress no principles, but it would be open to challenge by the conservatives that the government was ready to do everything the opposition proposed. "With such generalization we should gain nothing, even if everybody subscribed to it," Deák stated. If it went into detail, innumerable objections would be raised by the diverse liberal factions. "Believe me, my friend," he wrote Kossuth, "a detailed program would widen and multiply the breaches among us rather than promote unity." For the time being, the liberals would have to be content with the community of interests and basic ideas that had linked them in the past.

Deák's immobility did not stop the leaders of the opposition from acting. On November 18, 1845, twenty-eight leading liberals, among them Lajos and Kázmér Batthyány, László Teleki and Lajos Kossuth met in Pest. Adopting a brief resolution which was the genesis of the Statement of the Opposition, they referred to the need for the opposition to "organize itself within the bounds of loyalty as subjects, of the law and of the constitution, with the aim of promoting national welfare in a worthy manner." They also urged Deák, who did not attend the meeting, to take the helm and to come to live permanently in Pest. A delegation consisting of Lajos Batthyány, Kossuth, and two others went to Kehida November 22–24, 1845, to visit him in order to persuade him to compose a manifesto that would unite the opposition. He again declined on the ground that it was not feasible.[18]

In January 1846 Deák visited Pest, though he had no specific plans and was still set against the idea of a common liberal position. With the centralists and the radicals in a flurry of political activity, Deák's indecision hurt both his prestige and his influence. For a while the Progressive Conservatives gained in popularity as they pursued goals that were in keeping with the dynamism of the moment. The government itself was putting a lot of effort into controlling the Tisza river under the guidance of Széchenyi, who in the spring of 1846 launched the first steamer on the Danube. Had all the members of the government possessed Széchenyi's integrity, it is not unlikely that their supporters would have had a majority at the next diet. Despite some economic advances, however, the regime was reactionary. It believed the people could be bought with a few token improvements, but whenever it faced anything other than economic developments, its response was repressive.[19] No government can maintain a reform image when its basic intentions are as counter-reformatory as those of the Habsburg regime's in Hungary in 1846. Its momentary popularity soon began to wane and that of the opposition to increase. Deák meanwhile remained aloof, inactive, apathetic.

Like many other liberals who were standing on the sidelines, Deák was shaken out of his torpor by events in Galicia, where the peasantry and Habsburg army units bloodily forestalled a Polish national uprising by the local gentry.[20] In Hungary, fear of a similar peasant rampage, like the one in 1831, heightened the social and political tension. Apparently hoping that the Hungarian liberals would be chastened by what had happened to the Galician rebels the court however seemed disinclined to stir up the Hungarian peasants against the local gentry. It contented itself with declaring martial law and mobilizing the garrisons in Hungary.[21] The Hungarian liberals did indeed learn a lesson, but not quite what the dynasty had anticipated. Kossuth saw collusion between the court and the Galician peasants as underlining the need to agitate for far-reaching peasant reform in Hungary in order to ally the country folk with the liberal gentry. "The Hungarian nobility must anticipate such an act, a peasant revolt, if they wish to survive," he said.[22] Many Hungarian liberals' minds were preoccupied by the Galician incident throughout the rest of 1846.[23]

Deák himself at last dropped his opposition to discussion of a unifying liberal platform. On June 8, 1846, at the second meeting on the subject in Pest, he joined Lajos and Kázmér Batthyány and Kossuth among others. He still had doubts about too specific a declaration, but the meeting nevertheless adopted a fairly progressive statement including the more urgent practical reform measures. It called for land for the serfs, full compensation for landlords, introduction of universal taxation, and the requirement that the nobility should at once bear a fair share of Hungary's major burden, the war tax.[24] It also demanded popular representation first at the county level and then at the national level. Its adoption was due more to Kossuth than Deák.

A third meeting was held in November, but Deák did not attend. Kossuth became increasingly impatient at the lack of progress on preparing a formal platform and consolidating the liberals. Inspired by him, Pest county became more and more discontented. Finally Count Lajos Batthyány took matters into his own hands and on December 26, 1846, summoned a liberal constituent convention for March 1847. Twelve hundred liberals assembled from every corner of the country, and once more Deák failed to show up, this time claiming ill health. Kossuth presented his own draft, which he had discussed with Deák a few days earlier. It was debated, amended to accommodate all factions, and passed on March 15. Before dispersing, the convention elected a Committee of Six to compose a final version of the liberal platform on the basis of Kossuth's draft. The committee members were Kossuth, Eötvös, Pulszky, Teleki, Szemere and Deák, representing all three major liberal groups: the moderates, the center and the left-wing radicals. With this resolution, there emerged for the first time in the history of Hungary a party of the opposition, which aimed to lead the partisans of progress into battle under a centralized leadership. This was the feeling of many liberals at that time, but not of Deák. Still not convinced it was possible to find a program that would unite all progressives, he would have been content to move forward by easy stages so long as none of them compromised future progress.[25] It was his firm conviction that the forces of reaction in Hungary were so strong that the time was not yet ripe for concerted action. Is it any wonder that even his colleagues began in dismay to refer to him as Hungary's *Fabius Cunctator*? Indeed, he himself did not always observe his often repeated maxim: "One's duty must be done, regardless whether it will be a success or a personal fiasco."[26]

Deák was paralyzed by the same indecision that afflicted him when he was trying to make up his mind whether to go to the diet of 1843–44. The same political and psychological elements were at work on him. Still dreading a false step that might undo all the small gains that had been made and bring down ruin on the entire nation, he was scared by the radicalization of the liberals' tactics; yet his moral sense was offended by the idea of watering down their radical philosophy. He was still being asked to write a manifesto to create a united party, but the leadership of the liberals had fallen irrevocably to Kossuth, and Deák could not accept a secondary role. If he was really sick, as he said he was, then agonizing over his quandary was undoubtedly the cause. He went abroad to take the waters to restore his health.[27] Yet it is interesting to note that twenty years later, when he might have expected to feel the ills of the flesh, he was as dynamic as his fellow liberals had hoped he would be in the 1840's. When he alone led the liberals, his mind was sound and so was his body. In the 1840's he did not take the lead and his energies failed in feudal Hungary's last five years because he could not believe it was realistically possible for the liberals to achieve their goals in the face of stubborn Habsburg reaction. The only possible way was by violent revolution, and he eschewed violence. Events in 1847, however, forced him to play a principal part for a while.

Deák did as he was bidden and wrote the final version of the Statement of the Opposition for the Committee of Six, which adopted it at a meeting held in Pest on June 6. Zsigmond Kemény later commented: "Deák composed the declaration from other people's papers with such eclecticism that it satisfied every faction."[28] The leaders of the opposition issued a circular on June 7, 1847, giving Deák's manifesto the widest distribution possible. The circular emphasized that the manifesto had been written by Deák and unanimously endorsed by the other liberal leaders.

The manifesto was a work of compromise and common sense. It listed the reforms that were essential to transform feudal Hungary into a modern state. There were five basic ones: universal taxation and parliamentary supervision of the budget; representation of commoners; equality of all before the law; compulsory emancipation of the serfs in perpetuity with compensation for the landlords for their loss of income; and repeal of the entail system.[29] It is to Deák's credit that, broad as this democratic program was, he was at pains to reassure the crown that its aim was only to modernize Hungary, not to break with the dynasty. The manifesto declared: "We shall never forget those ties that exist between us and Austria on the basis of the Pragmatic Sanction, but we shall strictly insist on respect for Act X, 1790,[30] the provisions of which were consecrated in the words of the royal oath, which avow: 'Hungary is a free state and is independent in the entirety of its legislation, so that it is not subordinate to any other state or nation.'" It stressed that the

Hungarians did not want to start a contest between their interests and the unity and continued existence of the whole Habsburg monarchy, but it went on: "On the other hand, we consider it contrary to the law, justice and fairness that Hungary's interests should be illegally subordinated to the interests of the other several provinces, as has for long been the case in industry and trade." Thus while offering to harmonize Hungary's interests fairly with those of the Habsburg hereditary provinces, the manifesto gave notice that the Hungarians would never agree to surrender their fundamental interests, especially their constitutional right of self-government, for the sake of uniting the administrative system of the Habsburg lands. The attempt to impose administrative unity was seen by many in the court as an effort to achieve "the real unity of the entire monarchy," but the manifesto denied that they were one and the same thing. The dynasty's attempts to consolidate administration were not in order to unite the monarchy so much as to suppress Hungary's autonomy and the liberties of its citizens. "The ancient constitutional institutions of the Austrian hereditary provinces were sacrificed for the unity of the administrative system and that unitary administrative system was evolved on the basis of absolutism." To the Hungarians, however, their constitution was a precious instrument that must not be put in thrall to foreign interests or vague promises of material returns. On the contrary, it should be secured on an even broader base. "We are convinced," the liberals declared, "that, if the Austrian hereditary provinces were also to join the family of constitutional nations in accordance with the demands of justice and of the times, then the spirit of constitutionalism would inspire the government of the whole monarchy, the entire system and its component parts." Such constitutional governments on both banks of the Leitha could easily harmonize their interests. Such a transformation would unite the Habsburg lands not through a system of administration but by the community of their interests and increased mutual trust. "The spiritual and material energies of the monarchy would be strengthened and it would then be able to ride the storm that may some day break."

The manifesto thus advocated all the basic requirements to establish a classical liberal form of government. The ideology of the Hungarian liberals, whose spokesman Ferenc Deák was, reached its apogee with this demand to turn Hungary from a feudal into a modern state. Deák's hand can be clearly seen in the assurance that Hungary would remain loyal to the Habsburg system provided that the other provinces were granted constitutional governments of their own. This demand was one of the pre-conditions of the Compromise of 1867, but it was to be another twenty years before the dynasty would concede it and it became a cornerstone of the Dual Monarchy.

The Statement of the Opposition was a call for consolidation and unity, but its results were limited. Many liberals were seduced by the material gains already made; others succumbed to government pressure; yet others gave way to coercion, bribery, or blandishments. Some were too busy profiteering from the boom that closed the otherwise hungry 1840's; some had been scared by the events in Galicia and sought what protection they could behind the Habsburg Army's bayonets rather than through reform; some were satisfied by the government's own meager reforms; some were disillusioned by the scanty results of the liberals' reform measures that had taken so much to have enacted. Many were particularly disappointed that the most radical reform, the voluntary remission of serf dues, had had so little effect, for very few serfs had been voluntarily freed, and the continuation of the entail system had denied them full title to their land even if they redeemed all their obligations. Faith in gradual reform began to wane, and people either lapsed into apathy and despondence or turned to violent methods as the only way to effect change. How much unity the Statement of the Opposition really brought about is open to question. Deák's lack of enthusiasm may not have been so ill judged, for a paradox existed at the root of the reform movement: the privileged classes whose own privileges would have been forfeited if reform were successful were seeking fundamental social reform. It seems to have been proven that, because of its mentality, this class, though it gave to the country such splendid statesmen as Kossuth, Deák, and their colleagues, was incapable of stepping boldly ahead of its own free will. The shock of 1848 was necessary so that liberalism could achieve its breakthrough in Hungary.

CHAPTER 9

The Reluctant Revolutionary of 1848–49

FERENC Deák was anything but a revolutionary in the normal sense of the word. He feared and despised violence. By inclination he was a man of contemplation, negotiation, compromise, and peace. Yet paradoxically he played a significant part in the ideas and events of the revolution in Hungary and remained characteristically loyal to them. As the fever of revolt rose, Deák withdrew into seclusion, wanting no part of it. As so often in the past, he pleaded ill health, though it is open to question how much it was political indisposition and how much hypochondria.

It was during these hectic days that there occurred an episode typical of Deák the man, which Károly Eötvös recounted. Ever since Ferenc Deák's father had moved to Kehida following his wife's death, the house at Söjtör where Ferenc was born had scarcely ever been used. In view of this, László Stolczer, the leader of the Jewish community in Söjtör, approached Deák to rent the house or part of it for the community. Deák at first turned the request down, explaining that he wanted to keep the house exactly as it was in memory of his mother. Stolczer then told him how disappointing his decision would be for the community, which had wanted to use the house for divine worship because it had been unable to find suitable premises anywhere else in the area. "Well, that's a different kettle of fish," Deák had responded. "I'll lend it to you for prayer, for the worship of God, but I'll certainly not accept any money."[1] Deák the agnostic who never went to church so respected the religious sentiments of others that he readily made available his own property for use as a synagogue. Greater things, however, were soon to exercise Deák than such purely local acts of generosity. Even before the flame of revolution was lit in Palermo on

117

January 12, 1848, Hungary's last feudal diet was to pass significant
reforms and by April 11 the "April Laws" were to put an end
to feudalism, introduce a liberal form of government, and lay
the legislative foundations of bourgeois society. This momentous
diet was summoned by a royal writ of September 17, 1847,
which was read to Zala County Assembly on October 4. Deák
was at once elected the county's senior deputy, but he turned
the mandate down on grounds of his ill health, and two other
deputies were elected. When the diet was opened on November
7, the dynasty itself submitted a program of substantial reform.
From the rostrum of Zala County Assembly, Deák urged the legislators in Pozsony to take advantage of the opportunity they had
been offered, reminding them that what was of importance
was the reform, not who had proposed it: "There can be no
greater victory for the opposition than to bring matters to the
point where the cause for which it was once persecuted is
adopted by the government as its own."[2]

Revolution erupted in Vienna on March 13, 1848 and immediately spread to Hungary.[3] The news from Vienna reached the
diet the following day at the same time as the word that thousands
of discontented peasants were massing in the Hungarian capital.
By March 15 Pest, too, was in the grip of revolution, and a large
delegation from the diet set out from Pozsony to deliver to King
Ferdinand an Address to the Throne drafted by Lajos Kossuth
and passed by both houses. It proposed a program to transform
Hungary's government into a liberal one and modernize its
feudal society. Before the delegation left, the leader of the liberals, Count Lajos Batthyány, sent two trusted associates, Baron
Béla Winckler of the Upper House and Károly Tolnay of the
Lower House, to persuade Deák to join the diet without further
ado.[4]

Batthyány's emissaries and the local liberals finally prevailed
on Deák to accept election as Zala's senior deputy. His sweeping mandate directed that he was "to repair to Pozsony ... to
take part in the deliberation and passage of legislation as the
county's plenipotentiary representative, without instruction but
guided by his conscience and conviction, and to vote in like
manner."[5]

While Deák was readying his departure, the delegation from

the diet was received by the King in Vienna and presented the Address to the Throne. That same day, March 16, a royal rescript ordered the Palatine to appoint a ministry for the independent government of Hungary. Batthyány was named Prime Minister. By the time Deák reached Pozsony on March 20, the convulsion of the previous days had already accomplished much. While these achievements had been triggered by pressure from below, they had been realized from above, by legislative measures with the consent of the King—a great stride toward Deák's long-range goals. Deák had been drawn into the proceedings very much against his will, but he would now contribute richly to them both as a legislator and as Hungary's first Minister of Justice.

A chronological approach to Deák's dual role in the revolution would be confusing and clumsy. A brief summary of events, however, will aid in understanding a separate consideration of his two spheres of activity.

With the promulgation of the April Laws, the Hungarian revolution made sudden and significant progress toward the reshaping of society. Three local factors contributed to this success. The first was the happy chance that the last Hungarian feudal diet was already in session and so able to pass the reforms promptly. Both the other factors were the result of the long and patient work of Deák and the liberals: they were already a well-organized party and, with the Statement of the Opposition to hand, they had no need to improvise a program of fundamental social and political changes.

With Kossuth at the helm, the liberals led Hungary toward the modern age at a fast pace. For a while the dynasty cooperated. It had little choice. With the Habsburg possessions in Italy and the imperial capital of Vienna itself in rebellion, the court simply could not afford to oppose basically peaceful changes in Hungary. Count Lajos Batthyány's cabinet, inaugurated on March 17, started to implement the new laws at once, but ominous developments foreshadowed the revolution's doom.

The national minorities of Hungary organized themselves just as the Hungarian liberals had done and were entertaining maximalist goals of their own. The Hungarian liberals offered to share all the newly won liberties with them as co-citizens of

Hungary without regard to nationality distinctions, but the minorities were not satisfied with the offer. They sought their own territorial self-government. The liberals, on the other hand, saw such a reorganization of the unitary state of Hungary as the beginning of the partition of the lands of St. Stephen. Despite the determined efforts of many men of goodwill, the Hungarians and the national minorities were embarked on a collision course. A bloody clash seemed to be in the making, and in due time the dynasty began encouraging the minorities' demands in the hope of bringing it about.

Even before the June Days that marked the ascendancy of the counterrevolution in France—and, one might say, in Europe too—the Habsburg Empire had experienced its own June Days and counterrevolution. Prince Alfred Windisch-Graetz crushed the uprising in Prague and Field Marshal Josef Radetzky defeated the Italians at Santa Lucia. Though Radetzky then suffered several reverses, on July 24, 1848, he won the decisive battle of Custozza, and thus for the time being pacified northern Italy. In pace with the dynasty's successes elsewhere, its policy toward Hungary became more and more reactionary, and on September 11 it turned the arms of counterrevolution on Hungary itself. That day Count Josip Jelačić's Croatian troops crossed the River Drava and invaded Hungary. Repulsed at the battle of Pákozd, Jelačić fled to Vienna but two of his generals, many of his men, and much matériel were captured by the Hungarians. A second uprising broke out in Vienna on October 6, in part to forestall Austrian troop movements against the Hungarian revolutionary regime. After lengthy hesitation, Kossuth ordered his new armed forces to march on Vienna to aid the rebels. They were routed at Schwechat near the imperial capital.

On December 2 Ferdinand abdicated as emperor and king in favor of Francis Joseph I who did not, however, fulfill the constitutional requirements to become King of Hungary and was not acknowledged as such. In short order he launched an assault from four directions against Hungary, and by January 1, 1849, the Hungarian government fled from Pest to Debrecen. On March 4 Francis Joseph approved the Olmütz (Olomouc) Constitution drafted by Count Philipp Stadion, which partitioned the land of St. Stephen and for the rump of Hungary abrogated all the provisions of the old constitution that were contrary to the new one. The Hungarian Parliament responded by deposing the Habsburg dynasty on April 14, 1849. In the meantime the Hungarian armed forces had freed most of Hungary from the Habsburg grasp in the course of a remarkable spring campaign. On March 23, however, Field Marshal Radetzky conclusively defeated the Italians at Novara and permanently subdued northern Italy. Now a massive transfer of troops from Italy was possible and by mid-June these were reinforced by 200,000 of the Tsar's soldiers invading Hungary from the north. The Hungarian revolutionary army fought gallantly against the forces of the two great powers and an armed rebellion of the national minorities but lost battle after battle and finally on August 13 lay down its arms before the Russians at Világos.

Lajos Kossuth and many revolutionary statesmen found refuge at first in the Ottoman Empire, then moved on to the capitals of western Europe to continue their political struggle against the Habsburg dynasty from exile. Those who remained in Hungary faced terror. On October 6, 1849, Count Lajos Batthyány, the former Prime Minister, was shot and thirteen generals were executed in Arad—and this was but the beginning. Partitioned Hungary was to suffer under a regime of repression for many years.

This then was the background of events against which Deák's activities as a legislator and Minister of Justice must be viewed.

Deák's legislative activities during the revolution were the climax of his career as a social reformer. Afterwards his focus altered, and during the 1860's and after the Compromise he concentrated on constructing and then safeguarding the new relationship between Hungary and Austria and between Hungary and the Habsburg dynasty. The outstanding enactments of the revolution, the 31 April Laws, were all passed and promulgated within the brief space of two weeks. So rapidly were they enacted that they were inevitably less then perfect. There was no question in March about what needed repeal and about what social and political arrangements needed to be made, but drafting clear, comprehensive, exact laws in a bare two weeks was another matter. As a result, the April Laws, while they met the minimum needs of reform, fell woefully short of being a precise codification. They were haphazard, ambiguous, and deficient. The demise of feudalism and the inception of modern government and society in Hungary came about in a climate of confusion, and one of the first major tasks entrusted to Deák by his fellow legislators—and indeed expected of him by the man in the street—was to create order out of the legislative chaos.

Ferenc Deák's strategy was quite definite. He felt that his first duty was to maintain respect for the laws as they stood, regardless of their shortcomings. His second goal was to draft and have passed new laws that would eliminate ambiguities, extend benefits to as many citizens as possible, and eradicate every last vestige of feudalism. He believed that one of the foundations of society was not only respect for the law but also for order and for private property. "As God is my witness, I have been longing for conditions to change ever since my childhood," he told the Lower House on March 30, "but if the cost is anarchy, I shall have no truck with it. I realize that revival is associated with commotion, but the security of the individual and his property is sacrosanct ... and is to be respected, whatever the circumstances."[6] For a liberal statesman with a bourgeois mentality like Deák to speak or behave any other way would have been unthinkable, so his critics have some reason for accusing him of trying to end the revolution too early. In order to clear up the vagueness of the April Laws and to avoid similar confusion in any new legislation, Deák urged the deputies not to attempt to draft comprehensive laws but to pass resolutions only on principles of reforms.

Deák assumed it would not be a long process to adopt such declarations since the liberal majority was large enough to pass resolutions and solid enough to agree on principles. The hope of Deák, the ideological radical, was that a large number of such reform principles would be endorsed by the diet while the revolutionary wave was still at its peak, then, once it had subsided, several Parliaments would have time enough over a period probably of years to deal with their precise codification. In this way the need for further reform and the need for rigorous codification could both be met.

Deák followed the same tactics both in the last diet and in the first popularly elected Parliament, so that his strategy may be viewed as a single whole. He gave the first indication of the line he would follow almost as soon as he had arrived at Pozsony. In a letter to his brother-in-law, József Oszterhuber-Tarányi, on March 28, 1848, he wrote:

> I reached Pozsony on March 20 at one p.m. and found everything at fever pitch. Universal taxation and the emancipation of the serfs had already been passed by both houses. . . . Many of the lords and the Palatine himself asked me, if possible, to amend the law on emancipation. I told them, however, that, though I did not approve of this improvisation by the legislature and was not convinced that it had to take the form it did, since it had already been completed and passed by both houses, and since it had already been announced in many counties, any and every alteration would be dangerous and to take back what had already been granted would be tantamount to starting a bloody peasant war.[7]

Deák took his seat in the legislature on March 23 during the debate on abolition of the entail system. While it continued in existence, only the crown, the church and the nobility could own land (some towns were also entitled to and a few actually did own serf villages). To make sense of the emancipation of the serfs, it was imperative for them to be able to own land, and for this the entail had to go. Deák sensed that another ambiguous law was in the making and intervened to prevent it. His tactics gained their first success. The house adopted the basic principle, but left the government and future Parliaments to codify it.[8]

When the diet turned to Hungary's contribution to the costs of the court, common diplomacy, and common defense, a lengthy and contentious debate ensued and another ill-framed law began to take shape. Once more Deák intervened and pressed through a brief act granting three million florins as an advance for all three budget items, on condition that the court would account for it. The ministry of finance was instructed to elaborate a permanent solution.

The diet then began weighing Hungary's traditionally autonomous county system and the new system of ministerial government responsible to Parliament. "The county administrations and an accountable ministry are two mutually incompatible systems," Deák stated, "and we have reached the point where we must

opt for either local or responsible ministerial government."[9] Like
Kossuth, however, Deák believed that precipitate radical change
would be dangerous. For centuries the counties' autonomy had
been the most effective safeguard against Habsburg efforts to
extend absolutist rule to Hungary, and it might even now be
needed if the dynasty were to try its former despotic ways before
responsible ministerial government had become fully entrenched.
Deák and Kossuth therefore agreed that the system of county
self-government should not be modified more than absolutely
necessary.

The sum effect of the April Laws, in the passage of which
Deák had played no mean part, was to secure for Hungary an
independent administration with its own responsible ministry
free from imperial interference, a liberal form of government
with a built-in system of checks and balances. The monarch was
to reign, but not rule, and his decree was to run only with
ministerial countersignature. In short, the diet provided for the
legal foundations of a bourgeois society unrestricted by feudal
bonds where all men were free and equal before the law. The
April Laws did not challenge the Pragmatic Sanction, and they
also left intact such royal prerogatives as the investment of
bishops and archbishops, the commissioning of officers of the
armed forces, and even deployment of the army abroad, though
in each case ministerial countersignature was required so that
the prerogatives were far from absolute.[10]

The last feudal diet thus created a constitutional framework
within which peaceful progress was possible so long as both
dynasty and nation observed the laws promulgated on April 11.
It was agreed that Hungary's first popularly elected Parliament
should meet as soon as possible to continue and complete the
work of the last diet. Elections were held in June, and Parliament
assembled in Pest on July 5, 1848. This new legislative body
differed in origin from the diet. In the diet the counties had an
absolute monopoly of legislative power, for they had a total
of some fifty votes to the single one that the representatives of
all the towns could collectively cast. In Parliament every member
had one vote, whether his constituency was rural or urban. Deák
and the liberals deserve credit for curbing the Upper House by
raising even higher the already high property qualifications for

a seat, and also for legislating salaries for members of Parliament. In debate on the latter question, Deák said: "They [the lords] say that the poor should not be able to stand for election, so that membership would be limited to the financial aristocracy; the requirement that members should be unsalaried would in fact constitute a very high property qualification indeed."[11] An amendment by the lords was voted down, and members of Parliament were granted their salaries. In consequence several men of modest means were elected in June. In classic liberal tradition, property qualifications for the electorate were fairly high. The new franchise law extended suffrage to all those who had the right to vote in the past (the nobility, including the "slippered" nobility who, under the new property qualifications, would otherwise generally have lost their vote), townsmen owning real estate valued at 300 florins or more, independent merchants, artisans with at least one employee, farmers owning at least one-quarter of a session of land (land enough to provide for a peasant family and yield a marketable surplus), all graduates, ministers, priests and teachers, and finally rentiers with an annual income of at least 100 florins. The franchise was denied to all those under the authority of a "master" (employees).[12]

The new Lower House was still dominated by the liberal gentry, but they no longer had a monopoly of political power. The breakdown of its membership was 72% landed nobility, 25% townsmen, 2% junior clergy, and 1% peasants. By occupation rather than social standing, 30% of its members were officials of state, 12% county officials, 8% municipal officials, 12% lawyers, and 1% physicians.[13] The members of the house included one artisan (Mátyás Tanai), one butcher (József Zsitvai), and two peasants (Mihály Antal and Miklós Szivák).[14] Some 30 to 40 of the 426 members were radicals. Though a minority, they were extremely militant and cohesive and had the backing of pressure groups outside Parliament. One of the most prominent of these left-wing radicals was a member from Fejér county, László Madarász, who, to support the radicals, organized the Society of Equality, which rapidly acquired a membership of more than a thousand.[15] The radicals also had the support of an "official" group, the Committee of Public Safety in Pest. Both groups funneled pressure from below and lent the radicals considerable assistance.[16]

The spokesmen for the landed gentry with liberal sympathies were Ferenc Deák, Gábor Klauzál, and István Bezerédj. Unquestionably fighters for national independence, during the diet of 1832–36 the contemporary agents of the court had considered them the "extreme left." Now they were the arbiters of the proceedings: Kossuth had to lean on them for support. Many of their supporters sacrificed their lives for the goals of the revolution. Most of the members of Parliament from Transylvania and from the towns everywhere in the kingdom rallied to Deák. So did the two peasant representatives, who accepted Deák's leadership and frequently consulted him.[17]

The composition of the Upper House did not change. All adult male aristocrats, bishops, archbishops, heads of major religious orders, and the high sheriffs of the counties had seats in the senior chamber—800 in all. Both in its mentality and its source of power it remained a relic of the feudal past,[18] but its role declined as the revolution proceeded. In late March 1848 Emil Dessewffy noted: "Affairs in Pozsony go at a gallop. . . . The lords have degenerated into nonentities. They have had to reduce their activities to registering the resolutions of the estates [Lower House]."[19] Little changed with the advent of a popularly elected Parliament, neither the lords' feudal attitudes nor their devotion to the dynasty. But they did not oppose the revolution to a man. Even during its most radical period, 59 of them were fighting for the revolution, and 15 others were engaged on government assignments for it.[20]

Ferenc Deák's major effort in Parliament was to complete the emancipation of the serfs by eliminating the remnants of feudal dues and privileges. The April Laws had freed the peasants from hereditary servitude; released them from the lords' administrative, judicial, and moral authority; provided for state remittance of all their dues in money, kind, and services; and granted them title to the lands they worked "urbarially." In other words, they were given title to all lands registered as serf sessions, lands to which in the past they had had "strong" rights despite the fact that such land was the property of the lords. These "strong" rights included a ban on their eviction so long as they rendered their feudal dues to the landowners, the right of their issue to inherit the same rights, and the right to sell their rights and their investment in the land to other serfs. All those who had tilled such urbarial land now owned it completely. The same was not true for the former cotters, landless peasants who had been bound in their person to their lords. They had worked a tiny fragment of urbarial land, or none at all and had labored on allodial land (the lords' demesne land). The April Laws had freed the cotters in their person but had conferred no property on them—the most glaring shortcoming of the emancipation of Hungary's serfs. The lords had also retained several of their more exploitative and profitable monopolies, such as the rights to operate the taverns, mills, and butchers' shops. Finally, it was unclear whether the peasants still enjoyed such easements as gathering kindling in the lords' woodlands and cutting reeds in their marshlands, or whether they had been repealed. This ambiguous situation had caused widespread discontent and peasant seizures of allodial land were not uncommon. This was the immensely prickly nettle that Deák had to grasp. He set the Ministry of Justice to draft a precise and comprehensive law, since it would not have been enough to enact bare principles, as he recommended elsewhere. The busy months of summer and fall were coming, and answers had to be found promptly on who owned what and whose crops were whose.

The issue was all the more pressing because the number of landless freedmen was enormous. According to figures of Elek Fényes, the chief statistician of the Ministry of the Interior in 1848, 624,134 freed peasant families had been given title to land and 913,962 cotter families had been emancipated with no land.[21] Of Hungary's 1,732,713 serf families on the eve of emancipation, 33.6% produced a marketable surplus from the land they worked, 2.4% produced enough to support themselves, 1.9% worked less than a subsistence area of urbarial land, 44.6% had dwellings but tilled no urbarial land, 6.3% had neither dwelling nor land, and 11.2% were servants, domestic and field.[22] In other words, nearly two-thirds of the serfs could not provide for themselves from land to which they had "strong" rights. Meanwhile, after emancipation the latifundia survived, concentrating most of the land in the hands of the aristocracy and the Roman Catholic Church.

In fact, 72% of Hungary's population lived off only 37% of its arable land.[23]

Radical alteration of these property relationships was essential, and this was the goal of the draft prepared by Deák's ministry. It aimed to resolve two conflicting requirements: to get rid of the residue of feudal conditions and confer the maximum benefit on as many peasants as possible, and to preserve the lords' property rights that were based on past law and custom. The draft was a massive, all-encompassing opus divided into 77 paragraphs and was the most sophisticated social codification that Deák ever put together.[24]

Had the whole draft become law, the vast majority of the peasantry, though poor, would at least have had enough to subsist. As it was, because of the pressure of other business, Parliament began to debate the draft only on September 15, 1848. Unfortunately, the counterrevolution brought debate to a halt, and this remarkable draft, Deák's supreme effort as a social reformer, never was enacted.

The military forces of the counterrevolution were drawing ever nearer during Parliament's last days in session in Pest. By December 30, 1848, the main force under Prince Alfred Windisch-Graetz had reached Komárom, and the Hungarians under Arthur Görgey were in steady retreat. Another Hungarian army commanded by Lázár Mészáros, the Minister of Defense, had had to evacuate Miskolc before the advance of General Schlick from Galicia. In this dire situation the members of Parliament were busy discussing how much compensation the state should pay landowners for their lost incomes. Finally, Deák lost patience with his colleagues' self-centeredness and told them: "There is something repellent about discussing our own pockets at this time, especially since we should not forget that, although we have been elected on the basis of popular representation, probably most of the House consists of those who will receive compensation rather than those who will not." Deák proposed that the question be tabled. The House agreed, and three days later members were boarding trains for Debrecen, the new temporary capital to the east.[25] Ferenc Deák himself headed in a different direction to fulfill the mission he had been charged with by Parliament, his last action as a legislator and in behalf of the revolution. Before following him, however, the clock should be turned back to consider his policies and activities as Hungary's first Minister of Justice.

Scarcely had Deák's coach rattled into Pozsony on March 20 than he had been ushered into Count Lajos Batthyány's residence. Batthyány had been appointed Prime Minister on March 17 and had been authorized to present to the crown as many persons as he deemed necessary to form his ministry responsible to Parliament. Batthyány was thus in the process of putting together Hungary's government. A few hours later Deák left Batthyány's house designated Minister of Justice. Batthyány's ministry was installed by the King on April 7 and on April 14 moved to its permanent seat in Pest to take over the administration of Hungary independent of any imperial institutions.

Pesti Hírlap commented on April 21: "Ferenc Deák arrived here yesterday midday. The public views him with confidence and satisfaction.... Now everybody is forming imaginary ministries and from none of them is Deák left out.... The Prime Minister confers with him frequently and the results of these consultations can only be beneficial."[26] For Deák, however, Batthyány's offer was an agonizing one. Deák confided to his brother-in-law:

You might be able to guess how painful it was for me to join a ministry formed under the present circumstances in our country. I was obliged to do so by honor and duty, for Batthyány stated that he would not form a ministry without me in it. If he had resigned because of my refusal, there is hardly anyone else who would undertake to form a ministry instead of him. Then I should have been accused of preventing Hungary's first responsible ministry from being formed by my pusillanimous behavior. So perforce I have promised Batthyány my name and my cooperation for a few weeks, as long as my health permits.[27]

In the same letter Deák gave a very pessimistic appraisal of the situation in Hungary:

The situation in the country is very alarming. Up there [in Vienna] they cannot get used to the new order of things and they delay every

issue much more than is advisable under the present circumstances.
In Pest a sudden emotional outburst that would endanger the country could happen at any moment. For the time being, no one can
foresee or even guess at what the near future holds. Our country has
perhaps never faced greater peril. Whether the Russians will crush us,
or Austria's might again, or even anarchy possibly, God alone knows.[28]

Revolutionary conditions were indeed the worst possible circumstances for Deák to have to work in, but he served the
administration diligently and stood by its policies as long as
he was a member of it.

The ministry's fundamental policy was loyally to execute the
April Laws. Most of the ministers wished to consolidate the
achievements of the revolution rather than extend them and
hoped that this would ensure law and order in Hungary, regardless of the revolutionary fervor in the rest of the Habsburg
domains and elsewhere in Europe. They even dared to look
forward to the dynasty's eventual cooperation.

For Deák the name of the game was *Realpolitik* combined
with a determination to uphold the law, including unquestionably the April Laws, which were the basis for his words and
actions throughout the revolution and right up till the Compromise—a remarkable record of consistence. A no less solid foundation of his policy was respect for the Pragmatic Sanction, which
was for him as binding as any other law. Deák was at pains not
to collide with the dynasty, but this effort was subordinate to his
respect for the law. When the court finally moved to crush
Hungary's valid laws, Deák's loyalty went to the latter.

The most pressing problem facing Batthyány's ministry was
Hungary's nationalities problem. Like most of the classical
liberals of the day, the Hungarian liberals believed that all the
ills of the state and society could be cured by making the rights
and dignity of the individual secure. Kossuth was utterly convinced of this. To Pál Somssich, a member of the diet delegation
which left Pozsony on March 15 for Vienna, Kossuth said:
"Poltroon! You don't know the power of freedom. It is stronger
than nationality, religion, kinship or friendship. It can turn all
of them into patriotism."[29] Deák was of the same mind and,
with a little less bombast, might have said something similar.
In the beginning, the kingdom's national minorities with few

exceptions welcomed the Hungarians' success in March and gave them their support. Had Hungary's statesmen gone on to guarantee the specific national rights of all the minorities, they might well have enlisted them in the common defense of their freedoms. They concentrated instead on consolidating what they had won, and a few, including Deák, sought to expand the political, social, and economic rights of the individual. They did so in the belief that all the citizens of Hungary, regardless of their nationality or religion, would benefit and be satisfied. The national minorities, however, pressed their own demands, and, despite countless negotiations and plans, tension mounted and conflict increased. Perhaps the most tragic and unnecessary was the clash of the Hungarians with the Croats, a conflict that seriously jeopardized the April Laws. It was a collision that Deák tried hard to avert.

On Kolowrat's recommendation, the monarch on March 23 appointed Baron Josip Jelačić Ban of Croatia but without consulting the Hungarians. The Hungarian government wanted to come to an accommodation with the Croats, so early in June Batthyány went to Innsbruck to meet Jclačić, but the Ban failed to show up. Batthyány then arranged for the King to issue a rescript removing Jelačić from office. The rescript was gazetted in the *Wiener Zeitung* and published by the Hungarian ministry, but the Hungarians still hoped to reach a compromise. Archduke John was asked to mediate and set up a new meeting between Batthyány and Jelačić in Vienna for late July. Meanwhile it became clear that the court had prevaricated, for, despite the rescript, Jelačić was continuing to act as Ban and was receiving full financial and military assistance for future action against Hungary. When Batthyány finally met with Jelačić in July, the Ban declined to discuss Croatian grievances but affirmed instead that Croatia's troubles would be solved if the Hungarian ministry would refrain immediately from its preparations to establish an independent Hungarian army, desist from implementing that part of the April Laws instituting Hungary's independent financial system, and accept a share of the Austrian state debt. In short, Jelačić reiterated the court's own demands, which had nothing to do even indirectly with Hungarian-Croatian relations.[30] The Hungarians still did not give up, and Deák and

Szemere drafted a compromise agreement that would settle the Croatian affair amicably. The full Hungarian ministerial council endorsed their draft on August 27, 1848.[31] The resolution offered the broadest possible self-government for Croatia: "If all these conditions will not satisfy the Croats, Hungary is ready to recognize the full independence of Croatia and will be willing to conclude a free alliance with that free state. Fiume [Rijeka] and the Hungarian littoral will remain part of the Kingdom of Hungary with free access through Croatia," the resolution drafted by Deák and Szemere concluded.[32]

Once the draft had the ministerial council's endorsement, Deák and Batthyány took it to Vienna to seek royal assent. Their quest was fruitless, for the court had no interest in making peace but was preparing for war between the Croats and Hungarians. The Hungarians made a last-ditch effort to conciliate the Croats by issuing a manifesto proclaiming that Hungary had no wish to diminish the nationality and freedoms of the Croats but offered them peace and friendship. It was displayed in all the border areas, and government commissioners were named to negotiate with the Croats, but in the meantime Jelačić's army had crossed the Hungarian frontier.[33]

Unfortunately, the nationalisms of the Hungarians and the national minorities were self-seeking. None of them had the breadth of vision to see that their interests were the same vis-à-vis the counterrevolutionary regime in Vienna. The Hungarians overemphasized the idea of the freedom and equality of the individual and expected too much when they counted on the non-Hungarians to join in the defense of such rights. The national minorities expected too much when they put their faith in the court to defend their individual and national rights rather than the revolutionary Hungarian regime. The secessionist feelings of the national minorities grew steadily stronger through the summer of 1848, seriously undermining the Hungarian liberals' struggle against the Habsburg counterrevolution. By the end of that summer the non-Hungarian nationalists had become the court's allies.

Deák as Minister of Justice organized his ministry rapidly and enlisted men of talent for it. The first bill prepared by his ministry was a decree on press offenses. Work on it was rapid because

Deák's minority reports for the diet's subcommittee on reform of the criminal code in 1843 had contained provisions for exactly such a decree. By April 29 the draft was in the hands of the ministerial council, which duly promulgated it.[34]

Deák was an energetic administrator who kept his finger on the pulse of the nation. His door was always open to visitors and many peasants, in particular, called on him with grievances. On May 25 he issued regulations to improve the prison system by providing better conditions in the existing jails, building new, more sanitary correction facilities, and separating apprehended prisoners from convicted criminals. He also simplified the procedures of the Supreme Court. In short, he instituted reforms wherever his own ministry had power to do so.

Deák exerted himself to have the ministerial council adopt the policies he recommended, but when he was overruled, he stood faithfully by the council's resolutions. A case in point was the Austrian state debt. The court demanded that Hungary should take responsibility for 200 million florins of the Austrian state debt and the 10 million florins' interest they accrued a year. The demand came in the form of a royal rescript on April 7, 1848, as the new Hungarian ministry was being invested. Since Hungary's annual revenue was 28 million florins, the demand seemed excessive but, with better financial policies and organization, arrangements could have been made and a particularly sore point in the relations between the dynasty and Hungary could have been removed. It seemed a matter of common sense and in fact in 1867 Deák agreed to Hungary's taking over three times as much of the Austrian debt. The court demand in 1848 therefore could probably have been shouldered but, under pressure from below, Deák sided with Kossuth and voted to reject it.[35]

The Italian question was a much thornier one than the Austrian state debt. A royal rescript reminded Parliament that "the King of Sardinia and other powers have attacked the Habsburg dominions and it has not yet been possible to end that war." The Hungarian government began discussion of the issue on July 15 and took note that the Prime Minister had made a commitment in Vienna that Hungary would aid the Habsburg war effort and that the April Laws, especially Act III, 1848, acknowledged responsibility to "defend the monarch against foreign attack." Its view was that the dynasty should be asked to have the national minorities, in particular the Croats, end their rebellion against the Hungarian ministry so that with the restoration of order Hungary would be in a position to send troops to the King's assistance.[36] The extreme left saw the war in Italy as a fight for freedom against Austrian counterrevolutionary attempts to suppress it. Under these circumstances, it believed, Hungary could ally itself only with the Italians. Pál Nyáry, a leftist member of Parliament, told the Lower House on July 22 that the ministry's Italian policy was "the policy of reaction." In response Deák said: "The accusation that our policy is reactionary cannot be accepted in silence. Answer must be given. By reaction all the encyclopedias of the world understand the suppression of realized liberties and the reestablishment of absolutist rule.... The ministry can be accused of no such intention. If we recognize Italy as free and seceded from Austria, for that would be the outcome of our order to the military to withdraw from there, wouldn't that mean that we had allied ourselves with Italy against the Austrian Emperor? Whatever interpretation might be given to the Pragmatic Sanction, no man of sense could take it to mean that Hungary has a right to ally itself against the Emperor of Austria."[37] The Hungarians really had two alternatives. They could assume the left-wing radicals' position and take the Italians' part, winning victory or going down to defeat with the rest of Europe's revolutionaries, or they could follow Deák's recommendation to respect the Pragmatic Sanction and the April Laws, and in so doing, look like traitors to the European revolution by abetting the Habsburg counterrevolutionary effort against Italian freedom. Parliament chose a middle course that proved unacceptable to the dynasty and looked to revolutionaries elsewhere like a betrayal. By 233 votes to 36 it resolved: "When order and peace have been safely reestablished in Hungary and the country's material and spiritual integrity has been assured, we shall gladly lend Your Majesty aid to achieve a peaceful settlement that, on one hand, will secure the dignity of the throne, and on the other will respond to the Italian nation's constitutional liberties and reasonable desires."[38] This resolution simply furnished the Viennese counter-revolutionaries with another excuse to denounce the Hungarians for disloyalty and press on with preparations for a final settling of accounts. Meanwhile, Field Marshal Joseph Radetzky's victory on July 24 at the battle of Custozza settled the Italian question for good. Not only was there no longer a need for Hungarian aid, but troops were freed for use against Hungary, and the Habsburg court then launched the counterrevolution.

On August 31, 1848, the Palatine delivered a royal rescript to the Hungarian government demanding the restoration of the imperial government's authority over Hungary's independent ministry. The counterrevolution had come into the open.[39] The rescript ordered a Hungarian ministerial delegation to be dispatched at once to Vienna for negotiations. This last demand was hypocritical, for Batthyány and Deák were already in Vienna and had been trying for several days without success to gain an audience with the King.[40] István Széchenyi at last recognized the hostility of the dynasty, and, on realizing that his unfaltering belief in it for a whole generation had been only self-deception, suffered a nervous collapse.

The Hungarian revolution now faced its most serious crisis. Rather than weakening the Hungarians, however, it increased their resolve. Unlike the French bourgeoisie who, when faced with the proletarian uprising of the June Days, accepted a counterrevolutionary role, the majority of the liberal Hungarian nobles responded to the counterrevolution's threat by moving further to the left. Following the political leadership of Kossuth into a coalition with the left, they took a major part in organizing armed national defense of the first fruits of the revolution.[41]

This leftward trend was evident in the parliamentary resolution of September 4. On Kossuth's suggestion a hundred members of the Lower House and representatives from the Upper House were sent to Vienna to clarify whether the dynasty was willing to reign constitutionally. They left for Vienna on September 5, just one day after the King formally reinstated Jelačić as Ban of Croatia without consulting the Hungarian ministry again.[42] The Hungarian delegation, which included Deák but not Kossuth, received from the King on September 9 a meaningless reply that demonstrated clearly that the court had opted for counterrevolution rather than a constitutional course. On September 10 the

Batthyány ministry resigned because constitutional government had become impossible, and the majority did not wish to take the road of armed resistance. The following day the Palatine again named Batthyány to form a government. On the same day, September 11, Jelačić crossed the Drava and began the invasion of Hungary.[43]

This time Deák did not accept Batthyány's invitation to help him form a new ministry. As Habsburg armies rolled across the Hungarian plains, Deák abandoned his office as Minister of Justice. He explained his reasons for not joining the new ministry in a letter to Oszterhuber-Tarányi on September 22:

> You urge me to rejoin the ministry . . . but . . . Jelačić is fighting a war against us at the court's wish, with the knowledge and on behalf of the King, and His Majesty refuses even to issue an order to stop the war. Now, how could I be a minister and an instrument of the authority that is waging war against our country and that demands as the price of peace the surrender of the most important features of our national independence and constitutional liberties? . . . Not for a single hour could I identify myself with the court's policy.[44]

The hectic course of events in September and October swept away Batthyány's ministry, and executive power was vested in the Committee of National Defense. Deák had no part in this body but retained his seat in Parliament. On December 2 Ferdinand V abdicated and his brother Francis Charles, who was his rightful successor according to the Pragmatic Sanction, renounced his claims. Francis Charles's son, Francis Joseph I, was proclaimed Emperor of Austria and King of Hungary, a completely unconstitutional act since Francis Joseph did not swear the required oath of loyalty to the Hungarian constitution. The Hungarian Parliament declared the change of sovereigns null and void, and proclaimed Francis Joseph a usurper.[45] Deák voted for the resolution.

By mid-October the counterrevolutionary forces had retaken Transylvania. Early in December troops from Galicia invaded northern Hungary. The main force under Windisch-Graetz crossed the Hungarian border on December 13, driving for Pest and Buda with the objective of crushing the Hungarian forces and government. The second thrust of the counterrevolution had begun. The main Hungarian army did not give battle but instead withdrew from the Transdanubian region without a major encounter. By the last days of December the twin capitals lay exposed to an immediate attack by the enemy. Parliament resolved to move its seat to Debrecen and declared: "At this moment of decision for the country an attempt should be made to reach a peaceful solution on the basis of the nation's honor, constitutional liberties and welfare." The Lord Chief Justice, Count György Majláth, the former president of the Hungarian Royal Court Chancellery, Count Antal Majláth, Archbishop József Lonovics of Eger, Count Lajos Batthyány and Ferenc Deák were instructed to "seek an armistice from the commander in chief of the enemy in order to make arrangements for the intended peace and in addition, should circumstances permit, present themselves before His Imperial and Royal Majesty Francis Joseph. Parliament awaits their report on the results.[46]

Deák drafted the report dated January 1, 1849 on the meeting with Prince Windisch-Graetz at Bicske, which was read to Parliament on January 13. It stated:

> Prince Windisch-Graetz did not admit one member of the delegation, Count Lajos Batthyány; the other four . . . were received, but not as a delegation from Parliament because it had been dissolved by Ferdinand V. . . . He [Windisch-Graetz] answered the delegation's words about a peaceful settlement by saying that, after what had happened in the country, there could be no talk of an armistice or other form of bargaining: the only possibility is unconditional submission (*unbedingte Unterwerfung*).[47]

When Deák received no response to his report to Parliament, on January 14, 1849, he sent Parliament another report identical with his first, in case the latter had not been received. This was his last message to the assembly sent from the capital, which was occupied by the Austrian army. He did not go to Debrecen, because Windisch-Graetz would let him go only on condition that he would persuade Kossuth and Parliament to surrender unconditionally, and this Deák would not do. Later he remarked: "I was quite wise not to persuade my friends to let themselves be hanged."[48]

CHAPTER 10

Deák's Passive Resistance to the Counterrevolution

DEÁK was still in Pest when Francis Joseph proclaimed the Stadion constitution in Olmütz on March 4, 1849 and nullified Hungary's constitution.[1] The Hungarian Parliament's declaration of independence on April 14 was a response to the Olmütz proclamation, and April 14 in turn was the date, according to Austrian constitutional lawyers, on which the *Verwirkungstheorie* (forfeiture theory) became applicable to Hungary, the theory that Hungary had forfeited her constitutional status and rights because it was in insurrection. Deák's goal now became to restore Hungary's constitutional position.

Early in 1849 Deák went to Zala, where he spent some of his time at Kehida and some with his brother-in-law in Pusztaszentlászló. He made several attempts to rejoin Parliament in Debrecen but each time he was turned back by the Habsburg troops. Perhaps he was not trying very hard anyway. After the Hungarian Army had retaken the capital, Deák returned to Pest. There on June 4, 1849 he accidentally ran into Kossuth, but they seem to have had no political discussions. In fact they had very little to say to each other. Kossuth was basking in the glory of his temporary military victory, while Deák believed that with the declaration of independence the Hungarians had overplayed their hand.

On December 4, 1849, Deák was summoned before the counterrevolutionary military tribunal. Detained and investigated, five months later, after several hearings, he was completely exonerated on the ground that he did not vote for the dethronement of the dynasty. Nevertheless, in 1852, as despotism was tightening its grip, he burned all his correspondence in order not to implicate others were he again to be prosecuted.[2] While Deák

138

was under investigation in 1850, Anton von Schmerling, the Minister of Justice, called a group of legal experts together in Vienna to discuss ways of bringing Hungarian civil and criminal court procedures into line with the Austrian system. Deák was invited to take part, but on April 25, 1850 turned the offer down. "After the regrettable events of the recent past and in the prevailing circumstances," he wrote, "it is not possible to cooperate actively in public affairs."[3] This letter was Deák's first significant public avowal of passive opposition. He continued with it until late December 1860, when for the first time in his life he met with Francis Joseph and then took part in the Lord Chief Justice's conference from January 23 to March 3, 1861. But Deák warned those who wished to rush into an early settlement that ". . . we should seek not what leads sooner but without harm to our end goals . . . for the nation might if it must sacrifice its money even its sons' blood but not its rights . . ."[4]

Four factors require consideration in this period of Deák's resistance: the constitutional foundations of his attitude; the political, social and economic motives for his decision to move permanently to Pest in November 1854; his campaign in support of the widow and children of Hungary's poet laureate, Mihály Vörösmarty; and his activities as a member and director of the Hungarian Academy of Sciences. Until his move to Pest Deák remained completely inactive in national affairs; thereafter, though he still opposed the new order, he began to take part in public life.

One of Deák's contemporaries, Imre Halász, wrote of this period: "The shadows of the trees of Kehida saved for the future this extraordinary, valuable force, who could probably wait and persist like no one else, and who by his teachings and example could persuade others to wait and be patient, too."[5] At the heart of this perseverance was Deák's insistence on the continuing validity of the April Laws. Innumerable contemporaries attested to the fact that Deák's resolve remained firm even when all others did not dare to hope. Deák's family lawyer, Sámuel Szabó, wrote that to his intimates Deák always emphasized that the starting point for any settlement with the dynasty could only be 1848.[6] Another frequent visitor, Károly Kerkápolyi, a friend from Deák's law school days, reported that Deák was sure that the present regime was only provisional and would sooner or later come to an end, and that the basis for the return to normal would be the April Laws. He also quoted Deák as telling him that, once the April Laws had been revalidated, so that they could meet changed conditions "they could be altered with the consent of the legislative authorities," that is, the King and Parliament, the only authorities entitled to enact, amend, and repeal laws. Kerkápolyi stressed that Deák was very much alone in his intransigence and that most people, either out of opportunism or the desire for a speedy return to normal, would have been satisfied with the restoration of Hungary's prerevolutionary constitutional status as it had been in 1847. "Deák was the sole person of the opinion that the starting point that would tie together the future and the past could be nothing other than the most recent constitutional past and that was 1848."[7]

Deák's tenacity went back to the September crisis of 1848 when the counterrevolution came into the open. At that time he had written to his brother-in-law that he could not be a minister of the authority that demanded as the price of peace the surrender of the most important features of Hungary's national independence and constitutional liberties.[8] Both during the revolution and afterwards Deák found it unthinkable to cooperate with the dynasty as long as it violated Hungary's national independence and constitutional freedoms. Deák denied the court's insistence that the reestablishment of Hungary's constitutional rights might some time occur as a concession of the benevolent monarch. "It is not a concession but a duty," Deák said, "to fulfill that, the denial of which constitutes a breach of law."[9] That duty had to be performed by the monarch, an act which was the basis on which the Compromise of 1867 was negotiated.

This crowning success of Deák's policy, however, came only in 1867, nearly two decades after the revolution had been quelled. But was passive resistance the only line Deák could have taken during the 1850's? Even Deák himself sometimes doubted that he would achieve anything by it. Often despondent and pessimistic, he knew how weak Hungary was in comparison with the dynasty. This awareness did not raise his spirits. It was faith, not *Realpolitik*, that gave him the moral strength to persevere.

This faith was upheld by his conception of the sacrosanct nature of law promulgated by the proper "legislative authorities." Since the counterrevolution was built on violation of the law, its eventual fall was a matter of belief, and he was convinced that the fall would be hastened by the regime's own blunders. Pál Somssich remarked in his diary: "He [Deák] did not trust primarily to Hungary's strength but rather to Austria's weakness in general and to the megalomaniac attitude of its statesmen in particular."[10]

Blunders and megalomania may have been grounds for hope over the long run but they are not the stuff of *Realpolitik*. In fact, Hungary did not become a problem that demanded resolution until the four causes that had ensured Habsburg victory in 1849 began to disappear. These were Russian support, British interest in the maintenance of the Habsburg Empire to preserve the European balance of power, Habsburg ascendancy in Germany, and the absence of a domestic or foreign power capable of freeing Italy from alien control. In the early 1850's no one could foresee that any of these props was going to weaken, let alone collapse within two decades. So Deák was taking a chance. His political intuition, irrational but nevertheless the keystone of the "art" of politics, was teamed with his dogged rational insistence on the validity of properly promulgated law, and this combination of the irrational with the rational paid off.

For Deák it was an uphill struggle. That he was ultimately successful was due not to the fact that he was right but that the court was wrong. Hungarian political figures, many conservative but also some moderately liberal, gave the Habsburg court numerous opportunities to act generously and win the Hungarians' gratitude. As early as April 1850 the conservative Emil Dessewffy joined the distinguished liberal intellectual Eötvös in drafting a memorandum to Francis Joseph urging a return to the situation of 1847. How favorable their suggestion was to the dynasty was evidenced by the wide publicity the memorandum received in the Viennese press. Also in 1850 the conservative Somssich published in Vienna a pamphlet entitled *Das legitime Recht Ungarns und seines Königs* ("The Legitimate Rights of Hungary and Its King"), which followed the same argument. Somssich even went so far as to challenge the April

Laws on the grounds that they had been passed by legislators who had overstepped their county assemblies' instructions and were therefore invalid. Such a claim ought to have pleased the regime, but it remained unmoved. Almost alone, Deák dissented from both the memorandum and the pamphlet, contending that the April Laws were constitutionally valid in every respect because they had been universally approved by the Hungarian nation, the foremost source of validation for any law.[11] When he was urged to join political actions short of his own goals on patriotic grounds, he retorted: "The country might claim my life and properties but not my convictions."[12]

By 1857, two years before the outbreak of Austria's war with Sardinia and France, it looked as though Deák's policy of noncooperation had gone down to defeat. The court made gestures that appeared conciliatory and received positive responses from Hungarian statesmen ready to compromise on the basis of 1847. The most significant reply was again drafted by Count Emil Dessewffy. His new memorandum, issued on May 9, 1857, coincided with the announcement of a visit to Hungary by Emperor Francis Joseph and Empress Elizabeth. Signed by 129 persons, all of them aristocrats and senior clergy apart from three dozen minor noblemen and seven Pest merchants, it favored preservation of a unitary empire and within it the reestablishment of Hungary's constitutional status prior to 1848.[13]

In similar vein, Eötvös published in Leipzig in 1859 a pamphlet entitled *Die Garantien der Macht und Einheit Oesterreichs* ("The Guarantees of the Power and Unity of Austria"). It acknowledged the need to preserve the unity of the empire and proposed not a return to 1847 but the ratification of the Stadion constitution of 1849. That constitution, Eötvös wrote, though by no means perfect, "secures all the fundamental principles of constitutional liberty" and upholds all the prerequisites for imperial power and unity. He granted that it contained deficiencies in such areas as the autonomy of the crown lands, the rights of the nationalities and local government, which the events of 1848 had shown were a vital concern of all Austria's inhabitants, but he added: "I cannot see that the shortcomings of the Constitution of March 4 [the Stadion constitution] are irreparable. On the contrary, I am convinced that if the constitution were put into force they would soon be eliminated. Their amendment could make the constitution a basis for settlement."[14] Count Gyula Andrássy, who had returned from exile in August 1858, was provoked by the pamphlet into reproaching Eötvös for renouncing Hungary's rightful constitutional demands. Eötvös replied that he had sent the proofsheets to Deák who had returned them without comment, which Eötvös took for endorsement. Distressed, Andrássy then called Deák to account. Deák answered that "his policy was diametrically opposed to Eötvös's but that in the precarious situation of the country, he did not feel that he had the right to prevent the publication of opinions contrary to his own."[15] This was the Fabian Deák again, unsure of the outcome of his attitude of passive resistance and his maximalist position on a return to the conditions of 1848. While he did not believe in standing in the way of differing views, he was well aware of the need for wide support for his own views. Hence 1858 found him telling *Pesti Napló* ("Pest Diary"), the liberal daily that accepted his leadership: "The first priority is to keep alive in the nation an enthusiastic loyalty to constitutional freedom, so that at the opportune moment the Hungarian constitution can be restored at the stroke of a pen and we can have a free, constitutional state within twenty-four hours."[16] Another opportunity to state his position had come a few months earlier when he had replied to an address—in German—from the ladies of Zala county. Our nationality, he had told them, "is under repeated attack by the regime and is being eased out of public affairs. All we can do is cultivate it and preserve it where the power of the regime does not penetrate—in the private circle of our social lives. If even there we neglect it, it will be doomed forever."[17]

Deák, then, expected the nation, like himself, to hold the line in the struggle to defend its nationality, traditions, constitution and laws.

Deák considered his the most appropriate attitude under the conditions at that time. Should more propitious circumstances arise, he would be able to take proper advantage of them, since no previous actions could cause embarrassment or impose obligations. Indeed the propagation of these views was the most significant result of Deák's attitude during the absolutist regime.[18]

The importance of coincidence in Deák's decision to sell his estate and move to Pest should not be exaggerated, but neither should it be dismissed. One of those blunders that Deák counted on to hasten the downfall of the counterrevolutionary regime occurred on April 20, 1854. On that date the Habsburg dynasty concluded an alliance with Prussia clearly aimed against Russia, then involved in the Crimean War. It was then, A. J. P. Taylor wrote, that the phrase was heard in St. Petersburg "that the road to Constantinople lay through Vienna."[19] This change of heart in both Vienna and St. Petersburg eventually had a considerable impact on the relations between the dynasty and the Hungarians. Up to 1849 the moderate liberals' wish not to seek complete independence for Hungary but to effect political, social, and economic reforms within the Habsburg monarchy was based on the contention that union with Austria was the best protection against Pan-Slavism and, especially, against Russia. Russian intervention in 1849 in support of Habsburg rule in Hungary was the mainstay of the argument of the Hungarian exiles, particularly Kossuth, that the dynasty was more of a menace to Hungary than a defense against the Slavs, so that the only solution for the Hungarians was complete severance of all ties with the dynasty which was the ally, if not the tool, of the Russians. The divorce of Habsburg policies from Russia in 1854 gave the moderate liberals and Deák grounds to claim that Hungary's future might lie within the Habsburg domains, not outside as the exiles wished. This change of direction in the court was probably a major factor in Deák's gradual move toward a more active political part. Indeed, by July 31, 1854, the sale of Deák's estate had been notarized, and in November he was living permanently in Pest. His "total" passive resistance was over.

The wish to live at the center of things was by no means the only reason Deák moved to Pest. After all, had agriculture been profitable, he could probably have hired a steward for his estate or leased out the land to secure an income and free time for his political activities in Pest. In the 1850's medium-sized estates, such as that of Deák[20] and much of the Hungarian gentry, were not only unprofitable but many of them were in bankruptcy or verging on it, not unlike their peers in the neighboring countries. Their proper course should have been a rapid transition to a capitalist system of agriculture, but few of them had the means. Credit was advanced only to aristocrats loyal to the dynasty, and they alone were able to take advantage of the boom in the German food market in the 1850's and begin the mechanization and capitalist transformation of their estates.[21] The gentry was not.

Deák was not spared these general hardships, but complicating factors made his case disastrous. One of the first to begin paying taxes voluntarily, he offered his serfs very generous redemption terms well before emancipation was proclaimed. He was also a reluctant farmer who, because he did not like his calling, neglected his land. It was hardly surprising that he was heavily in debt when he decided to sell his estate. When István Széchenyi heard of this resolve, he came to Deák's rescue and looked forward to seeing him living in Pest at the center of Hungary's political life. Széchenyi bought all of Deák's real property on munificent terms for his son Ödön. It was valued at 50,000 florins, 10,000 of which were mortgaged and some 12,000 more owed in debt to his sister, Mrs. Oszterhuber-Tarányi. Széchenyi paid off the whole mortgage and offered Deák a life annuity of 600 imperial gulden a year, enough to keep him in comfort for the rest of his days.[22] The sale of Deák's chattels realized almost exactly what he owed Mrs. Oszterhuber-Tarányi who, however, refused to accept a penny from her brother and burned his promissory notes.[23] With the money he was able to establish himself well in Pest. But Deák's straits had been typical of much of the Hungarian gentry, with his debts amounting to virtually a half of all his assets.

On November 11, 1854 Deák moved into the Hotel Angol Királynő in Pest. He soon gave evidence that the period of his "total" passive resistance was over. In 1851 László Szögyény-Marich, the only Hungarian member of the *Reichsrat* (Imperial Council) and thus an open collaborator with the counterrevolution, had sought Deák's support for his appointment to the council. Deák's counsel was sought even by his opponents because, among other things, they appreciated that he was true to his own principle: "Whatever is truth must be told whether it heartens or hurts the listener, whether it promotes one's own interests or sets them back."[24] So Szögyény-Marich in 1851 expected and received Deák's frank opinion: "Even if I shall not understand some of your actions, I shall not misjudge Your Excellency."[25] It hardly amounted to enthusiastic encouragement, but three years later, on December 14, 1854, only a month after moving to Pest, Deák was able to write to the Imperial Councillor far more warmly: "I understand, appreciate and commend your view completely.... You are sacrificing your pleasures, your time, and your ease of mind only to be able to do something for the good of individuals and of the community, and you have not held back even though what can be achieved is very little."[26] Deák's tone may not have been very optimistic but he was giving proper credit for even the least advance as well as evidence that he himself was moving off the sidelines.

Deák's new home at the Hotel Angol Királynő was a modest three-room suite. There was a living room, and a bedroom, and in the third room "lived his loyal old friend Count János Mikes, who was quite inseparable from him."[27] The living room was frugally furnished, mostly with the hotel's own pieces. A large sofa, Deák's favorite seat, was flanked by two armchairs for guests. A smaller settee and several occasional chairs afforded further accommodation for visitors. Politicians, newsmen, friends, and relatives crowded the room every day except when Deák was working. Then he would shut himself up, and no one was admitted to the little third-floor suite.

On every piece of furniture wherever there was space would be a quantity of cigars and vestas. Deák was a chain-smoker and, whenever one cigar was finished, he wanted to be able to light the next without moving from where he was. Neatness does not seem to have been a feature of his bachelor suite. A few other things he also kept at his fingertips: the *Corpus juris hungarici* (the collection of Hungarian laws), a copy of the parliamentary rule book, and a flyswatter. Stating the obvious, he would tell visitors that the purpose of the flyswatter was to kill flies, but, as he did so, his eye would always light on the *Corpus juris hungarici* to indicate that the law, old and new, was the weapon he preferred to use on his "flies."[28] His library was now reduced to about fifty volumes, a mere fraction of what he had owned when he was younger, but he always seemed to be well informed about the latest literary and political books.

Deák rose between five and six every morning and strolled in the streets for up to three hours before breakfast. It was one of the most enduring habits of his life. Back in his suite by about nine o'clock, he received early visits by beggars to whom he doled out the same small sum of money that they knew he had already counted out to give them. His friends, particularly Andrássy, arranged with the hotel manager that not more than three of these paupers were allowed up to his rooms each morning lest Deák bankrupt himself again. Between 9:30 and ten his more respectable visitors began to arrive, but unless they had a luncheon invitation, they all knew that they had to leave by half past one, because at that time he invariably went down to the hotel restaurant to eat his one main meal of the day. It always included generous servings of meat, and he took his time over it.

In the afternoons, whenever he found time, Deák took up his favorite hobby wood carving. He particularly regretted that he had had to leave his larger tools behind in Zala. With only hand tools he could no longer make furniture but only whittle at small objects like pipes, canes, and small figures. His favorite subject was still Baroch, the Jewish merchant in Kehida, whose head ornamented many of his carvings. As soon as he finished each piece, he gave it away as a present.[30]

Despite the simple comforts of the Hotel Angol Királynő, Deák's heart remained in Zala at the Oszterhuber's home in Zalaszentlászló. He continued to send his sister Klára small gifts regularly. The letters he wrote to his brother-in-law, his closest friend after his brother Antal's death, are a treasure house of Deák's hopes, ideas, anxieties, and despairs. He wrote candidly what was on his mind, asking József Oszterhuber-Tarányi's advice and offering his own. In return he expected detailed accounts of what was happening at the Oszterhubers' home, the most important place on earth to him. When Klára fell seriously ill in 1854 (she died on Christmas Day 1859), Deák was consumed with worry. "For God's sake," he wrote to her husband, "tell her to take care of herself. She should beware of catching cold. Don't forget that your lives are vital to me, for I am all alone in this world."[31] This brief note points to an overriding fact of Deák's life. For all the countless persons who swarmed about him, glorified him, loved him, and sought his company, he always felt lonely outside the circle of the Oszterhubers and a handful of friends. In this respect he was still the schoolboy brooding alone on one side while the others played ball and teamed up for games.[32]

It was during this period of gradually increasing political involvement that one of Deák's special friends died. Mihály Vörösmarty was the leading romantic poet of his day, whose ideas and sense of nationalism were exactly in line with Deák's. For romantics like Vörösmarty, Kölcsey, and Széchenyi, humanity and patriotism were identical. Their most sacred symbol was the nation, and it was through love of the nation that humanity was served. The xenophobia and self-centered arrogance of the following generation were alien to them. Hungarian nationalism was never more universalist, never richer in human values, than during the era of Romanticism.[33] When Vörösmarty died on November 18, 1855, in Pest, he left his widow and children penniless and commended them to Deák's care. Seeing Vörösmarty as the epitome of Hungarian national consciousness, the regime was anxious to prevent any commemoration of his death from becoming an incentive for political protest. It banned individuals, the press and the Hungarian Academy of Sciences from organizing any sort of valedictory rites and even prohibited a public collection for the relief of the poet's family. Despite these precautions, however, the mourners at his funeral on November 21, led by Deák, made the occasion a demonstration of national solidarity and rejection of the counterrevolution. In the following months, having no other recourse, Deák wrote personal letters to hundreds of notables in royal Hungary and Transylvania on behalf of Vörösmarty's family. His appeal was passed on in chain-letter fashion and donations came pouring in. On March 14, 1857 Deák had the satisfaction of writing to one donor that to date 100,000 florins had been contributed.[34] The fact that Deák's own estate at Kehida had been valued at only 50,000 florins is a measure of the magnitude and success of this fundraising campaign, Deák's first semipolitical act since the collapse of the revolution.

Deák had been elected an honorary member of the Hungarian Academy of Sciences on November 23, 1839, but after 1849 he attended none of its sessions until February 23, 1855, some three months after his move to Pest. Thereafter he rarely missed a meeting. On April 17, 1855, he and Eötvös were both elected directors of the academy, and within months he was involved in a political wrangle over the academy's bylaws.

The Pest chief of police had notified the president of the academy on October 13, 1853, that, if the academy was to continue in existence, its bylaws would have to be drafted in German and officially approved. Although its constitution already had legal sanction, the academy complied. Four years later, on February 27, 1858, the academy received back its newly approved bylaws but with several substantial amendments by the government. A committee was elected to prepare an Address to the Throne requesting rescission of the arbitrary alterations. Deák wrote the petition, which was endorsed unanimously by the academy's directors and approved by a plenary session of the members.

The address recalled that the academy's original bylaws, which had been approved by its founders, the Hungarian diet and the King in 1827, had stated that the primary mission of the academy was the cultivation of arts and sciences in Hungarian and hence the perfection of the language. The bylaws as amended defined the academy's mission as the cultivation of arts and sciences and "at the same time" the promotion of the Hungarian language. This modification implied that arts and sciences could be pursued in any language and that eventually the academy would become just another imperial institution with little interest in the Hungarian tongue. The address requested restoration of the original wording.

It then pointed out that the academy had always been supported by private contributions with no state subsidy and had been autonomous, freely electing its own members and officials. The new bylaws granted the academy the right to propose its members and officials, who would then be appointed by the Governor General, making a mockery of the institution's autonomy. This restriction, the petition claimed, was more stringent than those the regime had imposed on any other organization in Hungary.

Finally, the address requested repeal of a provision permitting the local government Commisioner "to protest resolutions that conflict with high government goals" on the grounds that "high government goals" was too imprecise a concept. The address was signed by the president of the academy, Count Emil Dessewffy, and the secretary, Ferenc Toldy, on May 29, 1858 and presented to Francis Joseph on July 1 by a delegation headed by the vice-president, Baron József Eötvös. They were told that the petition would be taken under advisement, but on August 28 a rescript rejected it in its entirety.[35] At the same time Bach assured the academy that the government had no intention of curtailing the use of Hungarian in its endeavors. Nevertheless, Dessewffy stated in a speech on December 20: "The academy will function freely despite the brakes applied to it."[36] Such defiance became steadily more widespread as the decade of absolutism neared its close.

On March 16, 1859, Deák wrote to Ferenc Pulszky, who had been living in exile abroad since the revolution of 1848–49: "I am growing old, suffering from real and imaginary illnesses."[37] In July of this politically tense summer of 1859, Deák fell conveniently "ill" in Vienna on his way to spend several weeks as usual in Marienbad.[38] While recuperating in the imperial capital, he met the Imperial Councillor Szögyény-Marich who asked him whether he would accept an invitation to come to court and what he would propose to settle relations between Hungary and the dynasty. According to Szögyény-Marich's diary, Deák replied that he would not come to Vienna under any conditions whatsoever. "A Parliament summoned on the basis of the laws of 1848 is the only possible institution by which he would consider the legal order to have been reestablished and by which, in view of the changed situation, relations between Hungary and the empire could be settled," Szögyény-Marich recorded.[39] So Deák's attitude had not changed one whit between the moment of the counterrevolution's triumph and the time absolutism had proven bankrupt.

CHAPTER 11

From Opposition to Constructive Activism
Six Years of Turmoil (1859–65)

AUSTRIA'S military defeats at Magenta (June 4, 1859) and
Solferino (June 24, 1859) reflected the failure of the whole
system. Foster-Arnold commented: "The victories of Radetzky
in Italy in 1848 had once sealed the fate of constitutionalism in
Austria, so in 1859 the news of his [sic] defeat came like the
first dull crash of the long frost-bound winter and the advent of
the spring of freedom."[1]

Francis Joseph and his advisers were conscious of this and
recognized the need to put the system in order. They therefore
signed a preliminary peace with the Sardinians and French at
Villafranca on July 12, and three days later Francis Joseph issued his Laxenburg Manifesto. Announcing the conclusion of the
preliminary peace, he promised that he would use the "leisure"
provided by the cessation of hostilities in order "to place Austria's welfare on a solid basis 'by appropriate development of its
rich spiritual and material resources, and by modernizing and
improving its legislature and administration.' "[2]

Two weeks after the promulgation of the Laxenburg Manifesto, Bach was dismissed as Minister of the Interior, and an era
came to an end. As in Hungary, two opposing groups were competing to fill the gap in the empire left by Bach's departure.
The provincial aristocracies were pressing for a federal reorganization of the empire, based on its historic component parts and
their own domination of the new structure. The great liberal
financial bourgeoisie was pressing for German centralism and
its own primacy in the new regime. Both wanted to introduce a
measure of constitutionalism, mostly to institutionalize their own
share of power. The dynasty, Francis Joseph himself, the officers

151

of the court, and the representatives of bureaucratic absolutism had to choose one of these two groups as an ally, because they could not carry out the necessary consolidation alone. The choice, however, lay squarely with them, and this went hard with constitutionalism, for Francis Joseph stubbornly resisted any restriction of his power.[3] He yielded only to insurmountable circumstance.

A new ministry was formed under Count Rechberg, the Foreign Minister. Bach's office, with the new title of Ministry of State, was filled in August by Count Agenor Gołuchowski, a Polish aristocrat and advocate of federalism. Little by little the new government introduced changes to mollify the Hungarian public without, however, making any commitments to any specific future reforms. In April 1860 the much-disliked governor, Archduke Albrecht, was replaced by General Lajos Benedek, a Protestant Hungarian commoner, who immediately paid calls on Deák and Eötvös.[4] The previous month an imperial edict had set up a "reinforced" (enlarged) Reichsrat, but only a few conservative Hungarian aristocrats had accepted appointment to it. Among them were Counts Antal Szécsen and György Apponyi. On accepting appointment, Apponyi made a point of his determination to uphold Hungary's traditional constitutional rights.[5] Szécsen, Apponyi, and other Hungarian aristocratic conservatives were willing to cooperate with the dynasty in an attempt to reconcile the monarchy's great-power attitude with the historic constitutional traditions of its component territories.[6]

This was the group that backed the proclamation of the October Diploma which substituted historic federalism for German centralism and limited parliamentarism for absolutism.[7] The essence of the diploma was compromise reached among the dynasty, the traditionalist feudalistic political forces of the Habsburgs' hereditary provinces and the conservative Hungarian aristocracy.[8] The most important changes it made in Hungary were the convocation of Parliament, the reestablishment of the pre-1848 executive and judiciary branches of government, and the partial revival of the autonomy of the counties. As in the Reform Era, Pest county was again the bellwether of liberal sentiment. On December 10 the county assembly passed a resolution demanding the unconditional reinstatement of the laws of 1848. The resolution was printed and circulated throughout the country. In short order numerous other county assemblies followed suit and adopted the same resolution with few or no amendments.[9] Deák, however, remained skeptical. When Dessewffy rushed from Vienna to Pest to show him the issue of the *Wiener Zeitung* in which the diploma was published, Deák read it through and pronounced it unacceptable, and he also turned down the office of Lord Chief Justice.[10] Alive to public opinion, he expected the Hungarians to reject the October Diploma and was soon proved correct. Almost everybody objected to it, some intuitively, some because they believed it prejudicial. Concomitantly Hungarians refused to pay their taxes.[11] Ignaz Edler von Plener, the Minister of Finance, told the ministerial council on November 24 that Hungary was in a state of semi-revolution and could be considered lost as far as tax revenues were concerned.[12] The mood of revolt became so deep that counties and communities acted as though the absolutist regime had been abolished and, without waiting for instructions from above, elected new slates of officials.[13] They were encouraged by *.Pesti Napló*, whose editor, Baron Zsigmond Kemény, Deák's close friend, published a series of articles and editorials in the fall on the theme that this upsurge of national disobedience demonstrated Hungary's determination to settle for nothing less than a return to its status of 1848.[14]

Whether to return to the status of 1847 or that of 1848 was the main issue before a conference authorized by Francis Joseph and organized by János Szcitovszky, Cardinal Archbishop of Esztergom and Primate of Hungary, to decide on the legislative procedures for the forthcoming Parliament. Those invited to attend included 42 aristocrats, 21 lesser nobles, mostly from the gentry, 22 burghers, and 12 prelates.[15] Deák was invited but turned the invitation down.[16] He encouraged his colleagues to take part, however. Finally, out of the 100 persons invited to the conference, which was held in the archbishop's library on December 18, 1860, twenty-five absented themselves. The most active liberal to attend was Eötvös, whose advocacy of the status of 1848 was so persuasive that a leading conservative participant complained: "Eötvös has even won over the canons of Esztergom to support the electoral law of 1848."[17] In fact, this was precisely what the conference finally decided on—a stunning victory for the liberals.[18] Nevertheless, they still had a long way to go. On December 13, 1860, Gołuchowski was succeeded by Anton von Schmerling, a representative of the centralist German liberal bourgeoisie. For the provincial aristocracies and their federalist line, it was an ominous change, for it signaled imperial exasperation with their lack of success, especially their failure to placate Hungary.[19] Two weeks later Francis Joseph received Deák and Eötvös separately in audience. It was the first time that Deák and the King had met,[20] and they both came away with favorable impressions of each other. Deák was surprised to learn how well informed the King was. Francis Joseph commented to Baron Miklós Vay, the Hungarian Chancellor, after the audience: "Well, that is a man of honesty from top to toe and he has strong convictions. And how logical he is! Unfortunately, he considers too many things feasible that face insurmountable obstacles."[21] The audience was an exchange of information rather than an attempt at negotiation. Its one positive result was that two men who would come to depend on one another greatly in future felt they could respect and trust each other.[22] For the time being, however, Deák was still uneasy and he wrote to his brother-in-law: "Hungary is in a more precarious situation now than ever before."[23] He was as disheartened by Francis Joseph's reluctance to make constitutional concessions as he was dismayed at the continuing unruliness of the counties. After more than a decade of now discredited despotism, they were anxious to undo the absolutists' work. From county after county came resolutions demanding immediate reinstatement of the April Laws, dismissal of officials who had served under Bach, or organization of territorial forces on the basis of the National Defense Act of 1848. Prominent exiles such as Kossuth and Klapka were elected *in absentia* to the county assemblies. Imperial taxes went uncollected even while local taxes were paid. Deák disapproved of the turmoil and warned that anarchy bred despotism, but he also condemned the former regime: "These twelve years of absolutism have damaged every part of the organic life of the state, they have wasted the wealth of three generations to come and probably more, they have sapped our lifeblood, they have razed industry and commerce."[24]

He pursued a cautious policy between the heritage of the despised Bach ministry and the recalcitrance of the counties. Giving verbal support to the counties' maximalist demands to bring home to the government the need to reach a speedy settlement on the liberals' terms, he declined any state office for himself but advised other liberals to accept positions in order to take advantage of the constitutional opportunities offered by the diploma, however restricted they might be. He worked to defuse moves or demands that were too radical, revolutionary, or risky in order to prevent retaliation, which would undoubtedly have meant a return to unconstitutional despotism. He tried to keep the door open even for Hungary's representation in the *Reichsrat* if it were ever granted a much greater degree of self-government than the diploma afforded. He encouraged the conservatives to accept even the most meager concessions that they could pry out of the regime because the more they could achieve, the stronger would be the liberals' grounds be in the future when they were in a position to bargain for a settlement with the monarch. But for all this, he preferred personally to remain in the background.[25]

It was during this period that Deák accepted an invitation to attend a conference held by the Lord Chief Justice in Pest between January 23, 1861, and March 4, 1861. The purpose of the conference was to adjust the judicial procedures inherited from the Bach regime to the changed conditions of the times. It was here that Deák took issue with those constitutionalists who would return to the system in force before 1848 in order to nullify all that the absolutist regime had introduced. He based his objections on the fact that such a solution would have reversed such advances as equality before the law and would have restored some elements of feudalism. That would have been too high a price for the extinction of absolutist procedures. "The revalidation of traditional Hungarian laws is a guiding principle for me too," he commented, "but whenever their revival would in my judgment obstruct judicial relations or the democratic principles of our institutions, I shall set myself unhesitatingly against them."[26] The conference finally adopted the Provisional Rules for the Judiciary, a compromise between Hungarian feudal procedures, the April Laws and the innovations of the Bach

regime. The rules nicely complemented conditions in an embryonic capitalist economy. Endorsing the completion of the emancipation of the serfs by the Urbarial Patent of March 2, 1853, a
contemporary element, they also recognized the validity of entail-
ment, a feudal element. Deák's attitude to this compromise was
in dramatic contrast to his earlier radical social reformist bent.
His newfound social conservatism, however, probably did not
bespeak any basic change of heart but rather an anxiety not to
alienate the court and the Hungarian conservatives in order to
make some progress on the constitutional issue of Hungary on
which everything else depended. Whatever the actual reason
for his change, it is a pathetic fact that, after never having missed
an opportunity to push for an improvement in the condition of
the peasantry, this time he uttered not one word in its behalf.
Without demur he acceded to the Urbarial Patent despite the
fact that it fell miserably short of the legislative drafts that he
himself had presented to Parliament in the summer of 1848.[27]

On February 27, while the Lord Chief Justice's conference
was still in progress, the February Patent was issued, ostensibly
supplementing the October Diploma but in fact supplanting
many of its provisions. It embodied "Schmerling's political philosophy, the doctrine of bourgeois German centralism, which now
replaces the conservative concept of the historical rights of the
kingdoms and lands."[28] The patent seems to have been an attempt to satisfy the hopes of the Cis-Leithanian bourgeoisie,
since the diploma, contrary to expectations, had failed to satisfy
the gentry of Hungary.[29] The patent was the "charter of German
centralism" but it failed to put constitutionalism in Austria on
a firm foundation.

For Hungary it was a regression, since it turned it from a self-
governing state practically into an Austrian province. For three
centuries the Hungarians had been fighting the Habsburg kings
politically, intellectually, and even with arms to prevent precisely this change of status, so it was highly unlikely they would
acquiesce in it now. The day the patent was promulgated, Deák
quit the Lord Chief Justice's conference and indicated that there
was probably no way for Hungary to resolve the problem except
by revolution.[30] In the same vein *Pesti Napló* stated on March
24 that under no circumstances would Hungary surrender its

rights guaranteed by the Pragmatic Sanction, which was a bilateral contract between Hungary and the dynasty that neither could alter without the other's consent, and yet this was exactly what the patent had done.[31] The intransigence of Schmerling's patent swung Deák and the liberals back to an inflexible stance. Of all the events that followed in the wake of the Bach regime, the most important for Hungary was the Parliament of 1861. It was during the sessions of this Parliament that Deák gradually became the one preeminent national leader, but it did not happen overnight. It was also the first legislative assembly in which he did not represent his county of birth, Zala, but stood instead for the inner city of Pest.[32] The essence of his program, as he expressed it during his election campaign, was: "The constitutional status of our country, its independence, and its constitutional freedoms are the fundamental preconditions of our national existence which we must not surrender at any price and under whatever duress. Any damage that we ourselves do to them would be a wound fatal to the life of the nation."[33]

A royal decree of January 21 summoned Parliament for April 2, 1861. When Deák accepted candidacy, there was hope that a settlement on the basis of the October Diploma was possible. The promulgation of the February Patent before the elections made such a settlement very difficult.[34] The Schmerling regime countered the outburst of rage in Hungary that greeted the patent by stepping up its suppressive controls, but the elections were still held at the appointed time. Of the candidates who were returned 80% were country gentry or intellectuals of minor noble background, 12% were representatives of the national minorities, and 8% were of bourgeois origin.[35] The social composition of the legislature, then, was similar to that of the reform diets of 1830 to 1849. The overwhelming majority of the members were liberals, but, because they controlled the executive branch of government, the conservatives handled all the preliminaries of the session. Attempting to make certain of Hungary's entry into the *Reichsrat*, they hoped to assure their own future influence at court.

Parliament was opened on the King's behalf by the Lord Chief Justice, Count György Apponyi.[36] Even then there was a hitch. The radical wing of the liberals had aimed either to restore the situation of 1848 or to have no Parliament at all. Its leader, Count László Teleki, to whom Francis Joseph had granted amnesty only in December, insisted that under the April Laws the seat of Parliament was Pest, not Buda as the royal summons had stipulated. Convocation in Buda implied the *status quo ante* 1848, so Teleki urged members not to attend the opening or any other sittings there. He also urged that, until Parliament had resolved otherwise, King Ferdinand V's abdication should not be recognized nor Francis Joseph's reign accepted as valid even *de facto.* A caucus of all the liberal factions was held on April 4. Deák moved cleverly to forestall a revolt, insisting that Parliament must begin its deliberations. Hungary, he said, needed the sympathy of foreign countries, and Europe would never understand why, after a long period of absolutism, the Hungarians had thrown away the benefit of a Parliament simply because it had been summoned to Buda rather than to Pest. He would attend the inauguration even if he had to sit there alone. And so it happened that on April 6 only Deák and about another 50 of the 261 members of Parliament attended the opening ceremony in Buda, but as they were driving up the hill, a group of citizens greeted them with catcalls.[37] The subsequent regular sessions took place in Pest.[38]

Deák's first effort to prevent the wreck of Parliament was thus successful, but he was still far from controlling the body. During the five weeks of caucuses that followed the opening, the liberals split into two distinct groups that gradually began to act as separate parties. The names they took reflected the pressing constitutional issue over which they were divided: whether to deal with Francis Joseph as monarch.[39] If Parliament were to recognize him as *de facto* king, all dealings between Parliament and the sovereign would be in the form of petitions. If he were not acknowledged even as *de facto* monarch, then Parliament as the sovereign power in Hungary would pass resolutions. Proponents of the former position rallied round Deák and called themselves the Party of Petition; proponents of the latter lined up behind Teleki as the Party of Resolution and formed the majority. When the first official meeting of the Party of Petition was held on April 22, it could count on 130 members, while some 160 to 170 adhered to Teleki. Leadership of the house therefore went to the Party of Resolution, and Kálmán Ghyczy was elected speaker with Kálmán Tisza and Baron Frigyes Podmaniczky as his deputies.[40]

What were the bases of the policies of the Party of Resolution and Teleki? Were they simply troublemakers who did not understand the power relationship between the dynasty and Hungary? The answer is found in two major documents: Teleki's election victory speech at Nagyabony on March 30 and a speech he prepared for a full meeting of the Lower House of Parliament on May 8. Both made the same points.[41]

Parliament, said Teleki, should surrender none of Hungary's constitutional rights; reject the alien Austrian system, including the diploma, the patent, and the sentences on Hungarian patriots; and acknowledge all Hungarian laws, including those of 1848, as valid and in force. The 1848 laws should be considered the basis for further progress toward the complete equality of all citizens with the ultimate goal a true democracy free of discrimination on grounds of faith, language, or nationality. Freedom of industry and commerce should be established, adjusted to the general European economic system. Hungary should declare its good intentions toward the economic and spiritual interests of the other peoples of the Habsburg lands. It should acknowledge the autonomy and constitution of Croatia and revise its representation in the Hungarian Parliament through bilateral negotiation and agreement. All Hungarian citizens, including Jews, should be given completely equal political and religious liberties and civil rights. The national minorities should be conceded everything necessary to assure them of their national, linguistic, and religious freedoms and full equality of rights, short of partitioning the country. The last vestiges of feudal property relationships should be eliminated by giving fair compensation with regard to the interests of everyone. "We shall never let ourselves become tools to be used against others' freedom and independence. Once such a declaration has been made, come what may, I shall have no fear for the fate of the nation. If this Parliament were dissolved, if the absolutist regime were reimposed, we should face that power, whatever it might do, and being a power ourselves, we should prove the stronger of the two," Teleki concluded.[42]

The Party of Resolution had an absolute majority in Parliament and thus could pass any bill it wished. Aided by Teleki's prestige, it could have prepared a bill on the lines he proposed and prevented any negotiations with the court. But it was frightened by its power and by the possible consequences of a breach with the dynasty caused by its own intransigence and undoubtedly followed by a return to absolutism. Teleki himself was seized by a crisis of conscience, and on the night of May 7 he committed suicide. Beside him lay the draft of the program he was to present to Parliament the next day. His death caused dismay, shock, and confusion, and Parliament went into immediate recess. When it reassembled on May 13, Deák presented his own program in the form of a petition,[43] among hisses and gossips about his responsibility for Teleki's death. Deák needed all his energies and determination to go on. He had both. Placatory rather than provocative, Deák nonetheless criticized the diploma and patent as contrary to the Pragmatic Sanction and at odds with the April Laws. Alongside the criticism, however, was a proposal to settle three issues left more or less open by the April Laws, which should have appealed to the government. Deák suggested that Hungary should assume a share of the Austrian state debts, accept the defense of the Habsburg lands as a common responsibility, and contribute a fair share to the costs of defense. To negotiate acceptable terms, he proposed periodic consultations between representatives of the Austrian lands and Hungary, thus foreshadowing the dualism of the Compromise of 1867. His program recognized Francis Joseph as *de facto* king of Hungary, since the crown was hereditary, and moved that he should therefore be petitioned to reinstate the April Laws. Deák called for calm and reason rather than passion in the relations between Hungary and Austria. Parliament was an essential institution, he said, and ought not to be sacrificed for utopian dreams because there were many problems for it to take up, especially that of the national minorities.

One hundred thousand copies of Deák's speech were printed and in a single day in Vienna 24,000 were sold. The European press gave it extensive and sympathetic treatment and even the Hungarian conservatives welcomed it, although Deák constituted the single most serious threat to them. Rechberg was very worried about its impact abroad and circularized Austria's diplomatic missions to try to counter its effect.[44]

The main speaker for the Party of Resolution was Kálmán Tisza, a distant relative of László Teleki, who had stepped into the late leader's shoes. He was youthful, liberal, determined, and ambitious. Applauding Deák's constitutional arguments, he added to them a subdued version of Teleki's program on the nationalities, the peasants, and civil rights. He proposed that Deák's draft, amended in this direction, should be adopted as a resolution instead of a petition.[45] Debate on Deák's and Tisza's speeches continued from May 16 to June 4.

Since the Party of Resolution did not want to prompt a rupture with Francis Joseph, it did not insist on forcing Tisza's resolution through. Finally a parliamentary stratagem was agreed on to allow Deák's petition to pass by the barest possible majority. When the vote was called on June 5, 155 members voted for Deák's draft, 152 against, with 14 abstentions and the rest of the house absent on grounds of "illness."[46] The Upper House also passed the draft and on July 8, 1861, the chairmen of both houses of Parliament presented it to Francis Joseph, who signed his assent.

In the meanwhile however the regime consolidated itself, and instead of looking for a settlement with Hungary it renewed its suppression of any show of discontent and reimposed the forcible collection of illegal taxes.[47] At the inaugural session of the *Reichsrat* Schmerling declared that the Hungarians' repudiation of the diploma and the patent would be considered an offense against the monarchy's existence and against all the Habsburg lands and peoples, and that vigorous measures would be taken to prevent it.[48] The gap between the Schmerling regime and Hungary became wider, especially after a contradictory and authoritarian royal rescript of July 21, 1861. The Hungarian Parliament, which received it the following day, was commanded to send representatives to the *Reichsrat* forthwith. Austrian constitutional historians argued that Hungary was an integral part of the Austrian Empire, although their claim could never be substantiated in Hungarian law. Here the rescript was contradictory. "It is not our intention and it is far from our fatherly heart's desire," it said, "to incorporate into the Empire the lands that belong to the Crown of St. Stephen." Yet elsewhere it referred to Hungary which, "together with our other provinces, is included under the name of the Austrian Empire." And again, it stated that the October Diploma guaranteed the revival of Hungary's constitution "within the framework and under the conditions necessary to the interests of our throne and Empire." These circumscribed constitutional arrangements, it added, had been made on the basis of Francis Joseph's "absolute royal power."[49] Such tortured logic was only disillusioning when the ostensible object of the diploma had been to replace despotic rule by constitutional rule.

No less contradictory was the rescript's treatment of the April Laws, which it repeatedly stated to be invalid. In spite of this insistence, however, it demanded that all the laws of 1848 that conflicted wtih the diploma and patent should either be amended or annulled.

Some of the Hungarian gentry may have been unsophisticated, others may not have grasped the workings of international affairs, but they were all well versed in constitutional law and domestic politics. The contorted argumentation of the rescript jarred upon many. For this reason Count György Apponyi, a man loyal to the dynasty and interim chairman of the House of Lords, cabled the court requesting the immediate withdrawal of the rescript. It was a quixotic gesture.[50]

The increasing signs that the regime was determined to force Hungary into the *Reichsrat* on Schmerling's terms and the growing oppression in Hungary persuaded Deák that the time for compromise was over. He therefore swung back to his maximalist stance and prepared his second petition, which concentrated not on imminent settlement with the dynasty like the first petition, but on laying the groundwork for eventual settlement in the distant future and on preparing the nation for a new round of absolutism. His purpose was to define basic rules of conduct for the apparently inevitable new era of oppression.

Deák presented his bill to the Lower House on August 8.[51] The document was 16,000 to 17,000 words long and the summer heat almost unbearable, so he and another member, László Szalay, took turns in reading it section by section. It drew attention to the contradictions, prevarications, and hypocrisy of the rescript of July 21 and refuted each with careful legal reasoning. Deák cited numerous valid laws the Habsburg monarch had violated, in particular, the Pragmatic Sanction and Acts X and XII of 1790.[52] He noted that the Pragmatic Sanction of 1723 was a voluntary bilateral contract between the monarch and the nation with mutually binding commitments. It obliged the sovereign to reign strictly according to the laws of Hungary and not to introduce into Hungary the governmental practices of any other province. He was obliged to be crowned within six months of his predecessor's death and during the interim before his coronation to rule according to Hungary's laws and constitution. Before being crowned, he had to swear an oath to preserve the country's territorial integrity, rights, freedoms, and laws. If both the male and female lines of descent from Leopold I should become extinct, Hungary would be free to elect its own king. The Pragmatic Sanction established no link between Hungary and the hereditary provinces other than that of the person of the king. The indivisibility of all the Habsburg lands was predicated on this basis alone.

The other two acts to which Deák referred particularly were both promulgated by Habsburg kings of Hungary—as, indeed, was every other law he cited. Act X, 1790, declared: "Hungary is a free country, independent in its government and constitutional structure, subject to no other state or people and it possesses independence and its own constitution."[53] Act XII, 1790, stated: "The right to create, repeal and interpret laws in Hungary and its annexed territories is vested jointly in the legally crowned king and in the estates constitutionally gathered in the national assembly, and may not be exercised by any other."[54]

The bill announced that Hungary would insist on respect for the entire Pragmatic Sanction and all its provisions and would comply with nothing that conflicted with it. Neither the diploma nor the patent would be recognized as valid or binding on Hungary. No representative would be sent to the *Reichsrat*, and all laws, decrees and ordinances emanating from it and affecting Hungary or its annexed territories would be null and void. Its taxes and loans would be without effect in Hungary. Hungary would not be gainsaid on the legal validity of the laws of 1848,

because they had been properly passed by Parliament and promulgated by its constitutional king. Deák's petition concluded:

The nation will endure the hardships if it has to, in order to preserve
for future generations the freedom bequeathed to it by our ancestors.
It will endure without despair, as our ancestors endured and suffered
to protect the nation's rights, for what may be wrested away by main
force may be won back with time and good fortune, but what the
nation voluntarily surrenders for fear of suffering may not be regained, or only with great difficulty. The nation will endure in hope
for a better future and in trust in the justice of its cause.

Schmerling's policies had pushed Deák a long way from the
position he had held only six months earlier when he was considering representation in the *Reichsrat*. This time there was
no need to resort to a stratagem to secure the bill's passage. The
house gave it a standing ovation and passed it with unprecedented unanimity. The House of Lords did the same on August
10, 1861. Hungary's representatives were not about to yield to
absolutism in the guise of constitutionalism.

Before the court was able to prorogue the house, it issued a
protest against the anticipated absolutist policy written for it
by Deák. It declared: "We cannot resist armed might but we
solemnly protest against whatever may be perpetrated by force
and declare that we affirm all our laws inclusive of those promulgated in 1848. Only Parliament may change the law, so all acts
of force that suppress the law we shall deem unconstitutional
and invalid." Deák urged a policy of passive defense of Hungary's
laws and constitution. Under threat of arms Parliament was
prorogued on August 22, 1861.[55]

Four days later Schmerling read to a joint session of the
Reichsrat an imperial rescript denouncing the Hungarian Parlia-
ment and affirming the monarch's right of conquest in Hungary.
The *Reichsrat* responded with an Address of Homage to
Francis Joseph on September 8.[56]

A series of repressive decrees were issued and, to oversee
their enforcement, Count Mór Pálffy, a loyal Habsburg bureau-
crat, was appointed to head the Hungarian Viceregal Council.
Absolutism had been reimposed.

While Schmerling could claim with some justice that government was liberal in the Cis-Leithanian provinces, Hungary was once more under the thumb of military tribunals. According to the decree issued on November 5, 1861, Hungary was administered as a province of the Austrian Empire. The central government organs were the ones that had existed until 1848 and been revived by the October Diploma. The county assemblies and town councils were dissolved and local government was put in the hands of administrators handpicked by Schmerling. Though a liberal press law was introduced in the Cis-Leithanian provinces in 1862, Bach's censorship regulations of 1852 remained in force in Hungary.[57] In other respects, the new absolutism was different from the Bach years.

During the Bach era, many Hungarians clung to the hope, however utopian it might have been, that a revolutionary army would come marching in from Italy. Now even the dreamers expected no relief from abroad.[58] The Habsburg system seemed to have been accepted as a necessary, integral part of Europe. While the international situation offered Hungary's liberals little encouragement, the domestic scene was less bleak than a decade earlier. The liberals lionized the prorogued Parliament of 1861 and its principled defiance of the regime, and Deák's popular prestige had never been higher. He and his fellow members of Parliament were inevitably seen as the leaders of the resistance against the absolutist regime. Unlike the haphazard and uncoordinated resistance of the 1850's, the opposition also had an ideology in the form of two explicit and progressive petitions Deák had drafted. The advocates of the *status quo ante* 1848, the conservative aristocrats, lost influence not only in Hungary but also in Austria, while the prestige of the liberals grew rapidly both inside Hungary and out. Like the western European press, public opinion generally blamed the court for the failure of the constitutional experiment and considered Hungary victimized by Habsburg tyranny. Despite the controls imposed by the absolutist regime, local government became the center of political activity in Hungary. Shortly after the absolutist regime was introduced, almost all the county administrations published manifestos describing the provisional regulations as illegal, but adding that they would assume the burdens of local government for the sake of the public good.[59] The Hungarians' resistance was also reinforced by the fact that neither Croatia nor Transylvania sent representatives to the *Reichsrat*. Yet before Deák's policy could have any chance to succeed the Schmerling system had to demonstrate its impotence in foreign affairs and lose credit at home. Pressure had to build up behind the Austrian bourgeoisie's gradual recognition that a settlement with Hungary was in its interest. And finally Francis Joseph and the court had to be convinced that an accord with Hungary would redound to the glory of the dynasty and the monarchy's standing as a European great power. These preconditions were not fulfilled in 1863. Indeed, it was the year when Schmerling's power seemed to be at its peak. When at last the first political countermoves came, they were not made by Deák and the liberals but by the Hungarian conservatives, who feared that Schmerling would be successful in using the non-Hungarian nationalities to hold the Hungarians in check.

Schmerling had ousted these Hungarian conservative proponents of the October Diploma from their positions of power. Once dissociated from the government, they felt themselves free to criticize it and in due course to act. The most capable of them were Count Emil Dessewffy and Count György Apponyi, whose closest associates were György Majláth, and Baron Pál Sennyei. The first real plan came from Dessewffy in the form of a formal memorandum written in the winter of 1862–63 and presented to Francis Joseph. It pleaded for all the main principles of the Compromise of 1867: recognition of the April Laws, and of the indivisibility of all the Habsburg lands as laid down in the Pragmatic Sanction, a union of Hungary and the rest of the empire in a "dualism in equality" in which both parts would have their own parliaments and neither would be subordinate to the other, a separate ministry for each part except in those fields in which the nature of the Pragmatic Sanction made joint administration necessary. Those areas the memorandum defined as defense, international relations, commerce and finance. Legislative control over them would be exercised by a delegation composed of an equal number of representatives from both parliaments and executive control would be wielded by common ministries responsible to the delegations.[60]

Apponyi showed a copy of the memorandum to Schmerling,

who peremptorily brushed it aside. Another copy was shown to Deák, who realized the time was not yet ripe but who was much impressed. It was to the credit of these conservative aristocrats that they kept Deák abreast of what was happening. Another token of *noblesse oblige* was Apponyi's silence about the original authorship of the principles of the Compromise of 1867 when it was finally concluded and Deák was being lauded both for the idea and the political triumph of it.[61] The only effect of the memorandum was that the progovernment press played up the need to acknowledge the existence of common affairs, whatever the form of the monarchy. The liberal newspapers, on the other hand, Deák's mouthpiece *Pesti Napló* and Mór Jókai's *Hon* ("Homeland"), which followed the Party of Resolution's line, emphasized that the key to any settlement had to be unconditional revival of the April Laws.

No sooner did the Schmerling system reach what appeared to be the summit of success in 1863 than it began to disintegrate. Shortly after Transylvania on an arranged election had sent its representatives to the *Reichsrat*, both Bohemia and Galicia withdrew from it. The Czechs had maintained from the outset that the *Reichsrat* was incompetent to act in behalf of the whole Empire in the absence of the Hungarians and left in protest against discourtesy to their leaders by the president of the assembly. The Poles walked out, insulted when martial law was declared in Galicia in connection with the January Insurrection in Russian-controlled Congress Poland. By the summer of 1863 the completeness and representativeness of the *Reichsrat* was less than a fiction. The crisis in the *Reichsrat* was compounded by the Empire's continuing financial problems, tension with Prussia in the wake of Bismarck's appointment as minister president of Prussia, and differences with Russia over the Polish insurrection. As the underpinnings of the Schmerling system weakened, it became harsher. Inevitably, the Hungarians' reaction kept pace.

Most politically minded Hungarians looked to Deák to make the first move, but it was the conservatives who offered to mediate with the court. Many liberals gladly accepted the conservatives' offer. Not so Eötvös and his followers, who warned that the conservatives' initiative was a maneuver and that, instead of mediating, they would seize the chance to make their own compromise with Francis Joseph on terms that would not satisfy the liberals. To stop this, they pressed Deák to take action, but his fine sense of timing told him to wait a little longer. To be completely successful, he needed the undivided support of the mass of liberals, and if possible, of the majority of the nation. At present the economic depression was hurting the landed gentry so much that it would settle for virtually any solution that would ease the pressure, and under such circumstances it might be tempted to accept less than the maximum. If that were to happen, the radicals of the Party of Resolution could be expected to split away, and the divided liberals would then be easy prey to either Schmerling or the conservatives, or both. The years 1863 and 1864 were as much a time of crisis for the Hungarian liberals as they were for the regime. In this situation Deák was unwilling to move, and the strain between the activism of the fiery Eötvös and Deák's caution grew acute. In March 1863, when Deák was presented with an album of signed photographs of all the members of the 1861 Parliament, an occasion meant to rally all the liberals, he did not raise the banner of action but confined himself to the usual maximalist utterances about the unconditional reinstatement of the April Laws. He did not outline the conditions for a compromise because he knew the other party—the regime, that is—was not yet ready to bargain. In public Eötvös and Deák spoke in unison, but in private Eötvös angrily reproached Deák for ceding the field of action to the conservatives.[62]

It would be incorrect to see the Fabian Deák as completely inactive or anodyne. Had that been the case, he would long before have lost his standing as the foremost leader of Hungary's struggle for self-government. In fact, his residence at the Hotel Angol Királynő was as busy as any modern party headquarters. Sitting on his comfortable sofa, the air often heavy with smoke, Deák spent hours saying little but listening to his visitors talk. Now and again he interjected one of the stories or anecdotes for which he was known. The image of Deák the raconteur was a function of his alertness. Resorting to parable in case any secret police were present, he used his tales to explain or to mask facts, to calm or to inspire, and above all to raise flagging spirits. But more important was not what he said, but what he heard. He kept his finger firmly on the pulse of the nation, intently checking how far it had come and whether it needed inspiration or cooling. The news that interested him most was that from Vienna. His loyal conservative friends kept him advised and now more and more optimistic reports came in from liberals who were in Vienna to watch the *Reichsrat*. It was from there that the first sign came that the dynasty would sooner or later be ready to negotiate.

It came in the form of reports that the left-wing liberals of the *Reichsrat* were increasingly interested in a prompt settlement with Hungary and that the idea of dualism with common affairs administered by a joint body guided by constitutional principles was gaining ground. The Hungarian question was inextricably intertwined with the Cis-Leithanian bourgeoisie's economic interests in Hungary and its interest in a "greater German" settlement of the issues in Germany. The same Austro-German liberals who had welcomed the suppression of the Hungarian liberal republic in 1849 and voted homage to the monarch in 1861 for roughly treating the Hungarian Parliament and had seen Hungary as their own economic sphere of influence were in 1864 seeking an arrangement with a Hungary governed by fellow liberals, a settlement between two equal states bound together by common interests. They wanted a loyal, peaceful Hungary in their rear so that they could settle accounts with Prussia. The ephemeral success of the Danish war of 1864 and the subsequent signs that Bismarck was trying to find a "lesser German" solution to the problem of the fragmentation of the German-speaking lands, the evidence that Schmerling's policies were succeeding neither at home nor in Germany or elsewhere, quickly eroded his ministry's prestige. The liberals were also growing increasingly resentful of Schmerling's claim to be a liberal when the essence of his ministry was thinly veiled court absolutism. Gradually more and more liberals gathered round the "autonomist" group of Karl Giskra and Moritz von Kaiserfeld and pressed for a dualist compromise with Hungary.[63]

Harried from so many quarters, Schmerling, rather than yield, acted even more oppressively toward Hungary in an attempt to bring it into the *Reichsrat* and secure his own position. While Deák was still pondering whether the moment had at last come, the conservative aristocrats took the lead again to attack Schmerling frontally and discredit him before the court. The group around Count György Apponyi invited Mór Ludassy, a journalist, to write a critical pamphlet, *Drei Jahre Verfassungsstreit* ("Three Years of Constitutional Conflict").[64] As the title suggests, the Schmerling regime was condemned for bringing nothing but protracted tension. They also had him edit a newspaper they began publishing in Vienna, *Debatte*. It quickly rallied Hungarians of every stripe against Schmerling. Deák's closest associates, József Eötvös, Gyula Andrássy, Menyhért Lónyai, and Gábor Kemény became alarmed that the conservatives would win the day and negotiate an inadequate compromise. Now at last Deák saw his moment and began the series of actions that were to culminate in the Compromise of 1867. In this new process he became the dictator of Hungarian public opinion, a reluctant and compassionate one to be sure, but dictator nonetheless.

The deciding factor for Deák was the publication in late 1865 on Schmerling's initiative of a legal treatise by Wenzel Lustkandl, *Das ungarisch-österreichische Staatsrecht* ("Hungarian-Austrian Public Law"). Lustkandl's treatise was more sophisticated than the theory of forfeiture of all Hungary's rights used during the absolutist Bach regime. Making no claim that Hungary had ever forfeited its constitutional rights, he attacked Deák's petition of 1861 on the grounds that Deák had falsely interpreted Hungarian law. He asserted that the law acknowledged a real union between Hungary and the Cis-Leithanian provinces and thus was not incompatible with the February Patent. The prime significance of his assertion, however, was that it was the ostensible reason for Deák to move back into the center of the stage. Deák published his reply to Lustkandl in *Budapesti Szemle* ("Budapest Review") in early 1865 under the title: "Facts about Hungarian Constitutional Law."[65] In it he defended his petition, but the content and style of the article, admirable as they were, were secondary to Deák's purpose in publishing it and its actual repercussions. Deák's intention was to announce to all that he had taken up the political cudgels again and to alert Vienna to the Hungarian liberals' readiness to begin bargaining. His message came through unmistakably. From February through April 1865 Freiherr A. von Auguszt, vice-president of the Hungarian Viceregal Council and a confidant of the court, was in constant secret negotiations with Deák on the King's behalf.[66] Deák's article also touched off passionate public debate. Newspapers sympathetic to Schmerling, led by the *Neue Freie Presse*, launched a vitriolic attack against Deák. *Pesti Napló* replied in kind. Since Lustkandl's treatise was known to have been inspired by Schmerling, Deák's response pointed a finger not only at Lustkandl but also at the minister. The Cis-Leithanian liberals who wished for a settlement with Hungary welcomed Deák's return to action, and criticism of Schmerling's Hungarian policies mounted. Deák's article in *Budapesti Szemle* was only a beginning. It succeeded in drawing attention on both sides of the Leitha but it was only a legal polemic. Now statesmen and the public alike awaited constructive proposals for solving the Hungarian problem. On April 16, 1865, Deák anonymously published his "Easter Article" in *Pesti Napló* and followed it with a series of articles in *Debatte*. They, too, were unsigned but Deák virtually dictated them, and they became known as his "May Program"[67]—no one in Austria or Hungary doubted their authorship. It was no accident that the program was published in Vienna in German. Deák had no need to tell anyone in Hungary that a settlement was necessary or what terms it should be made on. It was others who had to be informed. But in Austrian-Hungarian relations it was not Deák's articles which turned the tide. Deák recognized that events were propitious and offered a solution. In Austria, the dynasty's centuries-old German imperial policy was bankrupt, and its collapse was the reason that in 1865 it began negotiating with Hungary again.[68]

The essence of Deák's program was insistence on Hungarian self-government and the validity of the April Laws, but he also declared: "We shall always stand ready, following the path prescribed by law, to concert our laws with the continued existence of the empire." He thus admitted that the April Laws could be modified. He also made it clear that Schmerling was not acceptable and that his policies would have to be reversed before negotiations could start.

The May Program proposed a dualistic monarchy in which Hungary would enjoy complete equality with the Cis-Leithanian provinces. In all its other details it agreed basically with the

Apponyi plan. The common affairs would be the royal household, foreign affairs, defense, and the upkeep of all three; customs and trade policy; indirect taxation and the general principles of commercial legislation. In addition to reinstatement of the April Laws, a Hungarian ministry responsible to the Hungarian Parliament was to be appointed, and the territorial integrity of the lands of the Crown of St. Stephen recognized. Once these prerequisites had been met, Parliament would be summoned on the basis of the laws of 1848.[69]

Deák had properly gauged the court's change of heart. On April 30, Francis Joseph in person paid an unannounced visit to Pozsony without his usual heavy military escort. He sent personal gifts to the Hungarian Academy of Sciences and then from June 6 to 9 he visited Pest, where he attended the annual fair of the National Agrarian Association. On leaving, the King made very optimistic comments about the likelihood and necessity of a settlement with Hungary.[70]

Late that same month of June György Majláth was appointed chancellor of the Hungarian Royal Court Chancellery and in mid-July Pál Sennyei took over as president of the Hungarian Viceregal Council. Both conservatives, they were, however, on the best possible terms with Deák. At the end of July Schmerling resigned, and Archduke Rainer, the minister president, "left on vacation." The Belcredi ministry was installed, and the negotiations that were to culminate in the Compromise of 1867 began in earnest.

CHAPTER 12

Climax and Anticlimax

I The Compromise of 1867

THE Belcredi ministry substituted for Schmerling's rigid policy one of settlement by negotiation aimed at reorganizing the Habsburg Empire "on the basis of conservative principles of historic rights."[1] The chief officers of state for Hungary as already mentioned were replaced by conservatives acceptable to Deák, but Móric Eszterházy, Francis Joseph's principal advisor, was as opposed as his master to the Hungarian liberals' dualist proposals.[2] Deák and his colleagues were well aware of the obstacles they still had to face, but "it became increasingly and painfully clear that the Magyar terms for dualistic partition of the empire would have to be met."[3]

The rescript summoning the new Parliament was issued on September 17, 1865, the same date as the February Patent was temporarily suspended.[4] At the general elections in November and December the "Deák Party" won an absolute majority.[5] Central Pest again returned Deák, and thus the Deák era commenced. It would be helpful had Deák left behind a diary, but he did not. "Only people conceited enough write diaries"[6] he said. Fortunately, however, many of his closest associates wrote diaries, thus we know the details of that monumental era, during which he indeed shaped Hungary's history.

Széchenyi, who inspired Hungary's liberal reforms, and Kossuth, who most effectively propagated them and led the revolution of 1848–49, both made history by stirring political and social forces into action. As these ran their full course, however, neither could control them, and history was shaped not by them but, contrary to their hopes and expectations, by others. Széchenyi, brokenhearted, watched events impotently from a sanatorium window; Kossuth looked on, equally powerless, from exile. Deák did not originate ideas or bring mass movements to life; he did not make history according to his own designs. He was able to recognize political, social, and economic forces and the power balance in the Habsburg lands, and, above all, to sense the moment he could harness these forces and use them to realize his goal, the realization of the ideas and designs of others that he had absorbed and made his own. Deák made history through *Realpolitik,* which consists not necessarily of unprincipled compromises but of the accomplishment of as many objectives at a time as circumstances permit and then waiting for the opportune moment to achieve more. Finally, by stages, the end result is achieved. Deák's successes were the result of such methods, a matter of strategy and tactics which alone responded to all the conditions of the time. It was the only possible course.

In the fall of 1865 Deák felt the time was ripe to achieve his long-term goals. Anxious not to let the opportunity slip, for the first time in his political career he exercised strong, dynamic leadership and demanded party discipline for the sake of effective concerted action. On December 20, 1865, a Deák Party Club was set up in permanent quarters where matters of organization and campaign strategy could be discussed and decided and from which party activities could be directed and controlled.[7] Deák laid down goals and principles and set the tasks that had to be fulfilled, but he avoided pettiness about discipline and made a point of neither humiliating nor excessively praising anyone.[8]

Francis Joseph opened Parliament in person on December 14. His Address from the Throne included the regime's proposals for settlement with Hungary, which bore some resemblances to Deák's May Program, though in other respects the two differed.[9] Like Deák, he made the Pragmatic Sanction the cornerstone of settlement and proposed that the common affairs that sprang from it should be defined as they were in the October Diploma and administered by the institutions set up by the diploma and the February Patent. While acknowledging that "their formal validity is unchallengeable," he emphasized that the April Laws would have to be amended before revalidation.[10] The main question was whether the new ministry was to be appointed at once, before amendment of the April Laws, as

Deák wanted, or afterwards, as the court wished. In other words, was the settlement to be arranged with a liberal Hungarian ministry in power responsible to a Parliament dominated by liberals, or under an executive of conservatives not responsible to Parliament and dependent on the court's pleasure? The issue was one of substance and the gap between the liberals and the court widened, but there was a major difference from the past. Now both sides sincerely sought a settlement.[11]

Deák drafted the reply to the Address from the Throne.[12] Stressing that the Pragmatic Sanction was a bilateral treaty which by nature was dualistic, he emphasized that on the one hand it assured the dynasty its hereditary rights in Hungary and the indivisibility of the Empire, and on the other, it guaranteed Hungary's constitutional independence and the inviolability of its constitutional freedoms. The latter the court had yet to acknowledge by its deeds. The reply agreed with the existence of common affairs but rejected both the diploma and the patent as alien charters that were not compatible with Hungary's liberties. Deák demanded that the laws of 1848 be reinstated, and if necessary amended, but only through regular legislative procedures. To put all this into effect, he urged the prompt appointment of a responsible Hungarian ministry. The position he took was thus a maximalist one, but the language of the reply indicated that he intended to build bridges, not burn them.[13]

The day the royal response reached Pest, March 3, 1866, Parliament on Deák's advice elected a Committee of Sixty-Seven as a token of its goodwill and readiness to bargain, to draft the formal Hungarian proposals for settlement. The royal response was conciliatory in tone[14] but neither appointed a ministry nor reestablished full autonomy of the counties.

The principal work of Parliament was now handled by the Committee of Sixty-Seven, which in turn elected a Subcommittee of Fifteen to draft the law on the common affairs of the future dualistic empire. The majority of both committees were from the Deák Party, including Deák himself, József Eötvös, Gyula Andrássy, Menyhért Lónyai, István Gorove, and Antal Csengery. The conservatives, led by György Apponyi, supported the Deákists. The representatives of the Left Center Party (Kálmán

Tisza, Pál Nyáry, Kálmán Ghyczy, and Imre Ivánka) functioned as little more than devil's advocates.[15] Deák's most loyal and hardworking partner, Csengery, kept a detailed and revealing record of the work of both committees.

Deák was most interested and active whenever matters of fundamental principle and policy needed to be clarified or made acceptable to the dynasty. Otherwise he stood back and did not intervene in day-to-day administrative affairs. When a financial question had to be settled with the Austrian authorities, Deák dumbfounded Csengery by commenting: "I couldn't be bothered with details."[16] When chairmen were to be elected for the committee and the subcommittee, everybody assumed Deák would be elected, but even before his name could be formally proposed, he declared: "I say the chairman should be Andrássy." He said it with such finality that Andrássy was duly elected to chair both bodies.[17] In the coming months Deák turned down similar positions in the same way. He declined to head the joint Austro-Hungarian committee that was to establish each country's contribution to the first common budget; he rejected leadership of the first Hungarian Delegation;[18] he refused the palatinate and the premiership. He simply was not interested in administrative work, in routine responsibility, in power, or even in recognition and reward. His natural laziness was part of the reason, yet he displayed enormous energy in working toward the fulfillment of the liberals' basic goals. Csengery's account of the work of the Committee of Sixty-Seven and the Subcommittee of Fifteen is full of such phrases as "Deák presents a detailed program," "Deák sets out the major objectives," "Deák is asked to draft the final resolution" and "Deák's draft is passed unanimously."[19]

Deák's exactitude in this sort of work won Csengery over completely, as it did others. "Deák dictates a text," Csengery wrote. "Sometimes he dictates it three times over, each time digesting it into a more and more condensed form, so that finally it is so precise and clear that it could not be faulted by the most demanding stylist." Csengery carped only at the dryness of Deák's expositions: "Deák carries simplicity to the point where it becomes the antithesis of artistic style."[20] These creations of Deák, however, were to become the final text of the Compromise of 1867 when they were incorporated into the code of Hungarian law.[21]

As tension between Austria and Prussia began to mount early in April 1866, Deák announced that in case of war Parliament would have to adjourn, but when war became imminent in mid-June, the subcommittee's work was so near completion that he decided to press ahead to produce a *fait accompli,* so that Parliament's position would be known before the results of the hostilities. Anticipating that an Austrian victory would lead to excessive Austrian demands, he sought to counterbalance them by Hungarian claims clearly stated before the war was over. In the case of Austrian defeat, excessive demands by Hungarian extremists could be tempered the same way. "We don't know," Deák said, "whether we should be glad or sorry if our army is beaten. It is uncertain which will be to the country's advantage."[22] The war broke out on June 17, and six days later Deák requested through the Hungarian Royal Court Chancellery that Parliament not be adjourned before June 30. Assisted by Csengery, Deák worked day and night to complete the draft. On June 24, the day of Austria's victory at Custozza, the Subcommittee of Fifteen met and endorsed Deák's draft in principle. Before the day was out, the full Committee of Sixty-Seven did the same. The text was published June 25 alongside news of the victory at Custozza. The following day Parliament was adjourned, but its committees had had time to prepare their legislative proposals for a settlement and publish them before the decisive battle of Königgrätz.[23]

On July 19, after the Austrian defeat at Königgrätz but before an armistice had been declared, Deák and Francis Joseph met for a second time. Still uncertain whether the war would be fought to a bitter end, the King wanted to sound Deák out in case worst should come to worst. Deák assured him that, come what may, Hungary would ask for no more than was contained in the subcommittee's draft. Urging the King to appoint a Hungarian ministry at once, nevertheless, in answer to Francis Joseph's inquiry, he said he would never himself accept the premiership. He suggested Andrássy for the office. The King told him that Count Belcredi had advised him to continue the war, which would require a second draft for the year. "What

is your opinion?" Francis Joseph asked. "In our country, Sire,
it would be impossible. In Hungary women have children only
once a year," Deák replied.[24] He advised the King to make
immediate peace and reestablish the Hungarian constitution.
Then, "your subjects, happy and contented, will restore the
prestige of the Empire and the power and glory of Your
Majesty."[25]

Aware that the Austro-Prussian war had brought Hungary
into the realm of European grand politics, Deák remarked:
"I don't know European affairs. I only know Hungary's laws.
I cannot accept leadership now." After the audience was over,
Deák left for Zala county, far away from the events of the
moment.[26] Meanwhile Andrássy had a series of audiences with
Francis Joseph while other Hungarian liberal statesmen were
in constant negotiation with Cis-Leithanian leaders, most of
whom accepted the subcommittee's proposals as the basis for
a settlement.[27]

The debacle of Königgrätz sharpened the appetites of Hungary's extremists. The preliminary peace of Nikolsburg on
July 21 and the definitive peace of Prague on August 23 encouraged the militarists, conservatives, and centralists. The court,
however, felt that appointment of a Hungarian ministry responsible to Parliament was now inevitable. "Austria . . . had to
yield to the demands of the well-organized, strongly nationalist
Magyar forces. None of the other nationality movements, including that of the Germans in the sixties, had the fighting spirit of
the Magyar middle and upper middle classes; none had a leader
equal in popular appeal and political ability to Deák."[28]

"The absolutist regime did not raise statesmen, only bureau-
crats," commented the contemporary observer Imre Halász. So
in its bankrupt military and financial circumstances the court
had to look elsewhere for leaders and invited the former Saxon
prime minister, Count Friedrich Ferdinand von Beust, to become
imperial foreign minister. According to the British ambassador
in Vienna, quoted by Halász: "Prussians in Bohemia meant a
major defeat, but a Saxon in the Foreign Office was an even
greater disaster."[29] But for the Hungarians the change was not
disadvantageous. A dissatisfied Hungary could not be reconciled
with Beust's revanchist policies. Besides, the wars of 1859 and

1866 had "finally shattered Metternich's old dream of a unified Austrian empire with a German superstructure."[30] The Hungarian Parliament was therefore summoned back to complete work on the compromise. Prodded by Deák, the Committee of Sixty-Seven completed a final draft law on common affairs. Deák made its passage by both houses of Parliament conditional on the appointment of a ministry responsible to Parliament and the revalidation of the laws of 1848.[31]

By this time, the Deák Party and the Cis-Leithanian liberals were in virtual alliance.[32] Belcredi, who opposed the proposal, was in retreat because he had failed to secure the only possible surety for his policies, the strengthening of the political influence of the Slav elements in the monarchy to offset the weight of the Hungarians and Germans.[33] The provincial assemblies of Styria and Upper Austria came out in favor of the dualist system. Beust and Andrássy pressed for a settlement, while Deák and Francis Joseph were oddly teamed to brake the headlong rush into it.[34] Beust, anxious to reconsolidate the monarchy's great-power position in Europe, in January 1867 accepted the Subcommittee of Fifteen's draft with only minor, inconsequential alterations. This was then adopted by the Committee of Sixty-Seven on February 6, 1867.[35] The die was cast so that Belcredi had no option but to resign. Gyula Andrássy was appointed Hungarian prime minister on February 7.[36] A royal rescript dated February 20 proclaimed the composition of Andrássy's new ministry. The king retained "complete prerogatives over the command, leadership and internal organization of the army" and the exact responsibilities of the Hungarian ministry of defense were to be legislated later.[37]

Parliament, meeting in plenary session, began debate on March 20 on the Committee of Sixty-Seven's draft bill on common affairs. It thus embarked on the final phase of the settlement with the monarch that was to culminate in Francis Joseph's coronation with St. Stephen's crown in Buda on June 8, 1867.[38] The settlement, usually known as the Compromise of 1867 (*Ausgleich* in German and *a kiegyezés* in Hungarian), was a complex covenant between Francis Joseph, the Hungarian legislature, and the Austrian Empire (formally and more properly referred to as "the lands represented in the *Reichsrat*"). The

principal documents were the enactments of the Hungarian
Parliament and the *Reichsrat* defining and ordering the administration of the common affairs of the two units. In the narrower
sense, these acts alone comprise the Compromise of 1867, but
in the Hungarian context they are irrevocably associated with
a series of companion enactments that laid the foundations
of the new Hungary. The latter, all bearing Deák's hallmark,
in chronological order were the emancipation of the Jews; the
Croatian-Hungarian Compromise of 1868; the Public Education
Act; the Equality of the Nationalities Act; and the Common
Defense Acts.

The definition and administration of the common affairs were
embodied in the Hungarian Parliament's Act XII/1867.[39] Rooted
in the Pragmatic Sanction,[40] it guaranteed the continuity of
Hungary's constitutional independence. The identity of the
monarchs of Hungary and the hereditary provinces was the
basis of the commonalty of defense and foreign affairs, which
were to be administered in concert by the cabinets of the two
associated states.[41]

In the absence of a common legislature, the two parliaments
exercised legislative control over the joint ministries through
the "delegations," which were commissioned by each sovereign
and independent legislature on the basis of equality and parity.[42]
The joint ministers of the common affairs could be called into
council under the chairmanship of the king-emperor, but they
did not form a constitutional corporate authority. All three
ministers remained individually responsible to the two parliaments through the delegations. Both "the Austrian and Hungarian prime ministers participated in the joint council of ministers."[43] This cumbersome and complicated machinery was
what brought into existence the dualist system of Austria-
Hungary called also the Austro-Hungarian Empire.[44]

The criticism of the Compromise of 1867 started in earnest
long before its promulgation, in fact as early as a chance for
its conclusion seemed probable. None other than Kossuth himself attacked the draft of the Compromise in an open letter
to Deák published in *Magyar Újság* ("Hungarian Journal") in
May 1867. Complaining that the April Laws had provided for
Hungary's finances and defense to be administered without

foreign interference, Kossuth pointed out that the Compromise was sacrificing this freedom. "Alas, you have no faith in the nation's energies. . . . The hub of your policy is that 'whatever can be realized should be accepted because nothing else can be achieved.' But I object to this for reasons of rights and policy. So to gamble with the nation is inadmissible."

Kossuth's main objection was that the association of Hungary with the other Habsburg lands made it subject to policies over which it had no control and would eventually leave it caught between inimical neighbors both in the east and west. The Compromise ruled out a fair solution of Hungary's nationality problems and the Croatian question. Hungary, Kossuth prophesied, would inevitably become the object of competing powers in some future European crisis. He also objected that the amendment of the April Laws eliminated from them precisely the provisions that were designed to keep a check on despotism, such as the National Guard system and the counties' function as a bulwark of constitutional government. Condemning the Compromise as inconsonant with the progressive trends of the age, he said that the concessions the Hungarians were making to the Habsburgs had neither the justification of force nor of the Habsburgs' position of power in Europe. "Do not drag the country to the point where it cannot be master of its own destiny," he begged Deák.[45]

At the same time as Kossuth, but from a different perspective, František Palacký, the advocate of a federal reconstruction of the Habsburg lands, attacked the Compromise. Deploring the hegemony of the Germans and Hungarians in the monarchy, he said: "The day dualism is proclaimed . . . will also be the birthday of Panslavism in its least desirable form, and the godparents of the latter will be the parents of the former. What will follow every reader can divine for himself. We Slavs will look forward to that with sincere grief, but without fear. We existed before Austria; we shall still exist when it is gone."[46]

Deák answered Kossuth's open letter in the May 30 issue of *Pesti Napló*. His policies, he said, could not dissemble less, for they were always explained fully to the public:

I have stated that it is my personal conviction that in our position it is better to make a peaceful settlement than to let our future depend on policies that are founded on vague promises, that would cause further delays and suffering, and that would probably depend on happenstance, on revolution and the dissolution of the empire, on foreign aid (for which our interests would certainly not be the main motive), or on new foreign alliances, the form, purposes and advantages of which cannot yet be known. I have also stated that the means I have proposed for settlement does not jeopardize our constitutional freedoms and, in many respects, is advantageous to the country. These statements of mine, which were never addressed to passions but rather to calm common sense, have always been made openly.

Deak emphasized that he had never tried to pressure anyone to follow him or to impose his will on others. "If, despite all this, the majority's opinion and mine have coincided, it can be simply explained by the fact that their convictions and mine were the same."[47] This clash between the two statesmen was but the climax of the Kossuth-Deák controversy, which had already a long history.

How similar were Deák and Kossuth, and how did they differ? Before 1849 they shared identical ideologies, but their styles could not have been more dissimilar. Both of them wanted to transform Hungary peacefully into a modern state with a liberal governmental system, a bourgeois society, and a population of equal, free citizens. Once Kossuth had accepted leadership of the armed defiance to the counterrevolutionary Habsburg regime in 1848, however, he was committed to a policy to which Deák could not subscribe. After the Hungarian revolution had been forcibly suppressed, their two names represented diametrically opposite concepts. Deák stood for the idea of '48: the reestablishment of parliamentary government in an autonomous Hungary. In order not to jeopardize this goal, he allied himself with the conservatives and apparently abandoned his earlier drive for social reform. Kossuth embodied the spirit of '49: a democratic Hungary at peace with, or, in later projects, in some sort of federal connection with, its neighbors and in complete secession from the Habsburg dynastic territories. With the passage of time Kossuth's social policies grew constantly more progressive.

Deák, who remained in Hungary after the revolution, was

the master of *Realpolitik*. He could not divorce himself from
the realities of life, nor did he wish to. Kossuth fled from
Hungary, and like so many other exiles through the ages lost
touch with Hungarian realities. He became the creature of
maximalist dreams and great-power politics. Certain great powers
rattled the specter of Kossuth to frighten the Habsburg dynasty
and, that done, abandoned him.

The two men were linked by a binding and rather paradoxical
interdependence. Without Deák's aid, Kossuth's rise to power
before 1848 was far from assured. Had Deák not stepped aside,
it probably would never have taken place. Without the specter
of Kossuth to scare the Habsburg regime, Deák's road to success
in 1867 would have been much more difficult. It is even debatable
whether 1867 would have been possible at all without 1849.

Kossuth, the flamboyant man of destiny, scintillated and then
faded from power like a passing comet. Yet he remained an
extraordinarily exciting source of inspiration and object of
passionate admiration because of his resistance to counterrevolution. Deák, the modest, gray, unaffected, and unimpressive
lawyer of his nation, won the Hungarians' vital suit. For this
the nation was grateful, but Deák never inspired its passion.
He was ever the sage, respected rather than admired. In 1867,
however, not only the legislators but also the vast majority of
the Hungarian voting public favored Deák's policies and supported the Compromise. Moreover, Deák did not consider the
Compromise an end in itself but a beginning, a groundwork on
which the enhancement of the rights of all could be built. It was
the maximum that could be realistically attained in 1867 as well
as the product of a righteous policy. Deák must be credited with
the arrangement of the settlement; its implementation was the
responsibility of those who came after him, and it is they and
other factors both internal and external that doomed the monarchy. In 1867 there simply existed no alternative to dualism
that could have brought the political and social forces under
control. There was no political, social and economic combination
capable of administering the monarchy other than the triad of
the Austro-German liberal bourgeoisie, the Hungarian liberal
gentry, and the dynasty with its traditional support from the
Roman Catholic church, the army, the conservative aristocracy,

and the bureaucracy. In addition, the European status of the
Habsburg dynasty itself was seen as necessary to the great-
power balance of Europe. During Deák's last years dualism
unquestionably secured the monarchy's position as a great
power.[48]

The constitutional niceties, rules, regulations, committees,
delegations, and all the other trappings of the Compromise must
not be allowed to obscure the fact that the creation of the Dual
Monarchy introduced a classic liberal form of government into
both parts of the empire. To be sure, it did not yet initiate
democracy, but, at the time, this was not unusual. The arrangement established a system of checks and balances and the
division of power among the three branches of government; it
installed legislative systems in which laws were made by the
representatives of a fairly large proportion of those governed;
it secured the freedoms of person, expression, assembly, and
association; and it laid to rest for good the enduring Habsburg
tradition of despotism and absolutism. The equality of all before
the law became a reality. For the rest of his days, Deák saw all
these principles wholly respected.[49]

The first of the liberal pieces of companion legislation to the
Compromise was the emancipation of the Jews. Act XVII/1867
realized one of Deák's and the liberals' cherished reforms. It
stated quite simply:

§1. It is hereby proclaimed that the Israelite inhabitants of the
country are entitled to exercise all civil and political rights equally
with the Christian inhabitants.

§2. All laws, practices and regulations contrary to these presents
are hereby repealed.[50]

The act was a model of precision that spoke for itself and needs
no analysis. It is to the credit of Deák and his fellow liberals
that it did not remain a dead letter but that for nearly two
generations the Jews found in Hungary a true homeland.

The second companion piece of legislation was the Croatian-
Hungarian Compromise,[51] often called by its Croatian name,
Nagodba.[52] It was as important in placing relations between the
two states on a new constitutional footing as its genesis was
characteristic of Deák's tactics and extraordinary influence over

affairs of state in 1868. During the preceding decades Deák had striven to preserve the territorial integrity of the lands of St. Stephen's crown but would have agreed to Croatia's secession rather than face a protracted Croat-Hungarian crisis; he had recognized that the Croats were a separate nation, equal in rights and privileges to the Hungarians, and would grant them complete autonomy in their internal affairs if they elected to continue their constitutional association with Hungary. In times of crisis Deák had said that his policy was to give the Croats the freedom to secede, but when passions were not running high, this stated policy had tended to fall into abeyance. Then his wish to continue the partnership had outweighed his willingness to consent to secession. The year 1868 was such a time.

On July 24, 1868, the Croat and Hungarian representatives endorsed the draft of their settlement,[53] which had in fact been composed by Deák in collaboration with Csengery. The settlement affirmed the indivisible community of the Hungarian and Croatian states. Croatia would be completely autonomous in the administration of all strictly domestic affairs, including local government, religious matters, public education, and justice, Its official language would be Croatian which its representatives would be entitled to speak in the Hungarian Parliament and the dualist delegation.

Hungary was to provide 93.56 percent of the budget for the common affairs of Hungary and Croatia and the Triune Kingdom the remaining 6.44 percent. This ratio, according to Macartney, "was generous towards Croatia, which was allowed to retain 45 percent of the yield of her taxes for her own *interna* [budget for domestic affairs]."[54] The Croatian Assembly endorsed the provisions of the settlement on September 24; the Hungarian Parliament passed it without debate on September 28. On November 17 it was promulgated as Act XXX/1868.[55]

The Croat nationalists were not satisfied, but they had let slip by two opportunities to outmaneuver the Hungarians. In 1861 they could have joined the *Reichsrat* and presented the Hungarians with a *fait accompli* by concluding a compromise directly with the court instead of following the Hungarian example of obstructing the October Diploma and February Patent and boycotting the *Reichsrat*. Again in 1866, when the

Hungarians' relations with the court were particularly delicate, Hungary would probably have agreed to much more advantageous terms for the Croats in order to secure its flank for its dealings with the imperial capital. The Croats, however, misjudged the situation by bypassing the Hungarian government and approaching the court directly. The court was much more interested in a reconciliation with the Hungarians, and the Croats found themselves out in the cold. They had to come to what terms they could with a Hungary that was being backed rather than checked by the court in the aftermath of the Compromise of 1867.[56] Under the circumstances it is hardly surprising that there are almost as many interpretations of the *Nagodba* as historians.

Once the Croatian-Hungarian settlement had been concluded, the Compromise was rounded out by two more companion pieces of legislation in Hungary, the acts on public education and the equality of the nationalities, both of which were fruits of the intellect and progressive liberal convictions of József Eötvös. In the passage of both of these bills Deák played as important a part as in the negotiation of the Compromise. It must be remembered that the great majority of the Hungarian Parliament was drawn from Deák's own social group, the landed gentry, who were the bastion of Hungarian liberalism but were also Hungarian nationalists. It was they who had pressed for the social and political modernization of Hungary, even at the expense of their own privileges, during the Reform Era of 1830–48. Nevertheless, their class loyalties prevented them from being true radical social reformers. Now they were debating legislation that would considerably broaden the rights of national minorities— Romanians, Slovaks, and Serbs—whose national ambitions were no less than the Hungarians'. In fact, these various nationalisms were at loggerheads, and the Hungarian liberals' success in concluding the Compromise had served to sharpen their own national consciousness, pride and self-esteem. They were to vote not ungenerous conditions for the other nationalities, but they could not be brought to alter nationality relationships in Hungary radically. Deák needed all his tact and prestige to overcome the obstructions of the reactionary nationalists and to temper his fellow liberals' nationalism. Both Deák and Eötvös were sincere in honoring the laws they created and steered into force, although their successors later violated them.

The Public Education Act[57] consolidated the establishment of modern primary schooling in Hungary, which was already well developed in the parochial sector. Eötvös's main purpose was to protect the plurality of forms and the freedom of education. His bill aimed to secure the right of churches, towns, nationalities, associations, communities, and individuals to maintain and run their own schools. In 1868 there were 13,789 elementary schools in Hungary, 13,319 of them parochial and 479 of them community schools.[58] Under such circumstances the prerequisite for variety was the protection of the existing autonomy of the church schools. The bill held that all private schools, including the parochial schools, were entitled to collect dues from their members for their own maintenance, to appoint their own teachers and determine their salaries, to select their own textbooks, to establish their own teaching methods, and, above all, to teach in the language of their choice. The state had the right to supervise these private schools by periodically inspecting them.

The bill made education compulsory for all children from the age of six through fifteen. In the first six years of school the pupils had to attend class regularly for twenty to twenty-five hours a week; in the next four years they had to attend five hours a week in winter and two hours a week in summer. The school year was to be nine months long in the towns and eight months long in the country.

The curricula of the public schools were regulated by the Ministry of Public Education and Churches. Paragraph 58 of the bill stated: "Every pupil shall receive education in his native tongue if that is one of the prevalent languages of the locality. In linguistically mixed communities, teachers shall be hired who can teach in the languages in use. In greater communities where there are larger numbers from differing linguistic groups, teaching assistants for the different languages shall be hired to the extent that the community's finances permit." The bill also provided for free education and textbooks for those who could prove their inability to pay.[59]

For all its shortcomings as enacted, the measure was the most progressive elementary-education law in Europe at that time. Austria made education compulsory in 1869, England in 1882; Italy passed a similar measure in 1904, Russia in 1912. Prussia to all intents and purposes had had a system of compulsory elementary education since 1815.[60] The crowning achievement of the Compromise was the equality of the nationalities bill, Act XLIV/1868.[61] It was the product of a troika: Eötvös with his intellectual gifts, Andrássy with his administrative skill, and Deák with his parliamentary tactics and personal prestige. The preamble, worded by Deák, affirmed the controversial principle of the indivisibility of the single Hungarian political nation:[62]

Whereas, according to the basic principles of the constitution, all the citizens of Hungary politically constitute one nation, the indivisible, unitary Hungarian nation, of which every citizen of the country is an equal member, whatever his nationality. . . .

The act prescribed that the state language of Hungary, of parliamentary debate, of the central government and of legislation was Hungarian, but that all laws would be published in official translations into all the languages in use in Hungary. In counties where one-fifth of the county assemblymen so wished, a second language could be made official for debate and records. Otherwise everyone could speak in his native tongue in the county assemblies. Communities, parishes, and church administrations could choose the language for their transactions. In communities one-fifth of the electorate could make a second language official. "All citizens of the state may petition their village, church, county, and the state administrations in their own tongue" (Paragraph 23). Paragraph 26 stipulated: "Every citizen of any nationality, community, church, or parish may establish on his own or in association with others elementary, secondary, or advanced schools and institutions to promote language, arts, sciences, economy, industry, and commerce . . . and administer them; he may associate freely with others, control his own institutions, collect dues to run them in order to achieve his legal national ambitions. . . . Private institutions may use the language of their choice."

Arthur J. May concluded: "The Nationality Act of 1868 was one of the most enlightened measures of its kind ever adopted, even more liberal than the minority safeguards incorporated in the peace settlements of 1919–20, which, indeed, were very largely modeled on the Hungarian precedent of 1868."[63]

With the enactment of the Compromise and its associated legislation Deák's political career reached its peak. He was a successful statesman, and in 1868 at the age of 65 he had become in his own lifetime the incarnation of his nation's ambitions. Climax, however, can be succeeded only by decline.

II Prestige Without Influence

Deák's decline after 1868 was a combination of physical factors and the nature of his party. In 1869 Deák's health began to break down and, physically exhausted, he fell ill more and more often. With the conclusion of the Compromise and its companion legislation, he concentrated on little more than the consolidation of his achievements. He would have liked to accomplish more, but he realized that his party would not sustain him in any more progressive legislation. At the end of the epochal Parliament of 1865–68, Deák told Somssich, the party chairman, what he believed should follow from the Compromise: "Our work is not yet finished. . . . Our program cannot but be to uphold the fundamental laws we have just created, to advance our constitutional life and institutions, and to promote the nation's economic and spiritual interests while safeguarding the people's rights and full equality before the law."[64] Thus Deák would have liked to transform the classic liberal form of government that had been established into a real democracy. It was the course that western Europe was taking. Deák's vision was not of a static society smugly satisfied with its achievements, but of a dynamic country that would keep pace with western European development. For the latter, however, Deák needed a vigorous liberal party willing to follow him as in the negotiation of the Compromise. Instead, the liberals were badly splintered.

The Deák Party that concluded the Compromise of 1867 never possessed any cohesion other than Deák's leadership and a common desire to reach an accommodation with the monarch on advantageous terms. During the crucial negotiations, it had attracted politicians of every stripe; once the Compromise was complete, disintegration set in and worsened as Deák's health and energy, and hence his leadership, weakened. The differences among the components of the party increased.

The most influential such group was that of the former centralists, above all, József Eötvös, Antal Csengery, and Ágoston Trefort. They were the most convinced liberals, cosmopolitan and vigorous champions of political and social reform, who became known as the Doctrinaires. The next group consisted of the liberal aristocrats, the great landlords led by Andrássy, many of whom were former exiles and Kossuthists. Their modern, capitalistic agricultural background made them *laissez-faire* liberals who wanted the settlement with Austria safeguarded. Their number included not only Andrássy but also Baron Béla Wenckheim and József Szlávy, each of whom in turn became prime ministers. In addition, conservatives who had seen power slipping from their grasp as Deák's liberals were taking the lead in 1865 had either retired from political life or had joined the Deák Party. Finally, representatives of large capital had also cast their lot with the Deák Party, which thus was an amalgam of great landowners, big capitalists and some of the medium landed gentry. The opposition then challenged Deák's national leadership, already weakened by internal dissent. The strongest opposition was Kálmán Tisza's Left Center Party, which had emerged from the Party of Resolution of 1861 and was composed predominantly of the reformist gentry, whose power basis was the ancient county system and who had sought liberal reform during the Reform Era. It included some aristocrats from the Trans-Tisza and Transylvania. Most of them, despite their aristocratic titles, were of the same economic level as the gentry and shared their outlook. Bourgeois from northern Hungary and Transylvania had also joined the Left Center Party.

The Extreme Left Party of '48, which later became the Independence Party, consisted of Kossuth's supporters—gentry and commoners who were professionals, writers, and intellectuals. They represented the petty bourgeoisie and Kossuth's spell made them also the party of the mass of mostly unfranchised peasantry.[65]

The Deák Party worked for the consolidation of the dualist system, the Left Center Party for its dissolution and replacement by a personal union with Austria, and the Extreme Left Party of '48 for secession from the empire, democracy, federalism, and the fairest possible solution to Hungary's nationality problems. Once the Compromise had been enacted, the gentry, whatever its party affiliation, felt secure and was content simply to reap the profit of its gains. Its liberalism was on the wane and its nationalism on the rise. This was already clear during the debate on Eötvös's draft of the Equality of the Nationalities Act. Most of the members of Parliament strongly opposed the maximum scale of the rights that Eötvös would have ceded to the nationalities, and Deák had to tone the bill down to save its major provisions. With his modifications it passed by 267 votes to 24.[66]

Immediately after its passage, Parliament took up the budget for 1869. It included a subsidy for the Hungarian National Theater, and the Serbian members therefore demanded a similar subsidy for the Serbian National Theater. Deák took the Serbs' part and stated that he would vote for both or neither. Increasingly self-confident and nationalistic, his party voted him down, approving the Hungarian subsidy while denying the Serbs'. It was Deák's first defeat by his own partisans and presaged their drift away from his principles.[67]

Deák's second defeat in Parliament came less than a year later, on July 8, 1869. At issue was a progressive measure to end the counties' authority over certain courts of law. The bill was killed when 110 members voted with Deák and 126 against him.[68]

In June 1870 Parliament defeated Deák's candidate for Hungarian state comptroller, Vince Weininger, whose expert knowledge and experience gained in the common ministry of finance admirably suited him for the job. The post was given to Salamon Gajzágó, a man with neither experience nor knowledge in the field. Gajzágó was voted in because the members of Parliament felt more comfortable with a member of the gentry than a sophisticated and cosmopolitan statesman like Weininger. Afterwards Deák remarked: "For a long time I haven't even considered myself a member of the party. . . . I have been treading a lonely road."[69]

It was, in fact, the beginning of the end of the Deák era. The following year was particularly disastrous for all that the states-man stood for. On February 2, 1871, Eötvös died. A fount of ideas and progressive plans, the intellectual pillar of the Deák system, he was irreplaceable. In May Boldizsár Horváth, the Minister of Justice and another staunch liberal, quit the party in disgust at its increasingly reactionary turn. There was no one of similar caliber to take his place. On November 13 Andrássy was appointed Austro-Hungarian minister of foreign affairs. His departure for Vienna was a major blow. Deák treasured his political skill, administrative talent, and excellent connections at court. Whatever Deák was not in a position to do, Andrássy had handled for him. With his departure, Deák felt isolated and help-less. To make matters worse, Deák and the new prime minister, Menyhért Lónyay, did not see eye to eye. They simply disliked each other. A ministry headed by someone with whom Deák could not work was calamitous for his influence and an unmis-takable sign that the party was already going its own way with little regard for his leadership.

Deák suffered another setback in March 1872, when the ever more reactionary Deákists filibustered against an electoral re-form bill that he had intended to strengthen Hungary's institutions "while safeguarding the people's rights and equality." Instead of taking a step toward the democratic ideal, the bill that was eventually passed restricted the franchise. Parliament had moved in a direction diametrically opposed to Deák's wishes. For days afterwards he kept himself locked away, buried in his books.[70]

Deák delivered his last major speech to Parliament on June 28, 1873, on the subject of church-state relations.[71] It was tan-tamount to a testament in which he indicated that Hungary's proper direction was forward toward democracy, not backward whence it had come. He made a few later interpolations on minor issues and appeared in Parliament for the last time on November 10, 1873. Illness kept him at home thereafter. During 1874 he was still able to receive Francis Joseph, Emperor Dom Pedro II of Brazil and other dignitaries at the Hotel Angol Királynő, but these were more visits to an honored relic of the past than to a person of real power.

The last political act of importance for Deák was the fusion of his party with Kálmán Tisza's Left Center Party, for which his advice and consent were sought. Deák's leadership was replaced by that of his former opponent Tisza and the new party's name, Parliamentary Liberal Party, made no mention of the former head. Not at all reluctant to agree to the change, Deák asked only that his own party should not be humiliated in any way and that the prime minister should at first be drawn from its ranks. So the fusion was effected and Deák signed his name first in the register of party members with the sardonic question: "Wasn't I liberal till now?" His irony was portentous. Previously "liberal" had not figured in the party's name, yet Deák and his colleagues had sought and realized liberal reforms. Now that the party was denominated liberal, liberalism was on the decline because of a paradox in the party structure and dualist Hungarian society.

This paradox was well described by A. Kecskeméthy, an opportunistic, reactionary journalist of great intellectual gifts, whose analyses, irrespective of his ideology, were perhaps the most penetrating of all of Deák's contemporaries':

In Hungary it would be reasonable to choose between two political directions. Either consider the weight of the Hungarian nation's historic supremacy, then the free institutions, autonomies, and adoption of the guise of liberalism and democracy should be discarded, and the nation itself should relinquish its enjoyment of certain political rights that the nationalities might use against it. In short: systematic dictatorship, strong centralism, the Hungarian language. Or else, start out from the conviction that the supremacy of the Hungarian language is untenable and that the nationalities simply cannot be dominated by bare institutional methods, then the principle of a multilingual state should be implemented through free institutions to the fullest degree. The Deák Pary with its ideological confusion is drifting right and left between these two. Nor is the opposition any abler. Only a handful sees the danger that arises from these contradictions and vacillations. The nation is incapable of the first alternative: it is too immature; but the impetus is also lacking for it to rise to the heights of the considerations in the second.[72]

For all his cynicism, Kecskeméthy was basically right. The Deák Party was unable to form an enduring, stable government because its heterogeneity did not give it a sufficient base either for a march toward democracy or for a move toward reactionary despotism. In fact, the nature of dualism tended to make the establishment of democratic institutions impossible. Dualism and democracy were poles apart. Dualism was rooted in the domination of the Cis-Leithanian provinces by the Germans and the Trans-Leithanian state by the Hungarians. Deák held up the illusion of democracy; Kálmán Tisza and the Left Center Party shared the illusion of augmenting Hungary's "independence" by undoing the dualist system and substituting a personal union between Austria and Hungary. Both these illusions were utopian. As the economic crisis mounted and the depression of 1873 struck, the Hungarian state verged on bankruptcy. Both the Deák and the Left Center Parties considered their fusion the sole solution to create a stable regime that would foster confidence among the big Austrian capitalists. These would then bail Hungary out of its financial straits. The only way this could be achieved was for the gentry to accept the dominance of the coalition of the great landlords and the big capitalists, and both parties therefore abandoned their utopian illusions. Andrássy and the Viennese financial circles pressed for this development in readiness for the impending reopening of the Eastern Question, that is, for a new Balkan crisis. The gentry of both parties acquiesced in their subordination to the great landowners and big capitalists in exchange for their own domination of the county administrations and of the constantly growing state bureaucracy.[73] The degeneration of the formerly conscientious and political independent gentry into a bureaucratic caste guaranteed the political and economic supremacy of the landowner-capitalist coalition and slammed the door on the evolution of the well-to-do peasantry into a petty bourgeoisie. The fusion of 1875 spelled the final demise of the Deák era, during which Deák and his closest associates could still honestly believe in their sincerely held but delusive goals of further fundamental social and political reform and the steady progress of parliamentary government toward real democracy. The advent of the Tisza era was the beginning of the steadily increasing subjection of the "lower" classes and the nationalities.

The elections of 1875 gave the new Parliamentary Liberal Party a landslide victory in which it gained 403 seats in Parliament to the combined right and left opposition's 50.[74] It was the last

Parliament of which Deák, despite his expressed wish, was a member. He was again returned by Central Pest but, as soon as the result was known, tendered his resignation because of sickness and debility. A new election was organized. Deák allowed himself to be persuaded by friends and various other groups to stand after all, and no one would run against him. The board of elections therefore declared him elected unopposed. The hero of 1867 thus for the last time in his life became a member of Parliament, a Parliament, however, in which he never once took his seat. In January 1876 he was failing fast. After a long life as a nonpracticing Roman Catholic, he received the last sacraments of his church, for, as he said, religion was a matter of sentiment, not intellect, and there were deistic sentiments he wanted to satisfy. As the clock on the University of Budapest Church struck a quarter before 11 p.m. on January 28, 1876, Ferenc Deák was pronounced dead.[75]

Deák's memory passed into the lawbooks on February 24, 1876, when Parliament passed Act III/1876:

> Whereas Ferenc Deák by the unalterable decision of divine providence has been called from the ranks of the living, the legislature resolves:
> §1. That the tribute due to Ferenc Deák after numerous years of service to the country is herewith made law;
> §2. That immediate measures shall be taken by the ministry to erect a memorial worthy of the deceased in the national capital out of funds raised by a nationwide collection;
> §3. That the ministry shall report on the matter of the memorial to both chambers at the end of every year until the memorial will have been completed. This act shall take effect as soon as it is promulgated and the ministry shall be responsible for its execution.[76]

The nation's tribute to Deák was indeed cast in bronze and set facing István Széchenyi's statue in front of the Academy of Sciences in Budapest. Parents and schools would take the children of later generations almost in pilgrimage to see the statue of Deák. Many fathers, like the author's own, must have pointed up at him and said: "Look, son, at the sage of the fatherland (*a haza bölcse*)."

Notes and References

Explanatory Note on Abbreviations in This Section

All Hungarian bibliographical sources in this section have been referred to in abbreviated form, beginning with the author's initials followed by the initials of the key words in the title. Refer to the Selected Bibliography for the expanded form of such entries and complete data.

Chapter One

1. *FZD*, III, 413–15.
2. *DFB*, I, 10.
3. Pre-revolutionary era or *Vormärz*.
4. *WGyDF*, pp. 93–94.
5. *DFB*, VI, 147.
6. Ibid., 411–12.
7. Ibid., 3.
8. *WGyDF*, pp. 10–11; *EKDF*, I, 18.
9. Béla K. Király, *Hungary in the Late Eighteenth Century* (New York: 1969), pp. 173–95; also C. A. Macartney, *The Habsburg Empire, 1790–1918* (New York: 1969), pp. 134–46.
10. Ibid., pp. 147–98.
11. Klára Deák died in 1859; her husband, József Oszterhuber-Tarányi, in 1869. *EKDF*, I 125, 127, 128, 148–50.
12. Ibid., I, 132–35, 218–44.
13. *AIDF*, p. 53.
14. *EKDF*, I, 225.
15. *Stimmungsreport*. *HHStA-GD*.
16. *EKDF*, I, 226.
17. *HILN*, p. 139; *GIGASz*, p. 294.
18. *AIDF*, pp. 190–91.
19. *WGyDF*, pp. 11–13. The teacher-student ratio varied from one religious denomination to the next, however. It was highest for the Jews, then came the Calvinists; the lowest ratio was among the Orthodox Christians. "Since even the poorest Jew knows how to read and write, it is safe to assume there is one teacher in every synagogue, which means a total of 410 Jewish teachers." *FEMST*, p.

113. In other words, there was a teacher for every 600 Jewish inhabitants of Hungary, almost twice the ratio for the population at large.

20. *Insurrectio.*

21. *PFEK*, I, 7.

22. Ferenc Pulszky wrote: "Deák often played bowls. During the meetings of the diet's Codification Committee [in the early 1840's] Deák used to get up at five a.m. and walk for three hours." *PFEK*, I, 14–15.

23. *Jurátus.* Emancipation of wet nurse *EKDF*, I, 24.

24. The total tax liability (5,200,000 florins) was increased illegally to 13,000,000 florins. *MSMT*, III, 181. See also Hugo Hantsch, *Die Geschichte Österreichs*, 2 vols. (Graz: 1968), II, 298–99.

25. This period of Ferenc Deák's life was analyzed by the present author in "The Young Ferenc Deák and the Problem of the Serfs, 1824–1836," *Südost-Forschungen*, XXIX (1970), 91–127.

26. *FZD*, I, 58–60; *WGyDF*, p. 12.

27. The Hungarian Reform Era is considered by many historians to have begun in 1825. They argue that the diet summoned in 1825 reestablished constitutionality after a decade and a half of Francis's extraconstitutional rule and that it was this diet that set up committees to recommend reforms. The liberals were then strengthened by the publication in 1830 of Count István Széchenyi's famous work *Hitel* ("Credit"), the reverberations of the Polish November Insurrection, and the Hungarian peasant rebellion of 1831. Encouraged by a broad sector of public opinion, the liberal reformers were then in a position to set to work in earnest. By the diet of 1832–36 the tide of liberal reform was flowing strongly toward its peak in the April Laws of 1848.

28. "There were a couple of hundred books on Deák's shelves." All these books were scholarly, for Deák did not read novels during this period of his life. *FZD*, I, 24, 52; *WGyDF*, pp. 13–15.

29. The *Auróra Kör* ("Aurora Circle") was formed around *Auróra*, a yearbook of *belles lettres* edited by Károly Kisfaludy. It was in circulation from 1821 to 1837, when it was succeeded by a much larger publication, *Atheneum. Auróra* was urbane, sophisticated and modern, addressed not only to the nobility, as late eighteenth-century Hungarian literature had been, but also to a wider, mostly urban readership. Around it revolved a new generation who became the leading intellectuals of the Reform Era: Mihály Vörösmarty, József Bajza, Ferenc Toldy, and others.

30. *FZD*, I, 63.

31. *Bene possessionati;* see Király, *Hungary . . .*, pp. 24–42.

32. On the functions and nature of the office of the *táblabíró* [magistrate] see Király, *Hungary* ..., p. 263.

33. *Sedria*; Deák never accepted *sedria* jurorship. *AIDF*, p. 18.

34. For the full text of Deák's speech, see *DFB*, I, 1–7.

35. *Ausgleich.*

36. The highest office in a county was that of the *főispán* (high sheriff) who was appointed by the king as his representative within the county's autonomy. In some cases the office was hereditary, and in all cases it was open only to the aristocracy and to a few prelates. The *főispán's* deputy was the *alispán*, who was elected by a special session (*sedes restauratoria electoria*) of the county assembly (*közgyűlés*). All the lesser nobility of the county were entitled to seats in the county assembly. The highest office to which a member of the gentry (*bene possessionatus*) could rise was that of the *alispán*, which was not, however, open to the *bocskoros nemesek* (slippered nobility), the lowest stratum of the lesser nobility, who were numerous, impoverished, often landless, and generally distinguishable from the serfs only by their tax exemption and their right to take part in the county assembly. The *surrogatus alispán* was an acting deputy high sheriff.

37. For a discussion of the status of the counties in the Hungarian governmental system, see Király, *Hungary* ..., pp. 108–13.

38. Quoted in *NID*, p. 253.

Chapter Two

1. County magistrate: *táblabíró*; County Court: *sedria*.

2. Credit: *Hitel*.

3. *AIMJ*, p. 435.

4. Galician Polish gentry: *szlachta*. The Galician upheaval of 1846 was complicated by racial tension between Poles and Ruthenians.

5. *AIDF*, p. 27.

6. Ibid., p. 12.

7. Habsburg provinces West of the River Leitha, e.g., Bohemia, the German Austrian Alpine provinces, etc. Cis-Leithanian Provinces is a term loosely used to cover all the Habsburg lands except Hungary.

8. The speaker of the House was the *Personalis* (*Személynök*), the highest state appointment accessible to a *bene possessionatus*. Appointed by the king, he was in principle the representative of the lesser nobility in all three branches of government. His main function was to preside over the *Tabula regia*, a branch of the supreme court that functioned as the court of the first instance for the nobility

and the highest appellate court in criminal cases for the commoners. The members of the *Tabula regia* sat as a body in the Lower House of the diet, of which the *Personalis* was the speaker *ex officio*. His third function was to sit in the *Consilium regium locumtenentiale hungaricum (Helytartótanács)*, or Hungarian Viceregal Council. The *Personalis* was Sándor Mérey from November 7, 1831, to June 15, 1833, and thereafter Pongrác Somssich (or Somsich). *PFD*, p. 11.

9. *DFB*, I, 37–38.

10. Unofficial session of the Lower House: *sessio districtualis*.

11. Plenary session of the Lower House: *sessio regnicolaris*.

12. *DFB*, I, 41, 16–18.

13. Ibid., I, 38.

14. *Tripartitum* ("Book in three parts") was the work of István Verbőczi (also Werbőczy) (d. 1541), a jurist and statesman. The *Tripartitum* was first published in Latin in 1517 and subsequently republished in Latin and Hungarian several times. The book was the exposition of the principles and practices of feudal society; it established noble privileges and the servile status of the peasants. The book was never promulgated into law, despite the author's intentions; nonetheless it affected the gentry's mind and policies just as strongly as if it had been the law of the land.

15. *DFB*, I, 34.

16. *AIMJ*, p. 48; *WGyDF*, pp. 17–20.

17. *Tagebücher* (2 vols.; Vienna: 1919), I, 508, 520, 618.

18. *Urbarium*: regulation of the obligations of the serfs and of their rights, issued by Maria Theresa in 1767 for Hungary, in 1756 for Slavonia, in 1780 for Croatia.

19. The hypocritical sentence that Deák referred to in the long royal rescript with which the King vetoed the liberal bills while posing as the protector of the peasantry read: "His Majesty wishes that all His subjects, that is, including the populous class of the peasantry, should live both individually and collectively in security, protected against all arbitrary acts against both their persons and their property, not only in their relations with their lords but also in all other relations." Deák, with no little irony, commented: "We find among Hungarian laws no principle more beautiful and more glorious than this. The estates should not hesitate to incorporate it verbatim into their Petition to the Throne." *NID*, p. 119. For the complete debate, see *KLOT*.

20. *SMDF*, p. 205; *CJH 1836–68*, p. 45.

21. *SMDF*, p. 205.

22. Ibid.

23. County high sheriff: *főispán*.

24. "Slippered" nobles: *bocskoros nemesek*, the poverty-stricken majority of the lesser nobility, or the Hungarian third estate.
25. *DFL*, p. 1.
26. Ibid., p. 7.
27. *DFB*, I, 48.
28. Ibid., I, 81.
29. Ibid., I, 82.
30. Property rights as legally defined at the time of the diet of 1832–36 involved two forms of landholding (*dominium*): *proprietas*, legal possession of the land, and usufruct (*usufructus*), the right to enjoy the product of the land. The serfs were entitled to the fruits of their labors on their urbarial holdings, and were said to have *dominium utile* of the land. When both ownership and usufruct were in the same hands, as was the case with the lords' manorial (allodial) land, the landholding was known as *dominium plenum* (full possession). Deák argued that in the case of urbarial land, the lords were entitled only to *proprietas*; *usufructus* was the serfs'. He did not, of course, challenge the lords' *dominium plenum* of their demesnes. *SMDF*, pp. 194, 206, 207; *CJH 1836–1868*, pp. 64–65.
31. The process was: the *concertatio*.
32. *EKDF*, I, 29.
33. The full report is in *DFB*, I, 264–312. "Deák's most remarkable work yet was his Report to the County Assembly (*Követjelentés*). This document gives an extraordinary portrayal of the state of contemporary legislative procedure in Hungary." *HILN*, p. 142.
34. *Törvényhatósági Tudósítások.*
35. On September 10, 1836. *DFL*, pp. 20–21.

Chapter Three

1. Deák's letter to Kossuth dated September 10, 1836. *DFL*, pp. 20–21.
2. Council of Regency: *Staatskonferenz.*
3. See note 34 in Chapter 2.
4. This and the following quotes from *DFB*, I, 241. See also *WGyDF*, pp. 35–39.
5. That branch of the Supreme Court of Appeal which dealt with the Wesselényi case was the *Judicum Septemvirale.*
6. The November Insurrection broke out on 29 November 1830, in the "Congress Kingdom," the Polish state set up by the Congress of Vienna. The King of Poland was Alexander I, Emperor of Russia. The insurrection was suppressed by October 1831. W. F. Reddaway *et al.*, eds., *The Cambridge History of Poland from Augustus II to Pilsudski (1697–1935)* (Cambridge: 1951), pp. 295–310.

7. Gentlemen's clubs: *kaszinók.*
8. *AIDF,* p. 80.
9. *MSMT,* III, 237.
10. Progressive Conservative Party: *Fontolva haladók pártja.*
11. Intellectuals of non-noble birth: *honoratiores.* See Király, *Hungary* ..., pp. 178, 225, 226, 257.
12. *EKDF,* I, 120.
13. *AIDF,* p. 133.
14. *EKDF,* II, 185–87.
15. *AIDF,* p. 244.
16. *FZD,* I, 248.
17. Provisions and fodder that communities were required to supply to military garrisons: *alimentatio.*
18. *FZD,* I, 259.
19. One of the chambers of the Supreme Court was the *Tabula regia* or the King's Bench, the High Court for the nobility.
20. The right of the nobility to resist by arms the illegal action of the crown: *ius resistendi,* was established by the promulgation in 1222 of the Golden Bull (*aranybulla*), the basic law of Hungary's feudal constitution. It was repealed by the diet of 1687–88.
21. *DFB,* I, 371–86.
22. Excerpts: *excerpta,* parts of a defeated major bill, enacted as law.
23. County magistrate: *táblabiró.*
24. *AIDF,* p. 136.
25. *DFB,* I, 491.
26. Report to the county assembly by the deputy to the diet: *követjelentés.*
27. This and all the remaining quotations in this chapter are taken (except if otherwise stated), from the text of Deák's *Követjelentés,* the full text of which is to be found in *DFB,* I, 488–553.
28. See Chapter 1, above.
29. See Chapter 5, below.
30. See Chapter 9, below.
31. *AIDF,* p. 73.

Chapter Four

1. *AIDF,* p. 18.
2. Ibid., p. 108, n. 2.
3. Ibid., p. 93. n.
4. Ibid.
5. *EKDF,* II, 36.

6. *AIDF*, p. 58.
7. *EKDF*, I, 180.
8. Ibid.
9. Ibid., I, 186.
10. Ibid., I, 187.
11. *KLF*, p. 59.
12. *MSMT*, III, 264 ff.; *WGyDF*, pp. 41–44; *PFD*, pp. 26–27; *HZTL*, I, 121–71; *PFEK*, I, 109–11.
13. The People of the East: A *kelet népe*.
14. *SzIKN*, p. 84.
15. *FZD*, I, 318.
16. Reply: *Felelet*.
17. Ibid., p. 20.
18. *EJKN*.
19. Ibid., p. 81.
20. *DFL*, pp. 81–82.
21. *AIDF*, p. 81.
22. *DFB*, I, 554; *TEML*, p. 39.

Chapter Five

1. Act V, 1840. *CJH 1836–48*, pp. 90–91; *WGyDF*, pp. 44–45; *PFD*, p. 14.
2. *FLA*, I/I, 26–29; *PFEK*, pp. 184–86.
3. Statement of the opposition: *Ellenzéki nyilatkozat*.
4. *PFD*, p. 15; *AIDF*, pp. 90–91.
5. *FLA*, I/II, 95.
6. Ibid., 139.
7. Ibid., 137.
8. Ibid., 242.
9. Ibid., 333; *AIDF*, pp. 92–93.
10. The King's Bench: *Tabula regia*.
11. *FLA*, I, 347.
12. *SBDV*, p. 24.
13. Ibid., p. 25.
14. G. J. Mittermaier, *Die Mündlichkeit, das Anklageprinzip* . . . (Stuttgart: 1845), p. 165.
15. *Francis Deák, Hungarian Statesman: A Memoir* (London: 1880), p. 49.
16. Deák's brother Antal died in 1842. From then on until 1854, when he sold his estate, Deák had to supervise the running of it. *EKDF*, p. 133.

Chapter Six

1. *EKDF*, I, 73, 196.
2. Ibid., II, 106.
3. Ibid., II, 109.
4. Ibid., II, 111.
5. Ibid., II, 113.
6. Ibid.
7. *AIDF*, p. 120.
8. *FZD*, I, 369, n. 1; *PFD*, pp. 16–22.
9. Domestic taxes: revenues collected by the counties to cover their own budget.
10. *FZD*, I, 372. The damage was so heavy that its signs were still visible in 1854. *EKDF*, I, 91.
11. *DFB*, V, 9–10.
12. *DFL*, pp. 94–120.
13. Ibid., p. 119; *WGyDF*, pp. 45–62.

Chapter Seven

1. The nationalities of Hungary at the beginning and the end of Deák's career were as follows. In the early 1840's the population (in millions) of Hungary, including Croatia and Transylvania, was 12.9, of whom 4.8 were Hungarians, 1.6 Slovaks, 1.2 Germans, 2.2 Romanians, 1.3 Croats, 0.8 Serbs and 0.4 Ruthenes. There were 60,000 persons of other nationalities (*FEMST*, p. 52, b). At the time of the Compromise, the total population was 15.5, of whom 6.4 were Hungarians, 1.9 Germans, 1.8 Slovaks, 2.4 Romanians, 0.3 Ruthenes, 2.3 Serbs and Croats, and 0.2 other nationalities (*HPMT*, IV, 619).
2. *DFB*, I, 306–307, 267.
3. Ibid., 268.
4. Ibid., 272.
5. Ibid., 270.
6. Ibid., 477.
7. *CJH 1740–1835*, pp. 407, 445.
8. The Slovak poet Kollár called the Hungarian language "barking." *SzGyI*, p. 134.
9. *DFB*, I, 268.
10. Act VIII, 1830, in *CJH 1740–1835*, pp. 400–503.
11. *CJH 1836–68*, pp. 14–15.
12. Act VI, 1840, in *CJH 1836–68*, pp. 91–92.
13. Act II, 1844, in *CJH 1836–68*, p. 198.
14. *SzLM*, I, 41.

15. *SzGyI*, p. 195.
16. Ibid., p. 198.
17. Act XLIV, 1868, in *CJH 1836–68*, pp. 490–94. See also Paul Bödy, *Joseph Eötvös and the Modernization of Hungary, 1840–1870: A Study of Individuality and Social Pluralism in Modern Politics* (Philadelphia: 1972), pp. 111–15.

Chapter Eight

1. Fiume: Rijeka. Following Deák's example two hundred nobles of Zala county renounced their tax-exempt status. *AIDF*, p. 120.
2. *DFB*, II, 57.
3. For an analysis of Kolowrat's position, power, and part in the Austrian Empire, see Egon Radványi, *Metternich's Projects for Reform in Austria* (The Hague: 1971).
4. *DFB*, II, 87, 91.
5. Ibid., 92.
6. Ibid., 96.
7. Ibid., 98.
8. Protection Association: *Védegylet.* See *AIDF*, p. 121.
9. *MEMT*, I, 459; *MJE*, p. 97; *MGyMI*, pp. 253–54, 378.
10. *DFB*, II, 62; *HZTL*, I, 121–70; *MGyMI*, pp. 254, 290, 393.
11. *DFB*, II, 63.
12. Ibid., *loc. cit.*
13. Ibid., 65.
14. Ibid., 66.
15. Statement of the Opposition: *Ellenzéki nyilatkozat.*
16. Pre-revolutionary era: *Vormärz.*
17. Conservative Evolutionary Party: *Fontolva Haladók Pártja.*
18. *FZD*, II, 19.
19. Ibid., 32.
20. The Polish gentry: *szlachta.*
21. *MEMT*, I, 474.
22. *FZD*, II, 38.
23. The Galician insurrection was sparked by the publication of the "Manifesto of the National Government of the Republic of Kraków" on February 22, 1846. See Appendix E in Stefan Kieniewicz, *The Emancipation of the Polish Peasantry* (Chicago: 1969), pp. 253–54.
24. War tax: *contributio.*
25. *MEMT*, I, 475; *MJE*, pp. 97–99; *FZD*, II, 43.
26. *EKDF*, II, 104.
27. From May 25 to mid-August 1847 Deák sought the cure in Germany and Switzerland in the company of his physicians, Drs.

Wurda and Attomyr, but what most engaged his attention during the tour was a meeting with Prof. E. J. Mittermaier, the leading contemporary expert on criminal law (see Chapter 5 above).

28. *DFB*, II, 162.
29. Full text in ibid., 163–68.
30. *CJH 1740–1835*, p. 159.

Chapter Nine

1. *EKDF*, I, 25.
2. *DFB*, II, 172; *PFD*, pp. 30–33; *SzETP*, pp. 89–102.
3. See R. John Rath, *The Viennese Revolution of 1848* (Austin, Tex.: 1957), pp. 84–85; Walter Rogge, *Österreich von Világos bis zur Gegenwart*, 5 vols. (Leipzig: 1872–79), I, 11.
4. *FZD*, II, 74.
5. *DFB*, II, 202.
6. Ibid., 209; Foster-Arnold, *op. cit.*, pp. 76, 79.
7. *DFL*, pp. 194–95.
8. *DFB*, II, 219.
9. Ibid., 220.
10. Acts I–XXXI/1848. *CJH 1836–68*, pp. 216–55.
11. *DFB*, II, 223.
12. *HSzMT*, V, 391; Acts IV and V/1848. *CJH 1836–68*, pp. 222–30.
13. *BJNO*, p. 17.
14. Ibid., pp. 15–16.
15. *MSMT*, III, 452. Society of Equality: *Egyenlőség Társulat*.
16. Committee of Public Safety: *Közbátorságra ügyelő választmány*. László Deme, "The Committee of Public Safety in the Hungarian Revolution of 1848," *Canadian Slavic Studies*, V, No. 3 (Fall 1971), 383–400; *MAFSz*, pp. 82–189; *SzETP*, pp. 36–87, 104 ff.
17. *BJNO*, p. 22.
18. Ibid., p. 25.
19. *DFB*, II, 203.
20. *BJNO*, p. 24, n. 6.
21. Ibid., p. 69.
22. *MSMT*, III, 411. The economic breakdown of the peasantry before emancipation was as follows (numbers of families):

Working one full session
or more (20–100 yokes)*   40,380

---

* [one yoke (*hold, Joch*) is equivalent to 0.57 hectares or 1.42 English acres]

Working 2/3 of a session (14–15 yokes of land)	6,458	
Working half a session (10 yokes of land)	281,264	
Working one-quarter of a session (5 yokes)	254,872	
Total families producing enough to market a surplus		582,974
Working one-eighth of a session (2.5 yokes of land) —subsistence farming producing no marketable surplus		41,872
Total number of serf families		624,134
Working less than one-eighth of a session (under 2.5 yokes)	32,120	
Working no urbarial land but having tenancy of a cottage	773,528	
Holding neither land nor cottage	108,314	
Total cotter (*inquilini* or *zsellérek*) families, landless or effectively landless		913,962
Total servant and field-hand families		193,905
Grand total of peasant families		1,732,713

23. Ibid., 411.
24. The full text in *BJNO*, pp. 621–32.
25. Ibid., pp. 79–80; *MAFSz*, pp. 40–54; *SzETP*, pp. 173–243.
26. *DFB*, II, 205.
27. Letter dated April 30, 1848. *DFL*, pp. 196–99.
28. Ibid., p. 194; *MSMT*, III, 406–407; *MAFSz*, pp. 21–23.
29. Letter of Pál Somssich to Manó Kónyi. *DFB*, II, 204.
30. *BJNO*, p. 60; Rath, *op. cit.*, pp. 317–18.
31. *BJNO*, p. 60, n. 185.
32. Ibid., p. 60.
33. *BJNO*, p. 61; Rath, *op. cit.*, pp. 267, 317–19.
34. *FZD*, II, 101. See also Chapter 8 above.

35. For the nature of Austria's state debt, see Rath, *op. cit.*, p. 7.

36. *DFB*, II, 267; *FZD*, II, 125; *MAFSz*, pp. 40–44;; *HZTL*, I, 187–96.

37. *DFB*, II, 282.

38. Ibid.; Rath, *op. cit.*, pp. 149–50, 150–51; *MLKLE*, II, 55–88.

39. *BJNO*, pp. 56–57; *HZTL*, I, 197–215.

40. *FZD*, II, 180.

41. *MSMT*, III, 462.

42. Interesting details of General Jelačić's aims and hopes in "Baron Jellačić Operationen gegen Wien und Ungarn." Fasc. VIII–X. *KA-FA48*. See also Foster-Arnold, *op. cit.*, p. 96.

43. The measures introduced by the Hungarian government in Fasc. III–XIII. *KA-KU*. Francis Joseph's "open order" in Fasc. XII/54. *KA-KU. DFB*, II, 319–22; B.F.D. Tefft, *Hungary and Kossuth or an American Exposition of the Late Hungarian Revolution* (Philadelphia: 1852), pp. 306–38.

44. *DFL*, pp. 208–209.

45. Minutes of Parliament, CXXXIVth Sitting, December 31, 1848; *BJNO*, p. 348; *MJE*, pp. 177–86; Fasc. XII/99 No. 181. *KA-KU*.

46. Minutes of Parliament, CXXXVIth Sitting, January 13, 1849; *BJNO*, p. 20; *KGyE*, pp. 71–78.

47. Fasc. XII/54 No. 181. *KA-KU*.

48. *DFB*, II, 375.

Chapter Ten

1. The Stadion constitution gave certain guarantees of rights of the citizens and nationalities of the Habsburg lands. This constitution decreed by the Emperor, however, deprived Hungary of her constitutional rights and self-government. Joseph Redlich, *Emperor Francis Joseph of Austria, A Biography* (Hamden, Conn., 1965), pp. 74–75. Robert A. Kann, *The Multinational Empire: Nationalism and National Reform in the Habsbury Monarchy, 1848–1918*, 2 vols., (New York: 1950), II.

2. Documents on his acquittal in *DFB*, II, 381. On burning his correspondence, see *EKDF*, I, 98. Constant police surveillance: Fasc. III/1850, Fasc. XLVII/January 16, 1853, Fasc. CCCLXXXV. Pr. II/1853 and No. 1106.GD/1853. *HHStA-GD*.

3. *DFL*, pp. 211–13; letters from Jakab Millasin to Aurél Kecskeméthy, Vienna, June 14, 1850 in *ADMF*, pp. 511–12, 514 n. 8. See also *PSVT*, pp. 58–70; *FZD*, II, 222.

4. *CsAHI*, pp. 44, 46. Lord Chief Justice's conference: *Ország-birói értekezlet.*
5. *HILN*, p. 175.
6. *DFB*, II, 406.
7. Ibid., 404.
8. Ibid., 320.
9. *CsAHI*, p. 89.
10. *DFB*, II, 397. See also Gorove's diary in *DFB*, II, 382. See also Julius Miskolczy, *Ungarn in der Habsburger Monarchie* (Vienna: 1959), pp. 90 ff. For general background, see *HZLT*, I, 291–306.
11. *FZD*, II, 242; *DFB*, II, 396–97; Foster-Arnold, *op. cit.*, p. 128.
12. *CsAHI*, p. 44.
13. Full text in *DFB*, II, 396–403. For a comprehensive analysis of the social and political forces of the time, see *LLMF*, pp. 11–186.
14. *DFB*, II, 404–405.
15. Ibid., 405.
16. Ibid., 396. Kecskeméthy commented: "Everybody knew that Ferenc Deák's views were expressed by what was said in *Pesti Napló*, and even more by what it did not say." *ADFM*, pp. 195–96.
17. *DFB*, II, 387; *DFL*, p. 236.
18. *HILN*, p. 175; *DFB*, II, 397; *FZD*, II, 240.
19. *The Struggle for Mastery in Europe, 1848–1918* (Oxford: 1960), p. 64.
20. After the family estate had been shared between Deák and his two sisters, Deák was left with 810 yokes of land, one flour mill and an inn, a typical medium-sized holding that, under normal circumstances, should have provided enough for the needs of a middle-class family. *FZD*, II, 226–27. Deák's own account contained in a letter dated November 1, 1852 lists the following items. (One *hold* yoke is 0.57 hectares, or 1.42 English acres. All items in *hold*.)

13 3/8 garden and orchard
402 4/8 plough land
152 pasture
167 hayland [presently bog]
567 6/8 forest
23 4/8 vineyard operated by Deák
272 vineyard rented out
5 pasture and ploughland belonging to mill and pub

Grand total of 1,614 *hold*

one flour mill
one inn and rented out houses

Cattle, 20 white oxen, 6 waterbuffalo oxen, 2 horses, 700 sheep, 24 milk cows. *EKDF*, I, 150.

21. *MAN*, pp. 270–71; *PFD*, pp. 34–35.

22. Deák's life annuity amounted to 3000 silver florins. At that time a county deputy high sheriff [*alispán*], the head of the county administration, received 1800 florins annual salary while the honorarium of a member of Parliament was 2200 florins a year. Deák thus spent approximately 250 florins a month out of which the following permanent items were paid (all in florins): 50 hotel rent, 50 monthly food bill, 25 for the valet, 25 cleaning, washing etc., a total of 150 florins expenditure, which left him with 100 florins balance. In addition, during the years when he was a member of Parliament he received 2100 to 2200 florins honorarium. Indeed his expenses were well covered, and he could afford to spend several summer weeks in expensive watering places, and to take care of three beggars a day. *EKDF*, I, 172–73, 189.

23. Ibid., I, 160.

24. Ibid., II, 90–91.

25. *DFL*, p. 216.

26. *DFB*, II, 385; *DFL*, p. 222. See also letter of Jószef Antumovics to Aurél Kecskeméthy, Szabadka (Subotica), June 15, 1850 in *ADFM*, pp. 515, 519 n. 7.

27. *AIDF*, p. 190.

28. *EKDF*, I, 305.

29. *AIDF*, p. 33.

30. *AIDF*, pp. 190–91; *EKDF*, I, 80–83, 90–91.

31. *EKDF*, II, 148.

32. *AIDF*, p. 10.

33. *SzAMI*, p. 330.

34. *DFL*, pp. 226–33. Károly Eötvös thought it to have been 112,000 florins. *EKDF*, I, 305.

35. Complete text of the address in *DFB*, II, 394–95.

36. Ibid., 395. Miksa Falk's assessment of Deák's strong influence over the Academy's proceedings in *ADFM*, pp. 334, 340, 357, 416, 418, 419, 426.

37. *PFEK*, II, 22.

38. *EKDF*, II, 38.

39. *DFB*, II, 404.

Chapter Eleven

1. Foster-Arnold, *op. cit.*, p. 134.

2. Macartney, *op. cit.*, p. 496; *Pesti Napló*, July 17, 1859.

3. Fritz Fellner, "Das 'Februarpatent' von 1861," *Mitteilungen des Instituts fur österreichische Geschichtsforschung*, LXIII (1955), Nos. 3–4, p. 549. László Szögyény-Marich, one of the most loyal Hungarian officials at court, reported that Francis Joseph considered any form of government other than autocracy dangerous. *SzLM*, III, 44–45.

4. His most recent biography is Oskar Regele, *Feldzeugmeister Benedek* (Wien: 1960).

5. *SzLM*, III, 32, 38–39, 188–89; *BAAM*, III, 101–102.

6. *FZD*, II, 244; *SzGyFK* pp. 14–16, 22–23. Before the government was formed, the court did not confer with the Hungarian conservatives, but after it had been installed in office, the ministers consulted them frequently. *SzLM*, II, 136–37; Redlich, *Das österreichische Staats- und Reichsproblem*, I/1, 464, 488, and I/2, 184–89. Eötvös was still advocating constitutionalism within a centralized empire in his book *Die Garantien der Macht und Einheit Österreichs*, published in Leipzig in 1859, but in 1860 he turned down an appointment to the *Reichsrat* and argued for reorganization of Austro-Hungarian relations on the basis of a personal union in a leaflet, *Die Sonderstellung Ungarns vom Standpunkte der Einheit Deutschlands*, also published in Leipzig.

7. *Wiener Zeitung*, October 21, 1860. The full text of the October Diploma in Redlich, *Das österreichische Staats- und Reichsproblem*, I, 228–34. The diploma, which in 1860 had simply been proclaimed, was presented by the court to the Hungarian Parliament in December 1865 and was published in the Parliamentary papers as document no. 6, *Az 1865 OI*, I, 7–8. For the most comprehensive legal and constitutional analysis and ideological background, see Kann, *op. cit.*, I, 18, 87, 127, 311 and II, x, 99–107, 115, 132.

8. *DFB*, II, 492–504; *SzGyFK*, p. 77.

9. *FZD*, II, 246; Rogge, *op. cit.*, II, 62–63; Redlich, *Österreich...*, I/1, 503, 526; *SzGyFK*, pp. 188–90, 158–73, 15; *KAN*, pp. 44–45. Supreme Court of Justice or Royal Curia: *curia regia*.

10. *FZD*, II, 245. Lord Chief Justice: *Országbiró*.

11. *SOMP*, pp. 291–92; *LLMF*, pp. 249–50; *SzGyFK*, pp. 80–83.

12. Redlich, *Das österreichische...*, I, 31, 677, 683–84.

13. *SzGyFK*, pp. 105–109.

14. *DFB*, II, 404–10, 508–509; *SzGyFK*, pp. 85–87; *SzLM*, II, 140–41; *BAAM*, III, 138; *BGKZs*, 206–208; *TLVM*, II, 208.

15. *SzGyFK*, p. 151.

16. Letter to Primate János Scitovszky dated December 3, 1860. *DFL*, p. 273.

17. *SzGyFK*, p. 152.

18. Ibid., pp. 155–57; *DFB*, II, 498–99; Rogge, *op. cit.*, II, 63; *BAAM*, III, 148; *SzLM*, III, 66–67; Redlich, *Österreichische* ..., II, 725.

19. *DFB*, II, 521; Redlich, *Österreichische* ..., I/1, 688–89 and I/2, 205; *BAAM*, III, 157–58; *SzLM*, III, 64–67; *SzGyFK*, p. 256.

20. *DFL*, pp. 273–74; *DFB*, II, 526–32; *BAAM*, III, 158–61; *SzLM*, III, 70; *SzGyFK*, pp. 221–24.

21. *HILN*, p. 187; *DFL*, pp. 286–87.

22. *FZD*, II, 252.

23. Letter to József Oszterhuber-Tarányi dated January 9, 1861. *DFL*, p. 279.

24. Ibid., pp. 279–86. See also *DFB*, II, 532–41; *KAN*, pp. 48, 66–73; *SzLM*, III, 70; *SOMP*, pp. 317–19; *SzGyFK*, pp. 191–206, 266–71.

25. *DFB*, II, 507–508; *SOMP*, pp. 291–94; *LLMF*, pp. 249–50; *SzGyFK*, pp. 83–85.

26. *SzGyFK*, p. 322. See also *FZD*, II, 264; *DFB*, III, 500–515; *SzLM*, III, 63, 235, 293 ff. For the participants in the conference, see *BAAM*, III, 142, 187.

27. For the full text of the drafts see *BJNO*, pp. 621–32. The 1861 Parliament resolved that the Provisional Rules for the Judiciary should remain in force until Parliament was in a position to pass definitive legislation, because the post-1848 economic changes ruled out the reestablishment of the old civil laws. *AOGyJ*, 48th Sitting.

28. Kann, *op. cit.*, II, 115, 118.

29. *SzGyFK*, p. 257. The February Patent, which was simply proclaimed in 1861, was presented to the Hungarian Parliament in December 1865 and was published in the Parliamentary papers as document no. 7, *Az1865 OI*, I, 9–13.

30. Richard Charmatz, *Österreichs innere Geschichte von 1848 bis 1895*, 2 vols. (Leipzig: 1918), I, 45; *DFB*, II, 592–93; *WEAGy*, I, 178.

31. *FZD*, II, 273; *WGyDF*, pp. 77–78.

32. *FZD*, II, 273.

33. *DFB*, III, 2; *AIDF*, p. 210.

34. *HILN*, p. 188; *SzGyFK*, p. 242.

35. *MEMT*, II, 55. Four out of ten of the members of Parliament had been members of Parliament in 1848; one out of seven had been imprisoned by Habsburg courts after 1848. *SzGyFK*, p. 421. Thirty-seven members of the Lower House had noble titles. *AOGyJ*, 4th sitting.

36. FZD, II, 276; SzLM, III, 276; BAAM, III, 214–15; DFB, III, 3–10; Redlich, Österreich . . . , II, 617–18; AOGyJ, 1st sitting.

37. FZD, II, 280. "There were only 30 members present." KAN, p. 122. Others claim there were as many as 80 present. SzGyFK, p. 436. By April 9, 296 members of Parliament had presented their credentials. AOGyJ, 2nd sitting; AIDF, p. 212.

38. The regular sittings began on April 6 in the National Museum, Pest. AOGyJ, 1st sitting.

39. SzLM, III, 208, 303; DFB, III, 25–26, 28–29; FZD, II, 284–89; SzGyFK, pp. 446–51.

40. For details see HZTL, I, 456; SzLM, III, 95, 298, 301; KAN, p. 129; DFB, III, 25–26; SzGyFK, pp. 438–40. The House had a quorum by April 17, when 261 members had presented their credentials. One member was a prince (Gyula Odescalchy). AOGyJ, 4th sitting. For the election of officers, see AOGyJ, 4th sitting. Party of Petition: Felirati Párt, Party of Resolution: Határozati Párt.

41. Both texts in TLVM, II, 232–37 and 237–53, respectively.

42. For different assessments of this program and its impact, cf. SzGyFK, pp. 450–51, 466–71; MEMT, II, 56–57; FZD, II, 292; HZTL, I, 471–72, 463–64, 459; DFB, III, 106–109; BAAM, III, 245; Rogge op. cit. II, 136. The new absolutist regime in Hungary: Provizórium.

43. Full text of Deák's petition in DFB, III, 34–60. The Parliamentary Record laconically reported: "László Teleki departed this life last night." The sitting then adjourned. AOGyJ, 20th sitting.

44. FZD, II, 58; SzLM, III, 304–14; DFB, III, 67–74; Redlich, Österreich . . . , II, 740; BAAM II, 255; György Szabad, "Kossuth and the British 'Balance of Power' Policy (1859–1861)," Studia Historica (Budapest), No. 34 (1960), pp. 44–45; AIDF, p. 227.

45. SzGyFK, pp. 478–80; KAN, p. 147; SzBÖM, V, 60.

46. AOGyJ, 37th sitting; DFB, III, 105–106, 115–16; FZD, II, 312; MEMT, II, 58; BAAM, III, 264; SzLM, III, 334–35. For the parliamentary debate on the details of the draft see AOGyJ, 39th to 44th sittings, inclusive. Deák's disclaimer of the draft in AOGyJ, 44th sitting. The passage of Deák's original draft with minor amendments by himself in AOGyJ, 55th sitting.

47. FZD, II, 289; HILN, p. 188. As early as May 3 protests began to come in from the Hungarian counties against the method of collecting taxes by armed force. AOGyJ, 17th sitting. One of the most vivid protests was from Somogy county: "The 'pious' regime in Vienna has sent in its bayoneted heroes to collect illegal taxes. They have been bivouacking all over the county ever since and have been taking out of the mouths of nigh starving people the food which has

been scarce since winter and is most needed at this time of their hardest labor. . . . Like usurers they are collecting three times the assessed value of the taxes." *AOGyJ*, 35th sitting. Esztergom county reported the case of a woman in childbirth who was evicted with all her other children for default. *AOGyJ*, 29th sitting..

48. Gustav Kolmer, *Parlament und Verfassung in Oesterreich*, 2 vols. (Vienna: 1902), I, 64–67; *SzLM*, III, 98–99; *BAAM*, III, 329.

49. Full text of the rescript in *DFB*, III, 193–202.

50. *DFB*, III, 193.

51. Full text in ibid., 220–72.

52. *CJH 1740–1835*, pp. 159, 161.

53. ". . . nulli alteri regno aut populo obnoxium. . . ." Ibid.

54. *AOGyJ*, 67th sitting.

55. Ibid.; *HILN*, p. 188; *DFB*, III, 139–43, 275; Redlich, *Österreich* . . . , II, 83–97, 740; *BAAM*, III, 272; *SzLM*, III, 109–12; *FZD*, II, 361; *AOGyJ*, 67th sitting.

56. *FZD*, II, 336.

57. *GJ67*, p. 43; *MEMT*, II, 63.

58. *HILN*, p. 189.

59. *FZD*, II, 376.

60. *DFB*, III, 302 ff.

61. Apponyi revealed his authorship twenty years after the *Ausgleich* was promulgated and eleven years after Deák's death. *HILN*, p. 197.

62. *FMKJ*, p. 68.

63. Erich Zöllner, *Geschichte Österreichs von den Anfängen bis zur Gegenwart* (Wein: 1961), p. 406; F. von Krones, *Moritz von Kaiserfeld. Sein Leben und Wirken* (Leipzig: 1888), p. 224; Lorenz, *Anton Ritter von Schmerling (1805–1893) und Freiherr von Bach (1813–1893). Gestalter des Geschicke Österreichs* (Innsbruck: 1962), pp. 422–23.

64. *DFB*, III, 414; (Mór Ludassy), *Drei Jahre Verfassungsstreit. Beiträge zur jüngsten Geschichte Oesterreichs.* Von einem Ungar (Leipzig: 1864).

65. "Adalékok a magyar közjoghoz" *DFB*, III, 344–78. It was also promptly published in German: *Ein Beitrag zum ungarischen Staatsrecht. Bemerkungen über Wenzel Lustkandls 'Ungarisch-österreichisches Staatsrecht'. Vom Standpunkte der Geschichte des ungarischen Staatsrecht.* Von Franz von Deák (Pest: 1865).

66. *WGyDF*, p. 82.

67. Easter Article: "Husvéti Cikk"; May Program: "Májusi Programm," full text of both in *DFB*, III, 396–410, 411–29. The content

of the Easter Article was approved by the court prior to publication. *WGyDF*, p. 183.
    68. *GJ67*, p. 62, and *HILN*, p. 190.
    69. *DFB*, III, 411–28.
    70. *GJ67*, p. 67. National Agrarian Association: *Országos Gazdasági Egyesület*.

Chapter Twelve

    1. Kann, *The Multinational Empire*, II, 125; *FZD*, III, 29.
    2. *BGFJK*, X, 636. "The new Cabinet, with Belcredi as Prime Minister, was entirely his [Eszterházy's] creation." Heinrich Friedjung, *The Struggle for Supremacy in Germany, 1859–1866* (New York: 1966), p. 80.
    3. Kann, *The Multinational Empire*, II, 125; *DFB*, III, 444–47.
    4. The rescript of summons: Document no. 1, Parliamentary Papers, *Az 1865 OI*, I, 1; *FZD*, III, 36; Friedjung, *op. cit.*, p. 82; Kann, *The Multinational Empire*, II, 126; *Wiener Zeitung* no. 215 (September 20, 1865). The *Landtage* of the Cis-Leithanian provinces were summoned the same day. *Wiener Zeitung*, no. 214 (September 20, 1865).
    5. The Deák Party won 180 seats, the Left Center Party 94, the Conservatives 21, and the Extreme Left 20. *FZD*, III, 36, 43, 48, 122; *GJ67*, p. 82; *GGDK*, pp. 27–37.
    6. *EKDF*, II, 104.
    7. *GJ67*, p. 83; *MJE*, pp. 354–61; *CsAHI*, pp. 36–37.
    8. *EKDF*, I, 306.
    9. The entire text: Document no. 2, Parliamentary Papers, *Az 1865 OI*, I, 1–3; *FZD*, III, 44.
    10. *FZD*, III, 45.
    11. Friedjung, *op. cit.*, pp. 83–84.
    12. Complete text: Document no. 11, Parliamentary Papers, *Az 1865 OI*, I, 26–30. Deák met Francis Joseph privately twice—on December 14 and 16. *FZD*, III, 45, 58–91; *KKPD*, p. 7; *CsAHI*, pp. 39–46. The secret police reported from Pest on February 28, 1866, that the public had reacted very favorably to the royal address. Fasc. LXXXI-1866 No. 1235 BM. *HHStA-IB*.
    13. *GJ67*, p. 88. The house adopted the reply on February 22, 1866. *FZD*, III, 91; *CsAHI*, pp. 48–53. The secret police reported to Vienna from Pest that the public at large considered the Upper House of Parliament inconsequential and that the "peers will stay silent when the House [Deák] speaks." Fasc. LXXXI No. 2725 BM. *HHStA-IB*.

216   FERENC DEÁK

14. Text of the royal reply: Document no. 14, Parliamentary Papers, *Az 1865 OI*, 33–37; *FZD*, III, 99–101; *KKPD*, pp. 11–12, 16 ff.

15. Ever since Kálmán Tisza had visited him on December 9, 1865, Deák had been convinced that there was no fundamental difference between the two liberal parties' views on basic questions. *CsAHI*, pp. 54–83.

16. Ibid., p. 175.

17. Ibid., pp. 14, 33, 97.

18. "Delegations": equal number of legislators from both the Austrian and Hungarian Parliaments whose duties were to supervise, on their individual Parliaments' behalf, the joint Austro-Hungarian Ministries of Foreign Affairs, Defense, and Finance. See note 42 below.

19. *CsAHI*, pp. 30–37, 55, 65, 67, 70, 71, 95.

20. Ibid., p. 51.

21. *GJ67*, p. 89; *FZD*, III, 138–60.

22. *EKHNH*, pp. 110–11; Friedjung, *op. cit.*, pp. 261–62. The secret police stepped up the surveillance of politicians. Fasc. LXXXI-1866 BM. *HHStA-IB*. A particular watch was kept on an 85-member "reading room." Fasc. LXXXI-1866 No. 2236 BM. *HHStA-IB*.

23. The rescript of adjournment dated June 24: Document no. 23, Parliamentary Papers, *Az 1865 OI*, I, 89–90; *FZD*, III, 116–22; *HILN*, p. 212; Zöllner, *op. cit.*, pp. 404–11; Friedjung, *op. cit.*, pp. 162–63.

24. *AIDF*, 242 n.

25. *EKDF*, II, 10, 1–92.

26. *FZD*, III, 169, 172; *DIHE*, pp. 171, 208, 210; Friedjung, *op. cit.*, pp. 261–62.

27. *GJ67*, p. 99, n. 12; Gerhard Ritter, *Staatskunst und Kriegshandwerk* (München: 1959), p. 252; *FZD*, III, 175–76; Krones, *op. cit.*, pp. 250–79.

28. Kann, *The Multinational Empire*, II, 128; *HILN*, p. 211; Friedjung, *op. cit.*, pp. 252–55, 261–62; *LLMF*, pp. 357–70; *KEAU*, pp. 142–82.

29. *HILN*, p. 212; *CsAHI*, pp. 84–91.

30. Robert A. Kann, *The Habsburg Empire: A Study in Integration and Disintegration* (New York: 1957), p. 34.

31. Documents nos. 24, 25 and 28, Parliamentary Papers, *Az 1865 OI*, I, 91–93, 94–101; *HILN*, p. 212; Kann, *The Multinational Empire*, II, 127; *GJ67*, p. 103; Fasc. LXXXI-1866 No. 857 BM. *HHStA-IB*.

32. *FZD*, III, 185–91; Hantsch, *op. cit.*, II, 374–78; Miskolczy, *op. cit.*, p. 138 ff.

33. Kann, *The Multinational Empire*, II, 127–29; *HILN*, pp. 209–10.

34. Zöllner, *op. cit.*, p. 411; Krones, *op. cit.*, pp. 253–58; *GGDK*, pp. 47–48.

35. Friedrich Ferdinand Graf von Beust, *Aus drei Viertel-Jahrhunderten Erinnerungen und Aufzeichnungen*, 2 vols. (Stuttgart: 1887), II, 66–70.

36. The royal rescript: Document no. 33, Parliamentary Papers, *Az 1865 OI*, I, 109–10; *FZD*, III, 216–50; Zöllner, *op. cit.*, pp. 411–13; Beust, *op. cit.*, pp. 83–96; Kann, *The Multinational Empire*, II, 127.

37. Document no. 35, Parliamentary Papers, *Az 1865 OI*, I, 112. At the same time 60 members of Parliament resigned to take up appointments in the ministry, as state secretaries or as county high sheriffs. All the byelections were won by Deák Party candidates. *FZD*, III, 267; *GGDK*, I, 38–40. Other members of the Cabinet were: Count György Festetics, high sheriff of Zala county, minister in waiting to the king; Baron Béla Wenkheim, high sheriff of Békés county, minister of the interior; Menyhért Lónyay, minister of finance; Baron József Eötvös, minister of public education and churches; Boldizsár Horváth, minister of justice; Count Imre Mikó, minister of public works and transportation; and István Gorove, minister of agriculture, industry, and trade.

38. Deák stiffly refused to act as palatine substitute in order to place St. Stephen's crown, jointly with the Primate of Hungary, on Francis Joseph's head. The act was performed instead by Andrássy. *FZD*, III, 275.

39. *CJH 1836–68*, pp. 333–34. See Kann, *The Multinational Empire*, II, 129–33; Beust, *op. cit.*, pp. 97–105; *GGDK*, p. 13.

40. Acts I, II and III/1723. *CJH 1657–1740*, pp. 563–69.

41. *NEMK*, p. 424. A résumé dated July 16, 1868, summed up all the basic agreements on defense questions signed by those who took part in the negotiations, most notably Andrássy and Beust. Fasc. XXIX.B, No. 6, July–December 1868, *KA-AMK*. "Entwurf: Die ungarische Landwehr," Fasc. XXIX.A, Nos. 1–5, 1868, *KA-AMK*. Count Gyula Andrássy's original proposals: *Promemoria hinsichtlich der Wehrfrage*, dated June 17, 1868 (Andrássy mistakenly wrote 1867), Fasc. XXIX.A, Nos. 1–5, 1868, *KA-AMK*.

Act XL/1868 covered the common defense forces, i.e., the Habsburg army and navy; Act XLI/1868 covered the Hungarian *honvéd*; Act XLII/1868 covered the popular levy. *CJH 1836–68*, pp. 470–85;

Documents nos. 295 and 298, Parliamentary Papers, *Az 1865 OI*, II, 401–402, 418; *TEML*, pp. 186–88. General Arthur Görgey had presented a memorandum on Hungary's defense bills to Deák in February 1867. Complete text in *GIGASz*, pp. 348–56. A second memorandum was sent Deák on May 8, 1867. Text in ibid., pp. 367–87. Beust's last résumé on the matter was presented to Francis Joseph on May 12, 1868. Fasc. XXIX.A, Nos. 1–5, 1868, *KA-AMK*. A recent review of the subject: Gunther E. Rothenberg, "Toward a National Hungarian Army: The Military Compromise of 1868 and Its Consequences," *Slavic Review*, XXXI, No. 4 (December 1972), 805–16. The prolonged tension between Hungary and Vienna over military matters is treated in *EKHNM*. Correspondence on the military oath that was to bind the troops' loyalty first to the king and only then to the laws of state: Fasc. XII/9, No. 766, March 7, 1869, *KA-AMK*. Military command of forts, garrisons, and bases in Hungary: Fasc. IX/4–1, No. 922, March 15, 1869, *KA-AMK*. Uniforms, equipment, and army regulations: Fasc. XII/2–5, No. 710, March 7, 1869, *KA-AMK*. *Honvéd* organizational regulations: Fasc. XII/2–8, No. 984, March 22, 1869, *KA-AMK*. Commissioning of *honvéd* officers, including Count Gyula Andrássy's colonelcy: Fasc. XII/2–15, No. 1290, *KA-AMK*.

42. Both delegations comprised 60 members—40 from the Lower House and 20 from the Upper House. Hungary's delegation included five Croats; Austria's 10 Bohemians, 7 Galicians, 4 Moravians, 3 from Lower Austria, and 2 each from Upper Austria, Styria, and the Tyrol. *NEMK*, p. 427, n. 1.

43. Kann, *The Habsburg Empire*, p. 80; *NEMK*, p. 431.

44. Institut für Österreichkunde, *Historisches Geschehen im Spiegel der Gegenwart: Österreich-Ungarn, 1867–1967* (Vienna: 1970); Anton Vantuch (ed.), *Der österreichisch-ungarische Ausgleich 1867: Materialen (Referate und Diskussion) der internationalen Konferenz in Bratislava, 28.8–1.9.1967* (Bratislava: 1971).

45. *DFB*, V, 1–8. Gen. Arthur Görgey also responded to Kossuth's letter on May 27, 1867. Complete text in *GIGASz*, pp. 388–89.

46. Joseph F. Zacek, "Palacký and the Austro-Hungarian Compromise of 1867" in Vantuch, *op. cit.*, p. 562.

47. *DFB*, V, 8–10.

48. István Diószegi, "Die politischen Probleme zur Zeit des österreichisch-ungarischen Ausgleich von 1867 aus ungarischer Sicht" in Vantuch, *op. cit.*, pp. 9–24. The Hungarian version in *DIHE*, pp. 129–52.

49. In the Cis-Leithanian provinces "the composition of the

house was to a large, though decreasing, degree (due to gradual franchise reforms between 1867 and 1906) dependent on the will of the government." Kann, *The Multinational Empire*, II, 130.
50. *CJH 1834–68*, p. 354. For the social and economic progress of the Jews in Hungary see William O. McCagg, *Jewish Nobles and Geniuses in Modern Hungary* (New York: 1972), in particular Chapters I–VI.
51. The use of the term Croatia in a constitutional sense refers to the Triune Kingdom, that is, the Kingdom of Croatia-Slavonia-Dalmatia, which had been constitutionally linked with Hungary since 1102. The nature of the link and the advantages or disadvantages of it to both parties are an issue hotly contested by both Hungarian and Croatian historians and are outside the scope of the present work.
52. Act XXX/1868 in Hungarian legislation. *CJH 1836–68*, pp. 422–39. See Kann, *The Habsburg Empire*, pp. 83–84; *GGDK*, pp. 57–68; *CsAHI*, pp. 179–239.
53. *FZD*, III, 348.
54. Documents nos. 117, 118, 221, 245, 251, and 252, Parliamentary Papers, *Az 1865 OI*, I, 258–61, and II, 136–37, 275–76, 281–90, 291–95. Macartney, *op. cit.* p. 558.
55. *CJH 1836–68*, pp. 422–39.
56. Oscar Jászi, *The Dissolution of the Habsburg Monarchy* (Chicago: 1961), p. 369; Ivo J. Lederer, "Nationalism and the Yugoslavs," in Peter Sugar and Ivo J. Lederer (eds.), *Nationalism in Eastern Europe* (Seattle: 1969), p. 421; A. J. P. Taylor, *The Habsburg Monarchy 1809–1918: A History of the Austrian Empire and Austro-Hungary* (New York: 1965), p. 137; Stavrianos, *The Balkans Since 1453* (New York: 1959), p. 268.
57. Act XXXVIII/1868. *CJH 1836–68*, pp. 449–69.
58. The first state schools were established by the Andrássy ministry. In 1874 there were 56 such schools in operation; 31 more were founded in 1875 and another 38 in 1876, so that by the time of Deák's death there were 125 state elementary schools all over the country, providing quality education and setting new standards. *KFMPL*, pp. 380–81.
59. Documents nos. 259 and 271, Parliamentary Papers, *Az 1865 OI*, 298–319, 350–51. See also Bödy, *op. cit.*, pp. 98–110.
60. Bödy, *op. cit.*, p. 108. The data on Prussia were supplied by Professor Christoph M. Kimmich of Brooklyn College.
61. *CJH 1836–68*, pp. 490–94; Documents nos. 274, 275 and 286, Parliamentary Papers, *Az 1865 OI*, II, 354–59, 389; *GGDK*, pp. 69–88; *KKPD*, pp. 29–40.
62. Original draft: *KGGIN*, I, 49–52.

63. *The Habsburg Monarchy* (Cambridge: 1951), p. 83.
64. *DFB*, VI, 147.
65. *KVPF*, pp. 24–27; *TEML*, pp. 299–332.
66. *FZD*, III, 361, 365.
67. *FZD*, III, 360; *TEML*, pp. 184–85.
68. *FZD*, III, 374.
69. *CsAHI*, p. 315; *KVPF*, pp. 74–81; *GGDK*, pp. 111–13.
70. *FZD*, III, 383. In the general election of 1872 Deák was once again returned by Central Pest. The Deák Party won 245 seats, the Left Center Party won 116, and the Extreme Left Party of '48 won 48 seats. *GGDK*, pp. 114–16.
71. *DFB*, VI, 408–16.
72. *KAN*, pp. 262–63.
73. The Andrássy ministry restored the counties' autonomy by a ministerial decree on April 10, 1867. It gave the counties far wider prerogatives than a ministerial system responsible to Parliament warranted, but it was a gesture the Deák Party had to make to the county gentry. Document no. 40, Parliamentary Papers, *Az 1865 OI*, I, 117–19. Aurél Kecskeméthy warned at once that the counties posed a greater threat to democratic progress than did Vienna. *KAPK*, p. 16; *GGDK*, pp. 92–94.
74. *GGDK*, pp. 126–44; *CsAHI*, pp. 332–46.

Social Background of Members of Parliament

| | Parliaments of | | | |
	1861	1865	1875	1881
Gentry	64.0%	62.4%	58.6%	64.0%
Aristocracy	13.3%	16.5%	10.8%	12.4%
Total	77.3%	78.9%	69.4%	78.4%

LEMPVR, pp. 29, 49, 50.
75. When Kossuth heard the news about Deák's death, he said "Deák practiced republican virtues in a monarchy." *FZD*, III, 413.
76. *CJH 1875–76*, p. 310.

Selected Bibliography

Explanatory Note on Abbreviations Used in This Section

To spare those who know no Hungarian the agony of unraveling the idiosyncrasies of Hungarian spelling, all Hungarian sources and archival material have been referred to in abbreviated form. The abbreviations for the Hungarian sources begin with the author's initials followed by the initials of the key words in the titles. The abbreviations for the Archival material consist of two groups of initials separated by a hyphen: the first group specifies the archive, and the second, the specific collection of documents in that archive.

SOURCES

There are several comprehensive bibliographies of the Deák era, two of which deserve particular mention. Domokos Kosáry's *Bevezetés a magyar történelem forrásaiba és irodalmába* ["Guide to Sources and Literature in Hungarian History"] (3 vols.; Budapest: 1954) has been revised and is being republished under the title *Bevezetés Magyarország történetének forrásaiba és irodalmába* ["Guide to Sources and Literature in the History of Hungary"]. The first volume was published in Budapest in 1970. The other outstanding bibliography is Zoltán I. Tóth, *Magyar történeti bibliográfia, 1825–1867* ["Hungarian Historical Bibliography, 1825–1867"] (3 vols.; Budapest: 1950–1952).

In the present bibliography, because of the large amount of material available, a selection was made in the following order of preference:
1. Ference Deák's own speeches, correspondence and publications.
2. Collections of documents.
3. Memoirs, reminiscences, correspondence, and other papers by Deák's friends and foes, associates and opponents.
4. Biographies of Deák.
5. Contemporary scholarly publications.
6. Modern scholarly publications.

The only English biography of Deák, that by Florence Foster-Arnold, has already been mentioned in the Preface. Among all the Hungarian biographies, which are listed below, three must be singled out. Manó

221

Kónyi's six-volume collection of Deák's speeches contains what amounts to a biography in its notes and glosses on the documents. With the political essayist's masterly pen, Károly Eötvös wrote a two-volume biography which includes much interesting political comment and many colorful sidelights on Deák and his family. The scholarly and objective three-volume biography by Zoltán Ferenczi was written three decades after Deák's death, when a substantial number of documentary sources had already become available. Now, seventy years after its publication, it has stood the test of time and still stands like a beacon in the sea of publications about Deák.

ARCHIVAL MATERIAL

Budapest, Hungary

Országos Levéltár (National Archives)

OL-ACsI   *Andrássy család iratai* [Andrássy Family Papers]
OL-KGy   *Kossuth gyüjtemény* [Kossuth Collection], 1851–63
OL-KI   *Kancellári iratok* [Chancellery Documents], 1865–67

Országos Széchenyi Könyvtár (National Széchenyi Library)

OSzK-KT   *Klapka-Teleki levelezés* [Klapka-Teleki Correspondence]
OSzK-PL   *Pulszky levelei Dunyovhoz* [Pulszky's Correspondence with Dunyov]

Hadtörténelmi Intézet Levéltára
(Archives of the Institute of Military History)

HI-64   *Az 1864-es év irományai* [Papers of the Year 1864]

(All the above are in the author's microfilm collection.)

Vienna, Austria

Haus-, Hof- und Staatsarchiv

HHStA-GD   *Gendarmerie Department: Polizeiakten*
HHStA-IB   *Informations Büro*
HHStA-IS   *Illyrico-Serbico*
HHStA-KA   *Kolowrat Akten*
HHStA-KF   *Kaiser Franz Akten*
HHStA-KK   *Kabinettarchiv: Konferenzakten*

Kriegsarchiv

KA-AMK   *Archiv der Militärkanzlei*
KA-FA48   *Feld Akten 1848–1849*

KA-KU   *Krieg in Ungarn: Akten der Insurgenten Armee*
KA-UK   *Ungarische Insurrektion*

PUBLISHED SOURCES

AIMJ   ACSÁDY, IGNÁCZ. *A magyar jobbágyság története* [The History of the Hungarian Serfdom]. Budapest, 1906.

AKMT   *1849–1866 Adalékok a kényuralom ellenes mozgalmak történetéhez. Az Asbóth-család irataiból* [1849–1866 Data on the Movements of Defiance Against Despotism. Selected Documents of the Asbóth Family]. Pest, 1871.

AIHB   ÁLDOR, IMRE. *A haza bölcse* [The Sage of the Fatherland]. Budapest, 1878.

AIDF   ————. *Deák Ferenc élete. Emlékkönyv* [The Life of Ferenc Deák: A Commemorative Book], Budapest, n.d. [1879].

ANDRÁSSY, JULIUS [Count Gyula]. *Ungarns Ausgleich mit Oesterreich.* Leipzig, 1897.

AGyB   *Andrássy Gyula Gróf beszédei 1847–1868* [The Speeches of Count Gyula Andrássy 1847–1868]. Edited by Béla Léderer. Budapest, 1891.

ADFM   ANGYAL, DÁVID, ed. *Falk Miksa és Kecskeméthy Aurél elkobzott levelezése* [The Confiscated Correspondence of Miksa Falk and Aurél Kecskeméthy] in the series "Fontes historiae hungaricae aevi recentioris." Budapest, 1925.

AJEJ   ANTALL, JÓZSEF. "Eötvös József politikai hetilapja és a kiegyezés előkészitése 1865–1866" [The Political Weekly of Joseph Eötvös and the Preparation of the Compromise 1865–1866]. *Századok,* 1965, Vol. VI.

AAEO   APPONYI, ALBERT. *Emlékirataim. Ötven év. Ifjukorom—huszonöt év az ellenzéken* [My Memoirs. Fifty Years. My Youth—Twenty-five Years in the Opposition]. Budapest, 1922.

APPONYI, ALBERT GRÓF. *The Memoirs of Count Apponyi.* London, 1935.

AOGyJ   *Az 1861. évi országgyülés képviselőházának jegyzőkönyve* [The Minutes of the House of the Representatives of the Parliament of 1861]. Pest, 1861.

Az 1865 ON   Az 1865-dik évi deczember 10-dikére hirdetett országgyülés képviselőházának naplója [Minutes of the House of Representatives of the Hungarian Parliament Convoked for December 10, 1865]. Pest, 1868.

Az 1865 OGy   Az 1865. deczember 10 dikére hirdetett országgyülés nyomtatványai. Képviselőház. Irományok [The Publications of the Parliament Convoked for December 10, 1865. House of the Representatives. Documents]. Pest, 1868.

Az 1865 OI   Az 1865-dik évi deczember 10-dikére hirdetett országgyülés Főrendiházának irományai [The Papers of the House of Lords of the Parliament Convoked for December 10, 1865]. 2 vols. Pest, 1868.

              BÁRÁNY, GEORGE. Stephen Széchenyi and the Awakening of Hungarian Nationalism, 1791–1841. Princeton, N.J., 1968.

BJNO   BEÉR, JÁNOS, ed. Az 1848/49. évi népképviseleti országgyülés [The Popularly Represented National Assembly of 1848/49]. Budapest, 1954.

BGMD   BEKSICS, GUSTÁV. Magyar doktrinérek [Hungarian Doctrinaires]. Budapest, 1882.

BGKZs   ——————. Kemény Zsigmond, a forradalom és kiegyezés [Zsigmond Kemény, the Revolution and the Compromise]. Budapest, 1883.

BGFJK   ——————. "I. Ferenc József kora" in Szilágyi Sándor, A magyar nemzet története ["The Era of Francis Joseph I" in The History of the Hungarian Nation]. 10 vols. Budapest, 1898. Vol. X.

              BERGER, PETER, ed. Der österreichisch-ungarische Ausgleich von 1867. Vorgeschichte und Wirkungen. Vienna, 1967.

              BERNATZIK, EDMUND. Die österreichische Verfassunggesetze. 2nd ed. Vienna, 1911.

BAAM   BERZEVICZY ALBERT. Az abszolutizmus kora Magyarországon 1849–1865 [The Era of Absolutism in Hungary 1849–1865]. 3 vols. Budapest, 1922.

              BEUST, FRIEDRICH FERDINAND GRAF VON. Aus drei Viertel-Jahrhunderten Erinnerungen und Aufzeichungen. 2 vols. Stuttgart, 1887.

Bödy, Paul. *Joseph Eötvös and the Modernization of Hungary, 1840–1870: A Study of Ideas of Individuality and Social Pluralism in Modern Politics.* Philadelphia, 1972.

Charmatz, Richard. *Österreichs innere Geschichte von 1848 bis 1895.* 2 vols. Leipzig, 1918.

Clark, Chester Wells. *Franz Joseph and Bismarck; The Diplomacy of Austria Before the War of 1866.* New York, 1968.

C.J.H.   *Corpus juris hungarici editio millenaria memorabilis.* Leipzig, 1902.

CsAHI   Csengery, Antal. *Csengery Antal hátrahagyott iratai és feljegyzései* [The Papers and Notes Left Behind by Antal Csengery] in the series of "Fontes historiae hungaricae aevi recentioris." Edited by Baron Gyula Wlassics. Budapest, 1928.

————. *Deák Ferenc Emlékezete* [The Reminiscence of Ferenc Deák]. Budapest, 1877.

DKKD   Dányi, Károly. *Kossuth és Deák-párt hirlapi vitája 1867-ben* [The Press Polemics of Kossuth and the Deák Party in 1867]. Kolozsvár, 1941.

DFDF   Deák, Farkas. "Deák Ferenc," *Magyar Helicon. Jeles magyar államférfiak életrajz- gyüjteménye* [Hungarian Helikon. The Collection of Biographies of Prominent Hungarian Statesmen]. Vol. II, No. 1. Pozsony, 1884.

DFB   Deák, Ferenc. *Deák Ferenc Beszédei* [The Speeches of Ferenc Deák]. 6 vols. Edited by Manó Kónyi. Budapest, 1903.

————. *Ein Beitrag zum ungarischen Staatsrecht. Bemerkungen über Wenzel Lustkandl's "Ungarisch-österreichisches Staatsrecht" vom Standpunkte der Geschichte des ungarischen Staatsrechts.* Pest, 1865.

DFL   *Deák Ferenc Emlékezete. Levelek 1822–1875.* [The Memory of Ferenc Deák. Correspondence]. Budapest, 1890.

DM   *Dembinski Magyarországon* [Dembinski in Hungary]. The leader's Manuscripts compiled and edited by Alfonsz F. Danzer. Budapest, 1874.

Deme, László. "The Committee of Public Safety in

the Hungarian Revolution of 1848." *Canadian Slavic Studies*, V, No. 3, Fall 1971.

Der oesterreichisch-ungarische Ausgleich von 1867; seine Grundlagen und Auswirkungen. München, 1968.

DIHE   DIÓSZEGI, ISTVÁN. *Hazánk és Europa* [Our Fatherland and Europe]. Budapest, 1970.

DPDF   DOBRÁNSZKY, PÉTER. *Deák Ferencz, Kor és életrajz* [Ferenc Deák, a Biography and an Analysis of the Era]. Budapest, 1877.

EIDF   EGRY, IRÉN. *Deák Ferenc. Történeti arckép* [Ferenc Deák, a Historical Portrait]. Budapest, 1941.

EISENMANN, LOUIS. *Le compromis austro-hongrois de 1867—étude sur le dualisme*. Paris, 1904.

EÖTVÖS, BARON, JÓZSEF. "Deák Ferencz üdvözlésekor" [At the Welcoming of Ferenc Deák]. *Beszédek* [Speeches]. 3 vols., III, 23–28.

EJR   ————. *Reform* [Reform]. Budapest, 1902.

EJKN   ————. *A kelet népe és Pesti Hirlap* [The People of the Orient and the Pest News]. Budapest, 1902.

EKDF   EÖTVÖS, KÁROLY. *Deák Ferencz és családja* [Ferenc Deák and His Family]. 2 vols. Budapest, 1905.

EKHNH   ————. *Harcz a nemzeti hadseregért* [Struggle for the National Army]. Budapest, 1906.

ETEROVICH, FRANCIS H., and CHRISTOPHER SPALATIN. *Croatia: Land, People, Culture*. 2 vols. Toronto, 1970.

FMKJ   FALK, MIKSA. *Kor- és jellemrajzok* [Sketches of an Era and Its Personalities]. Budapest, 1903.

FLA   FAYER, LÁSZLÓ. *Az 1843-iki büntetőjogi javaslatok anyaggyüjteménye* [Document Collection of the Criminal Judiciary Drafts of 1843]. 4 vols. Budapest, 1896–1902.

FEMST   FÉNYES, ELEK. *Magyarország statisztikája* [The Statistics of Hungary]. Pest, 1842.

FZWM   FERENCZI, ZOLTÁN. "Báró Wesselényi Miklós leveli Deák Ferenchez 1841–1850" [The Letters of Baron Miklós Wesselényi to Ferenc Deák 1841–1850]. *Történelmi Tár*. Budapest, 1904.

FZD   ————. *Deák élete* [The Life of Deák]. 3 vols. Budapest, 1904.

FOSTER-ARNOLD, FLORENCE. *Francis Deák Hungarian Statesman: A Memoir.* London, 1880.

FRIEDJUNG, HEINRICH. *The Struggle for Supremacy in Germany 1859–1866.* New York, 1966.

————. *Der Ausgleich mit Ungarn. Politische Studie über das Verhältnis Österreichs zu Ungarn und Deutschland.* Leipzig, 1877.

————. *Österreich von 1848 bis 1860.* Stuttgart, 1908–1912.

GJBG GAÁL, JENŐ. *Berzeviczy Gergely élete és müvei* [Life and Works of Gergely Berzeviczy]. Budapest, 1902.

GMDF GAÁL, MÓZES. *Deák Ferencz. Élet és jellemrajz* [Ferenc Deák. Life and Profile]. Budapest, 1900.

GJ67 GALÁNTAI, JÓZSEF. *Az 1867-es kiegyezés* [The Compromise of 1867]. Budapest, 1967.

GAPK GERANDO, ÁGOSTON. *Politicai közszellem Magyarhonban, A'Franczia forradalom óta* [Political Attitudes in Hungary Since the French Revolution]. Pest, 1848.

GIBM GONDA, IMRE. *Bismarck és az 1867-es osztrák-magyar kiegyezés* [Bismarck and the Austro-Hungarian Compromise of 1867]. Budapest, 1960.

GIGASz GÖRGEY, ISTVÁN. *Görgey Arthur a számüzetésben 1849–1867.* [Arthur Görgey in Banishment]. Budapest, 1918.

GGDK GRATZ, GUSZTÁV. *A dualizmus kora. Magyarország története 1867–1918.* [The Era of Dualism, A History of Hungary 1867–1918]. 2 vols. Budapest, 1933.

GULDESCU, STANKO. *The Croatian-Slavonian Kingdom 1526–1792.* The Hague, 1970.

GYULAI, PÁL. "Emlékezés Deák Ferencre" [Remembrance of Ferenc Deák]. *Budapesti Szemle.* Budapest, No. 118, 1904.

HILN HALÁSZ, IMRE. *Egy letünt nemzedék. Emlékezések a magyar állam kialakulásásnak ujabb korszakából* [A Generation that Passed Away. Memories of the Recent Era of the Evolution of the Hungarian State]. Budapest, 1911.

HPMT HANÁK, PÉTER, *et al. Magyarország Története 1849–1918* [A History of Hungary 1849–

1918]. Vol. IV of the official university text-book. Budapest, 1972.

HANTSCH, HUGO. *Die Nationalitätenfrage im alten Österreich; Das Problem der konstruktiven Reichsgestaltung.* Wien, 1953.

—————. *Die Geschichte Österreichs.* 2 vols. Graz, 1968.

HSzMT HÓMAN, BÁLINT, and GYULA SZEKFÜ. *Magyar Történet* [Hungarian History]. 5 vols. Budapest, 1938.

HM HORVÁTH, MIHÁLY. *Huszonöt év Magyarország történelméből 1823–1848* [Twenty-five Years of the History of Hungary 1823–1848]. 3 vols. Budapest, 1886.

HZTL HORVÁTH, ZOLTÁN. *Teleki László 1810–1861* [László Teleki 1810–1861]. 2 vols. Budapest, 1964.

Institut für Österreichkunde. *Historisches Geschehen im Spiegel der Gegenwart Österreich-Ungarn 1867–1967.* Vienna, 1970.

IVÁNYI, B. G. "From Feudalism to Capitalism: The Economic Background to Széchenyi's Reform in Hungary." *Journal of Central European Affairs*, XX, No. 3, October 1960.

JALAVA, ANTTI. *Franz Deák.* Helsinki, 1902.

JÁSZI, OSCAR. *The Dissolution of the Habsburg Monarchy.* Chicago, 1961.

KANN, ROBERT A. *The Habsburg Empire: A Study in Integration and Disintegration.* New York, 1957.

—————. *The Multinational Empire: Nationalism and National Reform in the Habsburg Monarchy 1848–1918.* 2 vols. New York, 1950.

KAN KECSKEMÉTHY, AURÉL. *Kecskeméthy Aurél naplója 1851–1878* [The Diary of Aurél Kecskeméthy 1851–1878]. Edited by Miklós Rózsa. Budapest, 1909.

KAPK —————. *Parlamenti kormány és vármegyei reactio* [Parliamentary Government and County Reaction]. Pest, 1867.

KAV —————. *Vázlatok egy év történetéből* [*1860 october huszadikától 1861 octoberig*] [Sketches from the History of One Year (From October 20

1860 to October 1861)]. Pest, 1862. [A German version was also published the same year.]

KFMPL KEMÉNY, FERENC, et al. *Magyar Pedagógiai Lexikon* [Hungarian Encyclopaedia of Education]. Budapest, 1933.

KGGIN KEMÉNY, G. GÁBOR. *Iratok a nemzetiségi kérdés történetéhez Magyarországon a dualizmus korában.* [Documents Related to the History of the Nationality Problem in Hungary during the Era of Dualism]. 2 vols. Budapest, 1952.

KKPD KERKÁPOLY, KÁROLY. *Publicistikai dolgozatok az 1865–68 évi országgyülés alatt* [Essays of Political Journalism during the Parliament of 1865–68]. Pest, 1869.

KERTBENY, KARL MARIA. *Franz von Deák. Biographische Charakteristik des ungarischen Staatsmannes.* Leipzig, 1868. [A pamphlet published also in English, French, Swedish, and Polish.]

KIENIEWICZ, STEFAN. *The Emancipation of the Polish Peasantry.* Chicago, 1969.

KIRÁLY, BÉLA K. *Hungary in the Late Eighteenth Century: The Decline of Enlightened Despotism.* New York, 1969.

————. "The Young Ferenc Deák and the Problem of the Serfs 1824–1836." *Südost-Forschungen.* Munich, Vol. XXIX, 1970.

KGyE KLAPA, GYÖRGY [General]. *Emlékeimből* [A Memoire]. Budapest, 1886.

KNATCHBULL-HUGESSEN, C. M. *The Political Evolution of the Hungarian Nation.* 2 vols. London, 1908.

KOHN, HANS. *Nationalism: Its Meaning and History.* New York, 1955.

KOLMER, GUSTAV, ed. *Parlament und Verfassung in Oesterreich.* 8 vols. Vienna, 1902–14.

KVPF KONDOR, VIKTÓRIA M. *Az 1875-ös pártfuzió* [The Party Fusion of 1875]. Budapest, 1959.

Kossuth and the Hungarian War, Comprising a Complete History of the Late Struggle of the Hungarians for Liberty. New Haven, 1852.

KLF KOSSUTH, LAJOS. *Felelet Gróf Széchenyi Istvánnak*

                [A Reply to Count István Széchenyi]. Pest, 1841.

KLIE   *Kossuth Lajos, Irataim az emigrációból* [Lajos Kossuth, My Papers from Exile]. 3 vols. Budapest, 1880–1882.

KLOT   KOSSUTH, LAJOS. *Országgyülési Tudósitások* [Reports from the Diet]. Edited by István Barta. In the series of "Fontes historiae hungaricae aevi recentioris." 5 vols. Budapest, 1961.

                KOSSUTH, LUDWIG. *Ungarns Auschluss an den deutschen Zollverband.* Leipzig, 1842.

KEAU   KOVÁCS, ENDRE. *Ausztria utja az 1867-es Kiegyezéshez* [Austria's Road to the Compromise of 1867]. Budapest, 1968.

KEMD   ––––––. *Magyar-délszláv megbékélési törekvések 1848/49-ben* [Hungarian–South-Slav Efforts at Reconciliation in 1848/49]. Budapest, 1958.

                KRONES, DR. F. VON. *Moritz von Kaiserfeld. Sein Leben und Wirken als Beitrag zur Staatsgeschichte Oesterreichs in den Jahren 1848 bis 1884.* Leipzig, 1888.

                KÜBECK, KARL FRIEDRICH VON. *Tagebücher.* 2 vols. Vienna, 1919.

LEMPVR   LAKATOS, ERNŐ. *A magyar politikai vezetőréteg 1848–1918* [The Hungarian Political Leading Stratum 1848–1918]. Budapest, 1942.

                LAVELEYE, EMIL. *Deák Ferenc.* Pest, 1869.

                Les Discours de M. Deák et l'état de la Hongrie. Bruxelles, 1861.

                LOFTUS, LORD AUGUSTUS. *The Diplomatic Reminiscences of Lord Augustus Loftus.* 2 vols. London, 1892.

                LORENZ, O. *Deák's Adress-Entwurf und das Staatsrecht Österreichs.* Vienna, 1861.

                LORENZ, REINHOLD. *Anton Ritter von Schmerling (1805–1893) und Alexander von Bach (1813–1893). Gestalter der Geschicke Österreichs.* Innsbruck, 1962.

                LUDVIGH, JEAN. *L'Autriche et la Diète de Hongrie, contenant l'adresse de M. Deák.* Bruxelles, 1861.

LLMF   LUKÁCS, LAJOS. *Magyar függetlenségi és alkotmányos mozgalmak, 1848–1867.* [Hungarian

Independence and Constitutionalist Movements, 1884–1867]. Budapest, 1955.

McCAGG, WILLIAM O., JR. *Jewish Nobles and Geniuses in Modern Hungary.* New York, 1972.

MJE MADARÁSZ, JÓZSEF. *Emlékirataim 1831–1881* [My Memoirs 1831–1881]. Budapest, 1883.

MARCZALI, HEINRICH. *Ungarische Verfassungsgeschichte.* Tübingen, 1910.

MSMA MATLEKOVITS, SÁNDOR. *Magyarország államháztartásának története 1867–1893* [A History of Hungary's State Finances]. Budapest, 1894.

MAY, ARTHUR J. *The Habsburg Monarchy 1867–1914.* Cambridge, Mass., 1968.

MSMT MÉREI, GYULA, and GYÖRGY SPIRA, eds. *Magyarország története 1790–1849* [A History of Hungary 1790–1848]. 4 vols. Budapest, 1961.

MGyMI MÉREI, GYULA. *Magyar iparfejlődés 1790–1848* [Hungarian Industrial Development 1790–1848]. Budapest, 1951.

MLKLE MÉSZÁROS, LÁZÁR [General]. *Mészáros Lázár külföldi levelei és életirata* [The Correspondence from Abroad and the Memoirs of Lázár Mészáros]. Compiled out of the original manuscripts by Viktor Szokoly. Pest, 1867.

METTERNICH-WINNEBURG, FÜRST CLEMENS L. W. VON. *Aus Metternichs nachgelassenen Papieren.* 8 vols. Wien, 1880–84.

MISKOLCZY, JULIUS. *Ungarn in der Habsburger Monarchie.* Wien, 1959.

MITTERMAIER, DR. G. J. *Die Mündlichkeit, das Anklageprinzip, die Oeffentlichkeit und das Geschwornengericht in ihrer Durchführung in den verschiedenen Gesetzgebungen.* Stuttgart, 1845.

MAFSz MÓD, ALADÁR, et al. *Forradalom és szabadságharc 1848–1849* [Revolution and War of Liberation 1848–1849]. Budapest, 1948.

MAN MÓD, ALADÁR. *400 Év küzdelem az önálló Magyarországért* [Four Hundred Years' Struggle for an Independent Hungary]. 7th enlarged edition. Budapest, 1954.

MEMT MOLNÁR, ERIK [Chief editor]. *Magyarország Tör-*

ténete [History of Hungary]. 2 vols. 2nd ed. Budapest, 1967.

NEMK   NAGY, ERNŐ. *Magyarország közjoga (Államjog)* [Hungary's Constitutional Law (State Law)]. Budapest, 1905.

NID   NEDECZKY, ISTVÁN. *Deák: A képviseleti alkotmány megalapitása* [Deák: The Foundation of the Representative Constitution]. Budapest, 1876.

OGy75   OLÁH, GYULA. *Az 1875-iki fuzio története* [A History of the (Party) Fusion of 1875]. Budapest, 1908.

PZSPE   PACH, ZSIGMOND PÁL. *Az eredeti tőkefelhalmozás gyarmati korlátai Magyarországon 1848 előtt.* [The Obstacles of a Colonial Nature, that Prevented the Original Capital Accumulation in Hungary Prior to 1848]. Budapest, 1950.

     PALACKÝ, F. *Österreichs Staatsidee.* Prague, 1866.

PSVT   PETHŐ, SÁNDOR. *Világostól Trianoning a mai Magyarország kialakulásának története* [From Világos to Trianon, a History of the Evolution of Contemporary Hungary]. 5th ed. Budapest, n.d.

     PETRIE, SIR CHARLES. *Diplomatic History 1713–1933.* New York, 1949.

PFD   PULSZKY, FERENC. *Deák Ferenc. Jellemrajz* [Ferenc Deák. A Sketch of His Character]. Budapest, 1876.

PFEK   ————. *Életem és korom* [My Life and My Times]. 2 vols. Budapest, 1958.

     RADVANY, EGON. *Metternich's Projects for Reform in Austria.* The Hague, 1971.

     RATH, R. JOHN. *The Viennese Revolution of 1848.* Austin, Texas, 1957.

     REDLICH, JOSEF. *Das österreichische Staats- und Reichsproblem.* 2 vols. Leipzig, 1920–26.

     REDLICH, JOSEPH. *Emperor Francis Joseph of Austria: A Biography.* Hamden, Conn., 1965.

     REGELE, OSKAR. *Feldzeugmeister Benedek.* Vienna, 1960.

     RITTER, GERHARD. *Staatskunst und Kriegshandwerk. Das Problem des "Militarismus" in Deutschland.* 2nd revised ed. München, 1959.

ROGGE, WALTER. *Oesterreich von Világos bis zur Gegenwart.* 5 vols. Leipzig, 1872–1879.

ROTHENBERG, GUNTHER E. *The Military Border in Croatia 1740–1881.* Chicago, 1966.

————. "Toward a National Hungarian Army: The Military Compromise of 1868 and Its Consequences." *Slavic Review,* XXXI, No. 4, December, 1972.

SVNM SÁNDOR, VILMOS. *Nagyipari fejlődés Magyarországon 1867–1900* [The Development of Heavy Industry in Hungary 1867–1900]. Budapest, 1954.

SBDV SARLÓS, BÉLA. *Deák és Vukovics két igazságügyminiszter* [Deák and Vukovics Two Ministers of Justice]. Budapest, 1970.

SMDF SARLÓS, MÁRTON. "Deák Ferenc és az urbéri földtulajdon az 1832/1836-i országgyűlésen" [Ferenc Deák and the Question of Servile Landownership at the Diet of 1832/1836]. *Jogtörténeti Tanulmányok.* Budapest, vol. I, 1966.

SOMP SASHEGYI, OSZKÁR, ed. *Munkások és parasztok mozgalmai Magyarországon 1849–1867* [Movements of Workers and Peasants in Hungary 1849–1867]. Budapest, 1959.

SCHUSELKA, FRANZ. *An Franz Deák.* Vienna, 1861.

SCHWICKER, JOHANN HEINRICH. *Franz Deáks politische Ideen vor 1848.* Vienna, 1882.

SGyMF SPIRA, GYÖRGY. *A magyar forradalom 1848–49-ben* [The Hungarian Revolution in 1848–49]. Budapest, 1959.

STEINBACH, GUSZTÁV. *Franz Deák.* Vienna, 1888.

SUGAR, PETER F. "The Nature of the Non-German Societies Under Habsburg Rule." *Slavic Review,* XXII, No. 1, March 1963.

SUGAR, PETER, and IVO J. LEDERER, eds. *Nationalism in Eastern Europe.* Seattle, 1969.

SG1848 SUPKA, GÉZA. *1848 A márciusi forradalom előzményei, lefolyása, társadalmi jelentősége* [1848: The Preliminaries, Events, and Social Significance of the March Revolution]. Budapest, n.d.

SzGyFK SZABAD, GYÖRGY. *Forradalom és kiegyezés válaszut-*

ján 1860–61 [At the Crossroads of Revolution and Compromise 1860–61]. Budapest, 1967.

SzETP   SZABÓ, ERVIN. *Társadalmi és pártharcok a 48–49-es magyar forradalomban* [Social and Party Struggles in the 1848–49 Hungarian Revolution]. Vienna, 1920.

SzIB   SZÉCHENYI, GRÓF ISTVÁN. *Gr. Széchenyi István döblingi irodalmi hagyatéka Blick és kisebb döblingi iratok* [The Döbling Literary Papers Left Behind by Count István Széchenyi, Blick and Minor Döbling Papers] in the series of "Fontes historiae hungaricae aevi recentioris." Budapest, 1925.

SzIKN   *Gróf Széchenyi István Munkái* [The Works of Count István Széchenyi]. Edited by Kálmán Szily. Vol. II: *A kelet népe* [The People of the Orient]. Budapest, 1905.

SzIVM   *Gróf Széchenyi István Válogatott Munkái.* [Selected Works of Count István Széchenyi]. Edited by Antal Radó. Budapest, 1903.

SzGyI   SZEKFÜ, GYULA, ed. *Iratok a magyar államnyelv kérdésének történetéhez 1790–1848* [Documents Related to the History of Hungarian State Language] in the series of "Fontes historiae hungaricae aevi recentioris." Budapest, 1926.

SzGyHK   ––––––. *Három nemzedék egy hanyatló kor története* [Three Generations: The History of a Declining Era]. Budapest, 1920.

SzBÖM   SZEMERE, BERTALAN. *Szemere Bertalan összegyüjtött munkái.* [The Collected Works of Bertalan Szemere]. 6 vols. Budapest, 1869–1871.

SzAMI   SZERB, ANTAL. *Magyar Irodalomtörténet* [History of Hungarian Literature]. Budapest, 1958.

SzMT   SZILÁGYI, SÁNDOR. *A magyar nemzet története* [The History of the Hungarian Nation]. 10 vols. Budapest, 1898.

SzLM   SZŐGYÉNY–MARICH, LÁSZLÓ. *Idősb Szőgyény-Marich László országbiró emlékiratai* [The Memoirs of László Szőgyeny-Marich, Sr., Lord Chief Justice]. 3 vols. Budapest, 1903–1918.

TMTA   TAKÁCS, MÁRIA. *Társadalmi állapotok és törekvések Magyarországon 1830–1847* [Social Conditions and Efforts in Hungary 1830–1847]. Budapest, 1909.

TAYLOR, A. J. P. *The Habsburg Monarchy, 1809– 1918.* New York, 1965.

——. *The Struggle for Mastery in Europe 1848–1918.* Oxford, 1960.

TEFFT, REV. B. F. D. *Hungary and Kossuth or an American Exposition of the Late Hungarian Revolution.* Philadelphia, 1852.

TLVM   TELEKI, LÁSZLÓ. *Teleki László válogatott munkái* [Selected Works of László Teleki]. 2 vols. Edited by Gábor G. Kemény. Budapest, 1961.

TL31   TILKOVSZKY, LÓRÁNT. *Az 1831. évi paraszt felkelés* [The Peasant Insurrection of 1831]. Budapest, 1955.

TIOT   TOLDY, ISTVÁN. *Öt év története (1867–1872)* [A History of Five Years (1867–1872)]. Pest, 1891.

TÖRS, KÁLMÁN, ed. *Deák Ferenc emlékezete* [Reminiscences of Ferenc Deák]. Budapest, 1876.

TEML   TÓTH, EDE. *Mocsáry Lajos élete és politikai pályakezdete (1826–1874)* [Life and Start of the Political Career of Lajos Mocsáry (1826– 1874)]. Budapest, 1967.

TAET   TREFORT, ÁGOSTON. *Emlékbeszédek és tanulmányok* [Commemorative Orations and Essays]. Budapest, 1881.

VANTUCH, ANTON (ed.). *Der österreichische-ungarische Ausgleich 1867: Materialien (Referate und Discussion) der internationalen Konferenz in Bratislava 28.8.-1.9.1967.* Bratislava, 1971.

WEAGy   WERTHEIMER, EDE. *Gróf Andrássy Gyula élete és kora* [The Life and Times of Count Gyula Andrássy]. 3 vols. Budapest, 1910.

WGyDF   WLASSICS, GYULA BÁRÓ. *Deák Ferenc* [Ferenc Deák]. Budapest, 1923.

ZOLGER, IVAN. *Der staatsrechtliche Ausgleich zwischen Oesterreich und Ungarn.* Munich, 1911.

ZÖLLNER, ERICH. *Geschichte Österreichs von den Anfängen bis zur Gegenwart.* Wien, 1961.

Index

Index